THE MANAGED CASUALTY

The Japanese-American Family in World War II

BY

LEONARD BROOM AND JOHN I. KITSUSE

UNIVERSITY OF CALIFORNIA PRESS

BERKELEY, LOS ANGELES, LONDON

University of California Publications in Culture and Society
VOLUME 6

UNIVERSITY OF CALIFORNIA PRESS
BERKELEY AND LOS ANGELES
CALIFORNIA
UNIVERSITY OF CALIFORNIA PRESS, LTD.
LONDON, ENGLAND

CALIFORNIA LIBRARY REPRINT SERIES EDITION, 1973
ISBN: 0–520–02523–7
LIBRARY OF CONGRESS CATALOG CARD NUMBER: 73–87134

PRINTED IN THE UNITED STATES OF AMERICA

PREFACE

THIS STUDY is an assessment of one major aspect of the adjustment of Japanese Americans to the series of events comprising their removal from the communities of the Pacific Coast early in World War II, their sequestration in temporary centers under governmental control, and their eventual release. It is in a sense an "impact" study in that attention is directed toward the effects administrative policies had on family groups and the resources these groups commanded to adapt to and ameliorate the conditions imposed upon them.

The preoccupation of the present study is easily justified. The importance of the family, in Japan as well as in the organization of the Japanese communities in the United States, makes this aspect of the social organization of the minority group a major concern for a rounded understanding of the evacuation. The relevance of the family as the unit of study is also indicated by the administrative policy which explicitly directed that family units be maintained in the processing of the population through the evacuation and relocation programs.

Although compilation of cases began at the outbreak of war, the evacuation and relocation of the families and the breaking up of some family units imposed progressive difficulties on the study. Cases would have been easier to complete if the unit of study had been the individual rather than the family, but the institutional focus of the research would then have been damaged. There was, therefore, some unavoidable attrition of cases, and in addition the loss of some cases which might have been saved if the study had not been meagerly staffed and financed.

Confronted by these limitations and opportunities, the study took the following form:

1. An account of the cultural and social origins of the Japanese family system, the immigration experience, the formation of ethnic communities, and the process of family building in the United States.

2. A summary of the conditions obtaining just before the outbreak of the war, giving a base line with which the wartime experience could be compared.

3. A minimal description of those administrative decisions and policies that set the conditions within which the families had to adjust.

4. Against this background the main alternatives available to the families and the adaptations made by them to administrative manipulations are described.

5. The case materials are presented as illustrative instances to give

substance and depth to the events being interpreted. It is not claimed that the cases are a random sample of the types of families constituting the Japanese-American population, but strenuous effort has been made to include families that represent the chief categories of religion, occupation, education, urbanization, degree of acculturation, and age and generation composition.[1]

Thanks are due Professor Ruth Riemer for help at all stages of the work, and to Professor E. Ashikaga for verifying the rendering of Japanese terms. Especially, we are grateful to those who collaborated with us in assembling the information for their family histories and for thoughtfully participating in the reinterpretation of their experiences. We have intended to give order to the events contained in the cases, but we have tried so far as possible to avoid the rewriting of reality. That is, we have had both documentary and analytic objectives, and our interpretations are intentionally set apart so that the reader may, if he wishes, use the cases for other lines of analysis.

---

[1] For note to preface, see p. 223.

L.B.
J.I.K.

CONTENTS

CHAPTER I

SOCIAL AND CULTURAL BACKGROUNDS OF THE JAPANESE POPULATION

THE PERIOD of Japanese immigration was brief and its termination abrupt. Miyamoto[1] divides the preëvacuation adjustment of the Japanese population into three intervals: (1) *The Frontier Period* ending with the Gentlemen's Agreement in 1907. During this time the immigrants, nearly without exception, planned to return to Japan. (2) *The Settling Period,* from 1907 to the Exclusion Act of 1924, saw the formation of Japanese ghettos, economic improvement, the balancing of sex ratios, and the founding of families. (3) *The Second Generation Period* beginning in 1924 found the people resigned to a life in America and orienting themselves to the rising *Nisei.**

The trends and adjustments were interrupted by the interlude beginning with the evacuation in 1942 and ending with resettlement in 1945. Our study concentrates on the wartime experience of the population. The postwar period, however, has opened a new chapter in which patterns of individual and community adaptation are being set for the next two or three generations.

We shall be concerned here with those aspects of cultural adaptation and family structure which affected the processes of decision-making and adjustment to the exigencies of the evacuation. In general, the most important of these fall into two parts: (*a*) cultural considerations, particularly as expressed in acculturation and cultural conservatism, and (*b*) family authority and dependency patterns, which comprise the critical context in which most decisions were actually made.

This treatment does not deal with traditional community forces, such as voluntary associations and prefectural organizations, which are commonly regarded as important for the Japanese-American population. The nature of the wartime handling of the population consistently undermined community resources, removed or weakened community leaders, and devalued many community institutions. Some 5,000 *Issei* males, comprising the bulk of qualified leaders, were removed to internment camps at the very outbreak of the war and, although many eventually were returned to their families in the relocation centers, they never recovered their prewar authority. The peremptory removal of the com-

---

[1] For notes to chap. i, see p. 223.
* See the glossary for the meaning of italicized Japanese words.

munity leaders weakened the organizations with which they were associated. The members failed to find new leaders and permitted the organizations to fall defunct. Except for the Christian churches, which were the most important agencies mediating between the Japanese and the *hakujin* population, and the Japanese American Citizens League (JACL), an organization of Nisei, the community was left without organizational resources.

For the sake of perspective, we must mention the chief features of the family system of the latter part of the nineteenth century in which the Japanese immigrants were reared. The native Japanese family was characterized by a strong solidarity expressed in "mutual helpfulness." It was patriarchal in form, and was colored throughout by the notion of male superiority and the correlative desirability of male children. The father symbol (*koshu*) was an object of respect, even awe; the mother symbol was one to elicit warmth and affection.

The individual matured in a role system in which the dominant themes were filial piety, seniority (more specifically, respect for the aged), masculine superiority, and ancestor worship. The imperative nature of deferential attitudes found linguistic expression in the use of honorifics (*keigo*) and in the emphasis placed upon verbal propriety in alluding to or adressing an elder.

Marriage was effected by family action for purposes of familial continuity. Through the oldest son family continuity would be achieved, parents would be protected in their old age, and obligations to the ancestors discharged. Marriage was usually arranged by a "go-between" (*nakōdo*) and there was small place for independent mate choice. In order to ensure continuity, families without sons commonly practiced adoption. If there was a daughter, the adoptee might be the daughter's husband (*yōshi*), thus assuring both ancestor worship and retention of property by the in-group. The adoption practices were capable of convenient variations such as the adoption of one's younger brother (*junyōshi*). Because the family's stake was so great, a careful scrutiny was made of the lineage or "blood" of the prospective in-laws. Tuberculosis, leprosy, inferior social status, or a prison record were disabilities.

Patently in such a system the family is the chief agency for social control, and the extension of family concepts and kin relationships into industrial and national spheres suggest their vigor. Miyamoto points out the functioning significance of this theme. "It is not so important that they speak of their community or nation as if it were a family;

what is really significant is that they act towards it in many ways as if it were a family."[2]

The rapid acculturation of the Japanese population in America and Hawaii and its adjustment to the dominant society have frequently been noted.[3] Considering the differences in the details of the American and Japanese cultures and the differences between the English and Japanese languages, the speed of this acculturation is impressive. It is not appropriate to review here the reasons for this adaptation, an achievement perhaps rarely equaled in the history of migration. We should observe, however, that great differences in cultural details need not be accompanied by equal differences in the less tangible aspects of culture and society—those aspects related to valuations, motivations, and the like. Indeed, it may be hypothesized that American and Japanese cultures are quite similar in the emphasis placed upon societal instruments, e.g., formal education.[4]

The geographic distribution and age structure of the population deeply influenced problems of adjustment and their characteristic solutions. The Japanese population in the United States has been characterized by progressive urbanization and progressive concentration in the Los Angeles area. In 1940 the Japanese population in the Continental United States was about 127,000 of whom 47,000 were aliens and 80,000 their American-born children. Approximately 90 per cent of this population resided in the four western states of California, Washington, Oregon, and Arizona. Thirty-nine per cent of the total lived in Los Angeles County, and there were other substantial settlements in Seattle and the San Francisco Bay area.

The population pyramid (fig. 1) shows a great preponderance of foreign-born males in the group over fifty years of age, a considerable proportion of foreign-born females in the forty to fifty age group, and an abrupt cleavage between the native- and foreign-born groups at the thirty to thirty-five year level. This age-generation cleavage reinforced culture conflict and increased the tendency to express culture conflict in generational terms. The cleavage lends a concrete group-formed reality to the "problem of the second generation."

The speed of Japanese acculturation has produced within the population individuals varying widely in their degree of acculturation. Abrupt termination of immigration from Japan created the following situation: a native-born (Nisei) population with an intermediate to high level of acculturation standing beside an immigrant population (Issei) with low to intermediate acculturation. "The Nisei problem,"

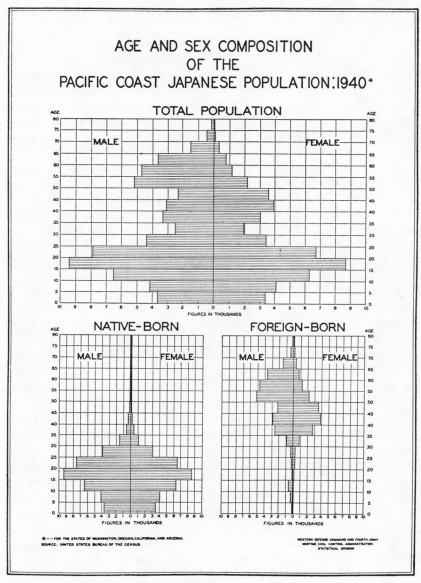

Fig. 1

the repeated concern of the Japanese community in the United States for more than thirty years, is the expression in societal terms of this cultural cleavage.

In the prewar period a number of forces impeded contact between Japanese and hakujin and therefore affected the rate and character of acculturation. Whether rural or urban, the majority of the Japanese population lived in segregated areas, although these were by no means as large and homogeneous as in the case of Negroes. In urban areas there were no schools attended exclusively by Nisei, although there were some primary schools in which Nisei were the largest single ethnic element. The usual pattern of urban residence was ethnic concentration in areas undergoing ecological change.

Within the ethnic enclaves the Japanese-language schools were the most important culturally conservative agency. The schools were centers of community activities embracing the whole locality and cutting across religious divisions, prefectural origins, and social strata. Here Japanese films were shown, speakers from Japan addressed the community, and the *engeikai* (a kind of dramatic club) displayed their skills in Japanese art forms. The language schools included some instruction in Japanese culture and history, and in some instances this was chauvinistic and militaristic. For the most part, however, schooling was conducted by untrained part-time teachers and the curriculum contained little more than routine instruction in reading and writing. The schools were often strongly resisted by the Nisei who, attending both public and language schools, had little time for other social activities. Wherever there was an appreciable amount of neighborliness between the Japanese family as a group and Caucasians, it was largely through the play activities of the children, and language-school attendance reduced the opportunities for such association.

Another conservative influence was the practice of visiting Japan. By going to Japan the Issei gained rewards and satisfactions for their achievements in America and exposed their children to Japanese culture. For the Issei, social status was measured by Japanese standards. Large sums were spent for American goods to be distributed among relatives in Japan; this show of wealth increased the prestige of the family.

Frequently parents left their Nisei children with relatives in Japan, and when these visits were prolonged to years and the children attended Japanese schools, the consequences were often culturally decisive. Such Nisei came to be known as *Kibei* when they returned to the United

States. The term Kibei refers to those whose cultural orientation had been decisively shaped by prolonged stays in Japan. Kibei is often misapplied to Nisei who made relatively brief visits to Japan. There is ample evidence that Nisei who visited Japan for short periods during their school years were actually alienated from Japanese culture. (See cases 3 and 6.)

Parents believed that by leaving their children in Japan or sending them there to study the family would be strengthened through cultural continuity. Plans were usually made for the family to rejoin the children in Japan or to send for them to return to the United States (*yobiyose*). Such plans often miscarried and children might be separated from their parents for years. When the parents failed to fulfill their plans, they had feelings of doubt and guilt about leaving their children in Japan. (See case 6, sec. i.) Even when the children rejoined the family in the United States, a sense of integration and solidarity often was not achieved. The Kibei, an "alien" within his family, was a source of embarrassment. Both parents and siblings were often unable fully to accept him with affection and respect. A full generation of dramatic change and increasing militarism separated the Kibei experience of Japanese society from that of the Issei. Most important, the militant component in prewar Japan instructed the Kibei to defend their Japanese cultural identity in aggressive ways, and this set the pattern of their interaction when they returned to the United States. Thus, contrary to parental expectations, the children's experience in Japan did not facilitate their communication with the Issei. But it did effectively reduce communication between the Kibei and their Nisei siblings and other contemporaries. The problem generated by these culture conflicts were so severe that the Kibei were isolated from the rest of the ethnic community.

By and large, Nisei associational activities were American both in form and content, and the Nisei were thus provided with a setting that was relatively free of traditional Japanese controls. In these associations, the Nisei explored and internalized American values. Even in such organizations as Buddhist churches which might naïvely be assumed to be agents of cultural conservatism, there rapidly emerged a set of Nisei forms and associations indistinguishable from their equivalents in the Protestant churches of middle-class white communities. Within these ethnically circumscribed associations the Nisei played acculturated roles which in interethnic situations would have required more aggressive self-confidence than they were able to marshal. In the

ethnic peer groups the Nisei found support for new standards and definitions of behavior which caused much intergenerational conflict in the
family and community. However, informal association with hakujin
was largely limited to the public-school environment.

ECONOMIC ADJUSTMENT

In the processes of economic adjustment, the Japanese had concentrated their activities in a few occupations (small-scale business in
ethnic enclaves, contract gardening, domestic service, fishing) and had
achieved a most important role in the production and distribution of
truck-garden crops.[5] The flow of Nisei into the occupations developed
by the Issei was a result of the convergence of several factors: the depression, which limited occupational opportunities that normally would
have been open to Nisei; the inability of the Nisei to break away from
the ethnic community, and the concomitant availability of relatively
secure employment in ethnic occupations; and the pressures toward
ethnic coherence in a period of crisis. Viewed in this light the apparent
choice for the Nisei of staying in the ethnic community or breaking
away was in fact no choice at all.

However, many Nisei who graduated from high school in the early
'thirties, encouraged by the high value given to education in the Japanese culture, chose college education as an alternative to entering ethnic
occupations. The convergence of economic conditions and cultural orientation raised the educational level of the Japanese Americans as a
group to the highest in the country. Although education was viewed
instrumentally, it provided an objective index of family status, prestige, and honor. Children were often educated at the cost of imposing
severe strains upon the family. (See case 5, sec. i.) *Gisei* (altruistic
sacrifice) is highly esteemed in the Japanese culture to compensate
family members who are deprived of benefits bestowed upon others,
and high expectations are placed upon the recipients of the benefits to
bring honor to the family through success in occupation and marriage.

A college degree offered no guarantee of securing the white-collar
jobs to which the Nisei as a group aspired, and the incongruity of college graduates taking employment in produce markets, gardening
routes, and small shops with scant prospects of advancement led to a
growing pessimism in the Japanese population. The Issei pointed to
this state of affairs as evidence that the Nisei must maintain their
Japanese identity. The Issei asserted they would be treated as Japanese
however they might deny this in their thoughts and actions. When the

Nisei were rebellious, they were reminded that despite their education they had failed to surpass the Issei's economic achievement. The flow of Nisei labor into ethnically defined occupations had important consequences for the group's adjustment to the society at large, for it restricted interethnic participation.

POLITICAL AND RELIGIOUS PARTICIPATION

The political participation of the Japanese population was limited and immature. Discriminatory legislation against the Japanese denied Issei the rights of citizenship. Consequently it remained for the Nisei to assume political leadership in mediating the group's relations with the dominant society. The extreme vulnerability of the population in an historically anti-Japanese region defined an ethnic-centered, defensive political strategy. Opportunities for participation in dominant political organizations were consequently limited to the race leaders at the level of the ward worker.

Although the Issei were reluctant to acknowledge the Nisei's increasing demands for adult status, they could not deny the fact that the community's representation within the dominant society would have to be mediated by the more acculturated Nisei. Because the Issei were ambivalent about granting Nisei leadership, the Nisei were largely excluded from decision-making responsibilities and restricted to performing an interpretive function. The importance of denying status and responsibility to the Nisei became immediately evident upon the outbreak of war when community leadership was destroyed by the FBI roundup of prominent Issei.

The permissive orientation of the Japanese culture toward religion favored the adherence of Japanese Americans to the dominant religious denominations. For many Nisei, church activities were more nearly a matter of sociability than of religious conviction. This attitude was reinforced in the home where religious forms were not closely integrated. Church membership was one way to relate the Nisei to the Japanese community.

The number of Christians in the Japanese population nearly equaled the Buddhists. However, as early as 1900 the Methodist Church, the denomination with the largest number of Japanese members, effectively separated the Japanese from their coreligionists. The occasional "interracial" meetings of Nisei and Caucasian youth groups were designed for group rather than individual interaction and emphasized the separation of Japanese from Caucasians within the same denomination.

FAMILY ADJUSTMENT

The Japanese family in America rarely participated as a unit in the larger society. We have already noted how the differential participation of its members in the dominant institutions created a wide range of acculturation in the population. Within the ethnic enclaves the family was a major conservative influence, and in most families acculturation of the Nisei was accompanied by conflict. Community and institutional supports, so essential to the maintenance of the Japanese family system in Japan, became less effective as the Nisei carried their acculturative influences into the family. The patriarchal family pattern was consequently attacked from within and without, and traditional authority and dependency relationships were strained.

This was emphasized by the generational division in the Japanese population. The Nisei entry into the ethnic job system had serious consequences for their ability to cope with intergenerational conflicts. The Issei were firmly in control of the ethnic economy, and the Nisei were dependent upon their patronage. This dependency tempered the Nisei's ability to challenge Issei authority. The Issei tended to view Nisei criticism of Japanese customs and practices as irresponsible if not impudent. Nisei organizations such as the JACL, which tried to cope with intergenerational problems, were defensive and in the final analysis dependent upon the Issei's tacit approval.

A comparison of the authority pattern of rural families with that of urban units suggests that the acculturative influences were less marked in rural areas, where the constraints imposed upon the Nisei by the internal structure of the family were strengthened by the community. The Issei controlled the agricultural economy and dominated the conservative rural community organizations. Even in farm families, however, where economic activity demanded a relatively high degree of supervision and coördination, the father was rarely able to obtain complete acceptance of his authority. (See cases 2, sec. i, and 5, sec. i.) Disagreements not only about the father's demands for work but also about the conduct of work were not infrequent. As the children gained economic maturity, their better knowledge of English facilitated transactions with the dominant society and placed them in a potentially superior position vis-à-vis their Issei fathers. This superiority was reinforced by the fact that the Issei farmer was legally prohibited from owning the land he operated. The California Alien Land Law, passed in 1913 and directed primarily at the Japanese,

made all Issei and any Nisei under twenty-one years of age ineligible
to own, buy, or lease land. The intent of this law was to relegate the
Japanese to the class of farm laborers or tenant farmers. Some Japanese circumvented the law by buying or leasing land through an
eligible agent. When their children came of age, the property could
be transferred, but the procedure, of course, entailed risks. The Alien
Land Law undermined the prestige and authority of the Issei. However, the increasing economic importance of the Nisei was not acknowledged by a corresponding degree of influence in the community. The
Nisei were confined to a junior status among the powerful Issei and
there was little encouragement for an independent Nisei community.

The relative absence of overt conflict in the transition from Issei to
Nisei control over farm enterprises is a testimony to the cultural conservatism of the rural domestic economy and the degree to which economic activity was woven into the fabric of family life. Where the farm
activity was concentrated in a few acres, it was, for the greater part
of the year, strictly a family enterprise in which the activities of its
members were adjusted to the demands of the work. This joint effort
was coördinated by the parents so that farm duties were associated
with obedience.

In the urban areas there were fewer family enterprises, and most
of these were small shops attached to residences. The more diversified
social and economic structure of the urban Japanese community provided less support for Issei dominance in home and community. When
the Nisei contributed economically to the family, their employment (in
fruit stands, nurseries, garages, etc.) enabled them more accurately
to measure their individual contributions. Furthermore, their work
was independent of the family head and free of his supervision. In
these circumstances urban Nisei could challenge the authority of the
father in their interpersonal relations without seriously disrupting
the family economy. This was not so in the rural setting where the
father's supervision of the closely interdependent economic activity
was the basis of his authority. Weakening of paternal authority over
the Nisei's noneconomic activities (education, peer group, dating)
necessitated fundamental changes in parent-child relations which
could threaten family integration. Thus, emancipation entailed more
conflict for the rural Nisei than for their urban counterparts who drew
support from an articulate peer group. By discussing their common
intergenerational problems urban Nisei gained a sophistication that
was lacking among rural Nisei. The adjustment of the latter to the

authority and dependency relationship was consequently more accommodative, and ordinarily entailed a gradual assumption of responsibilities for the farming enterprise under the father's over-all leadership. (See cases 5, sec. i, and 8, sec. i.)

In brief, the Japanese immigrants brought to the United States a set of cultural and social forms characteristic of Japan of the turn of the century. A racially visible group in a region of high sensitivity to Orientals, they experienced more than the usual stresses of immigrant life. Nevertheless, they integrated rapidly into the economic order and more than either the Chinese or Filipinos built stable family units. The children acculturated with great rapidity, achieved a remarkable educational level, and were the chief agency for the acculturation of their parents. The original Japanese family forms, therefore, underwent change and all but the most conservative rural families lost authority. Families often became the scene of culture conflict. The population was still undergoing critical change when it was suddenly confronted by the war and the consequent experiences referred to as evacuation and relocation.

CHAPTER II

THE ADMINISTRATIVE CONTEXT OF EVACUATION AND RELOCATION

IMPACT OF THE WAR

THE OUTBREAK of World War II found the Japanese community ill-prepared to meet the sudden stresses imposed upon it. Internal strains of group loyalties and identifications had eroded consensus and emphasized intergenerational conflicts. It is not certain—even though it is generally assumed—that the Manchurian invasion and the Sino-Japanese War resulted in an increase in either latent or manifest aggressions against the Japanese population on the West Coast. It is almost certain, however, that the Japanese had become highly sensitized to the ambiguity of their status, and the Alien Registration Act of 1940 underlined the defective status of the Issei.[1]

The growing crisis in the Pacific during the summer of 1941 precipitated a series of "loyalty demonstrations" and formal renunciation of dual citizenship status[2] by anxious Nisei under the leadership of the JACL. The loyalty issue raised before the war by the Nisei themselves was a recognition of their vulnerability. Despite the prolonged diplomatic crises, the Pearl Harbor attack found the Japanese on the West Coast psychologically and organizationally unprepared, and the most common reaction was one of utter disbelief followed by an acute sense of exposure. Movement was voluntarily restricted and, whenever possible, travel was avoided. Rumors that Japanese were being attacked and insulted heightened their feelings of fear and anxiety, but during the month of December the Japanese were comforted by the sympathy of their hakujin friends. In the first month of the war organized anti-Japanese sentiments were exceptional.[3] However, the serious consequences of the war for the Japanese population were dramatized by FBI raids, which resulted in the internment of some 5,000 Japanese during the first few weeks.[4] About one Japanese home in six had one member, usually the Issei father, interned. Issei were designated enemy aliens, their funds were impounded, the vernacular press was suspended, and travel was limited.

The major ethnic institutions collapsed, and community resources were dissipated. Language schools, Buddhist temples, *Nihonjinkai*, and other organizations were closed. The Japanese population indiscriminately destroyed possessions (art objects, letters, magazines,

[1] For notes to chap. ii, see p. 223.

photographs, etc.) which they feared might be suspect. Even those Issei who were not involved in nationalistic organizations searched their homes for evidence that might incriminate them. The destruction of Japanese items symbolized the population's awareness of their extreme vulnerability.

The Japanese population had hardly begun to adjust to the initial impact of the war when anti-Oriental elements on the West Coast began their activity.[5] Newspapers headlined the FBI raids for contraband, and reported and expressed increasing support for the evacuation of all Japanese aliens from the West Coast. Scattered acts of violence against Japanese, mostly by Filipinos, were magnified, distorted, and multiplied by rumors that swept through the Japanese community. Raids and arrests by the FBI in February, 1942, further demoralized the Japanese population. In almost every home Issei fathers were prepared to be picked up. The Japanese community was without leadership except for the Nisei-led JACL, which advocated full coöperation with the American authorities.[6]

However, rumors were already being circulated that the JACL leaders were turning informers in order to secure special treatment by the authorities and to gain possession of Issei holdings.[7] The focus of group hostility and resentment was sharpened by the JACL's declaration that it was the duty of the Japanese in America to prove their loyalty by aiding the authorities to apprehend suspicious persons. Arguments raged about whether Nisei could betray their Issei parents. From this it was a short step to open accusation of *inu* (dog, informer) against pro-American Nisei, and when the JACL urged the Japanese to coöperate in the evacuation, the majority of the population rejected its leadership and isolated its leaders. These preëvacuation events laid the foundations for acts of violence against some JACL leaders in the relocation centers.

The foundations of the JACL leadership were weak and could not sustain the internal stresses that were aggravated by the threat of the evacuation. Nor was the dominant community any better organized to cope with the sudden crisis of civil liberties. Groups that ultimately worked vigorously to ameliorate the status of the evacuees were unorganized or silent.

THE EVACUATION

By the end of January, 1942, two congressional committees, activated by West Coast pressure groups, were investigating means of evacuating the Japanese, including American citizens of Japanese ancestry.[8] On February 13 a joint meeting of the Congressional Committees on

Defense and on Alien Nationality and Sabotage passed a resolution recommending "... immediate evacuation of *all persons of Japanese lineage* and all others, aliens and citizens alike, whose presence shall be deemed dangerous or inimical to the safety of the defense of the United States from all strategic areas."[9] General DeWitt of the Western Defense Command was already drafting a memorandum in favor of mass evacuation. He issued it on February 14,[10] and five days later the President issued Executive Order No. 9066 authorizing the action.

The Tolan Committee hearings (February 21–March 12, 1942) were instituted at the behest of Carey McWilliams, Chief of the California Division of Immigration and Housing, with the intent of forestalling mass evacuation by giving a forum to moderate voices.[11] The hearings boomeranged, and testimony chiefly supporting evacuation was reported by the press. But these unanticipated consequences were irrelevant, for the Executive Order had been given and the administrative acts were being instituted. The most effective opposition could have done no more than ameliorate the terms of the evacuation. It is just possible that the detention of United States citizens in relocation centers might have been prevented.

The events immediately following Executive Order No. 9066 comprised the most confusing of the many wartime experiences encountered by the Japanese. General DeWitt did not immediately use the power given him by the Order but awaited Congressional endorsement.[12] On February 23 (four days after Executive Order No. 9066 was issued) the California coast near Santa Barbara was shelled by an unidentified vessel. This was the occasion for the publication of "eyewitness" accounts identifying the craft as a Japanese submarine and reports of signaling activities on shore. Two days later, on February 25, in the "Battle of Los Angeles" one to five unidentified planes were reported over the city which was blacked out. Antiaircraft guns were fired. Neither the vessel that reportedly attacked the Santa Barbara coastline nor the planes (if any) over Los Angeles have ever been identified as Japanese.[13] However, the two incidents were dramatized and gave new support to demands for the immediate removal of all persons of Japanese descent from the West Coast. In response to these demands, General DeWitt issued the following statement:

Military necessity is the sole yardstick by which the Army has selected the military areas from which the exclusion of certain groups will be required.

Public clamor for evacuation from non-strategic areas and the insistence of local organizations and officials that evacuees not be moved into their communities cannot and will not be heeded, for considerations of national security must come first.[14]

Grodzins asserts that DeWitt was very responsive to local interest groups and that military necessity was not the sole yardstick by which he arrived at his decisions.[15] On March 2, DeWitt issued Proclamation No. 1 designating the western halves of Washington, Oregon, and California, and the southern part of Arizona as Military Area No. 1, from which Japanese, German, or Italian aliens and *persons of Japanese ancestry* would be excluded. He announced that an evacuation program was being planned and advised the Japanese to evacuate the area voluntarily to "save themselves possible future trouble."[16]

After hastily liquidating their businesses and properties, some Japanese moved into the interior agricultural regions of the three western states. Their reception by local residents was frequently hostile. Some evacuees attempting to cross state lines into the Rocky Mountain states were met and turned back by vigilantes. The resulting confusion was so great that on March 27, roughly three weeks after he had advised voluntary evacuation, DeWitt issued Public Proclamation No. 4 forbidding further migration of Japanese from Military Area No. 1.

Forbidden to move, and faced with the prospect of being moved into detention centers at a proximate but unknown date, the Japanese communities were disorganized. To continue work in such circumstances seemed futile, and many Japanese quit their jobs or closed their businesses. Many Nisei children withdrew from school. Military curfews imposed upon the Japanese curtailed ordinary travel and visiting, hindered those who continued to work, and handicapped those who attempted to make arrangements for the disposal of their property. Idleness increased the sense of self-consciousness, exposure, and vulnerability. Widespread and acute insecurity deterred the people from group activities which might have ameliorated the accumulating tensions or have enabled them to explore a new basis of community solidarity.

THE RATIONALE OF ADMINISTRATIVE POLICIES

We shall not review here the long sequence of administrative decisions, their varied implementation, and their consequences. The interested reader is referred to a number of works for a view of this aspect of the evacuation.[17] A thoroughgoing treatment of the decision-making process and the assumptions and evaluations that directed the decisions has not been written. It is probably the most difficult and challenging task remaining for the social scientist interested in the evacuation.

An organizational analysis of administrative actions in the evacuation and detention of the Japanese population might well center on two irreconcilable approaches: (1) the logistical orientation which regarded the movement of a civilian population in its homeland as if it were a military operation; (2) a humanistic attitude which quite self-consciously rejected the concentration camp idea and was expressed in such decisions as the maintenance of the family unit and the ultimate objective of reintegrating the population into the national life. Some actions, such as General DeWitt's surprising utterance,[18] were in diametric opposition to American conceptions of due process and evidence, not to mention logic. On the other hand, when the administrative agencies dealt directly with individuals and families under their control, the strictures of humanity and respect for the individual strongly conditioned decision and act.

In the main, our analysis is based upon two kinds of documentation in addition to rather extensive observation, participant and otherwise. One kind is embodied in family histories that comprise the bulk of the work. The other documentation is drawn from official and semiofficial histories and records. In the remainder of this chapter we shall use this latter kind of documentation in unadorned form. We have done this despite the fact that it would have been easier for us and the reader if we had paraphrased the record rather than quoted it. The extensively quoted material is intended to minimize the intrusion of bias. It seems by all odds wiser in dealing with an historical event so recent and so tension-laden to let the record speak for itself when it can do so easily and clearly.

In the following pages we summarize very briefly the overt announcements and actions as they appeared to the Japanese population, setting the limits and the atmosphere within which the population had to adjust. The official histories often place a more than favorable construction on the course of events, but they are by and large remarkably frank. The presentation is chronological rather than topical in order to present a more accurate picture of the cumulative impact of administrative acts upon the decisions and adjustments of the Japanese population.

THE WARTIME CIVIL CONTROL ADMINISTRATION

The task of executing the unprecedented evacuation order was assigned to the Wartime Civil Control Administration (WCCA), created by the Commanding General of the Western Defense Command and Fourth

Army on March 11, 1942.[19] Tom C. Clark, then a special assistant to the Attorney General, was assigned to coördinate the many federal civilian agencies that took part in the evacuation program. The WCCA was held responsible for the first phase of the evacuation. The *Final Report* by the Western Defense Command and Fourth Army reads:

... The mission was clear cut: To devise and operate an evacuation and temporary settlement plan which would remove substantial numbers of people from strategic areas rapidly and safely, and with as little disturbance and loss as practicable to the evacuees and the coastal communities.[20]

Early in the development of WCCA policies the evacuation was separated from the problem of removing evacuees to more permanent relocation centers:

... It was concluded that evacuation and relocation could not be accomplished simultaneously. This was the heart of the plan. It entailed the provision for a transitory phase. It called for establishment of Assembly Centers at or near each center of evacuee population. These Centers were to be designed to provide shelter and messing facilities and the minimum essentials for the maintenance of health and morale. ...

... The program would have been seriously delayed if all evacuation had been forced to await the development of Relocation Centers. The initial movement of evacuees to an Assembly Center as close as possible to the area of origin also aided the program (*a*) by reducing the initial travel; (*b*) by keeping evacuees close to their places of former residence for a brief period while property matters and family arrangements which had not been completed prior to evacuation could be settled; and (*c*) by acclimating the evacuees to the group life of a Center in their own climatic region.[21]

Dispatch in the evacuation of the Japanese population was the overriding concern of WCCA, and this led to dislocation and demoralization. The Administration might better have served the objective of evacuating the population "with as little disturbance and loss as practicable to the evacuees and the coastal communities" had it properly assessed the problems of completing family and business arrangements and extended more effective service and assistance before the population was summarily evacuated.

The "operational technique" of the evacuation proceeded, in brief, according to the following plan:

1. "Registering and servicing" of the population at civil control stations located in various centers of Japanese concentration.

2. Movement of the population from civil control stations to assembly centers, which were constructed at race tracks, fairgrounds, and other facilities. This phase was completed by the end of August, 1942.

3. Movement of the population to more permanent relocation centers, most of which were situated east of the three West Coast states. The newly created War Relocation Authority (see below) assumed the responsibility for this phase of the evacuation which was not completed until November, 1942.

The "flow of evacuees" outlined above proceeded with few exceptions. Temporary deferments were issued to isolated individuals who were unable to complete settlement of personal or business property affairs. The bulk of deferments, however, were issued for medical reasons and to individuals of mixed ancestry or to non-Japanese married to Japanese. Approximately 1,740 evacuees were released directly from assembly centers as part of a farm labor recruitment program centered in the Rocky Mountain area.[22] These evacuees were given "furloughs" and were legally in the custody of the War Relocation Authority (WRA). With the exception of 332 persons who returned to the assembly centers to be transferred with their families to relocation centers, the farm labor recruits did not enter the centers operated by the WRA.

The assembly-center interval afforded the opportunity for a fresh assessment of the "military necessity" for continued evacuation. If "military necessity" was hard to justify at the beginning of the evacuation, it was even harder to defend in August, 1942, at the close of the assembly-center period. Nevertheless, the plans had been set for moving the population to the relocation centers, the program inexorably was put into operation, and the opportunity for a critical reëxamination of "necessity" and an early reversal of the program was ignored.

THE WAR RELOCATION AUTHORITY

Executive Order No. 9102, issued on March 18, 1942, created the War Relocation Authority, a civilian agency, to assume the responsibility for the care and administration of the Japanese population evacuated by the Army. The WRA was the administrative heir of the WCCA, the Army agency that administered the first phase of the evacuation. The Army terminated its responsibility for the evacuated population with the transfer of the final contingent of evacuees from Fresno Assembly Center to the Jerome Relocation Center on November 3, 1942. WRA was faced with developing policies to deal with a population that had been subjected to a mass manipulation without precedent in American history since the Indian removals of the nineteenth century.

Milton Eisenhower, Director of WRA during the first three months of its existence, issued the following policy statement on May 29, 1942:

By terms of the Order, the Authority is responsible for: (1) aiding the Army in carrying out the evacuation of military areas, (2) developing and supervising a planned, orderly program of relocation for evacuees, (3) providing evacuees with work opportunities so that they may contribute to their own maintenance and to the national program, and (4) protecting evacuees from harm in the areas where they are relocated. The first specific task of the Authority is to resettle some 100,000 alien and American-born Japanese evacuated from military areas of the far western states.[23]

The set of functions enumerated provided a wide latitude for the formulation of policy. The Authority could have viewed itself as an administrative agency, tacitly accepted the legitimacy of the notion of "military necessity," and governed the centers accordingly. Such an orientation would have sensitized the agency to the sort of pressures that had precipitated the evacuation. If the Authority endorsed the legitimacy of the evacuation, it would have been defined by the evacuees as a symbol of their incarceration. Under these conditions the Administration-evacuee antithesis would have been inevitable and extreme.

The second alternative would have taken the evacuation as *fait accompli* and would have striven for a neutralist role. The Authority would have neither justified nor rejected the rationale of the evacuation, and it would have dealt with the evacuees in a strictly legalistic fashion. This might have proved in the long run a better protection for the evacuees' interests and might have sustained the evacuee's capacity for independent judgment and independently initiated activity. It also might have protected the Authority against pressure from politicians and the press.

A third policy could have denied the legitimacy of the evacuation. This position would have been most responsive to the psychological conditions of the evacuated population. It would have interpreted the function of "protecting evacuees from harm" to include protection from further psychological and social stress. The Authority might then have asserted that although it had accepted the responsibility for administering the centers, the evacuation itself was not justified, the ambiguities and contradictions of the situation were not to be resolved by rationalizations of "military necessity," the principle of due process had been violated, and the evacuated population had a legitimate claim against the government for damages suffered. With such a policy the Authority would have assumed an elite function of defending democratic values. The Authority would then have been allied with the evacuees in pressing their demands for equitable treatment; and it would have counseled them about opportunities and limits of action at a particular time. It would have paid a heavy price for this policy in that it would have been vulnerable to charges of mollycoddling and subversion.

The official reports of the Authority indicate that the administrators of the program attempted to incorporate aspects of the first and third policy orientations and the inherent contradictions were too great to reconcile. The policy statement of May 29 illustrates this point and demonstrates an unawareness of the extent of disorganization and financial loss in the evacuated population.

> The objective of the program is to provide, for the duration of the war and as nearly as wartime exigencies permit, an equitable substitute for the life, work, and homes given up, and to facilitate participation in the productive life of America both during and after the war.... Initially, the Government will provide the minimum essentials of living—shelter, medical care, and mess and sanitary facilities—together with work opportunities for self-support.[24]

No matter how WRA conducted the centers, the question of the legality of detaining the evacuees concerned the Authority during its first months of existence.

> There were two questions which WRA had to face in connection with the detention issue: (1) whether the agency had legal authority to detain the evacuees without bringing charges against them; and (2) if such authority could be found, whether it was necessary and desirable to exercise it....
>
> By April 15 the Solicitor had produced a series of confidential memoranda which explored carefully the question of how far the courts might be expected to sustain the detention of the evacuees if circumstances should force upon the Authority a policy of detention....
>
> Detention of American citizens, however, was a vastly more complex, delicate, and debatable kind of question [than that of detaining aliens]. While it was clear that the rights and immunities of citizenship as set forth in the first Ten Amendments and spelled out by the courts were not lightly to be infringed, it was equally plain that the Constitution had not been devised to serve as a strait-jacket in time of global war.
>
> [The Solicitor concluded that the war powers of the President] are sufficiently broad and flexible to include the detention of American citizens "to whatever extent is *reasonably* necessary to the national safety in wartime...." On the additional question of whether citizens of Japanese descent could be singled out and treated as a class differently from all other citizens, he concluded that this could be done "if the discrimination can be shown to be related to a genuine war need and does not, under the guise of national defense, discriminate for a purpose unrelated to the national war effort."[25]

Internal Organization of the Centers

The assurance of the Solicitor's report, although not unqualified, defined the effective status of the evacuees over whom the Authority had assumed control. Barbed wire and watchtowers around the centers were constant reminders of this power, to the administrators as well as to the evacuees. The euphemism of "relocation center" was a feeble countersymbol to the immediate reality of physical constraints.

Beyond minimum essentials of life and protection, concessions were tendered at the pleasure of the Authority. The introduction of community participation and a degree of self-government were among these concessions. The first policy statement in this regard was issued on May 29, 1942. It called for

the election of a temporary council to advise the project director. It also provided for the selection of a chairman and other officers and the appointment of an executive and a judicial committee. Voting was extended to everyone eighteen years of age or older, but only citizens of the United States twenty-one years of age or over were eligible to hold office.[26]

Early discussions of community government indicated that the evacuees would have a degree of power and responsibility, and "each relocation community will be approximately what the evacuees choose to make it."[27]

A community government shall have as its objectives the training of residents of the community in the democratic principles of civic participation and responsibility; it shall assume the responsibility for the regulation of community life; it shall assume much of the responsibility for the formulation of policy and administrative direction of services and supply.

During the initial stages of settlement and community organization, it is recognized that the inexperience of the colonists and the exigencies of the administrative situation prohibit any broad delegation of authority. However, the success of project administration should be considered a direct expression of the delegation by the project director and the assumption by the community of the responsibilities of self-government.[28]

The initial policy, however, was radically revised at a conference in August, 1942.

As issues were clarified and decisions made, the earlier objectives of self-contained and self-supporting communities became subordinated to the point of view that the relocation centers were to be primarily temporary havens until it was possible for their residents to establish themselves in new communities or to return to their West Coast homes. There were to be created no incentives or symbols that would deter the outward movement.[29]

WRA's intial program for a War Relocation Work Corps proposed to develop suitable work projects for the evacuees at or near the centers. Such a program was to utilize the manpower in the centers in "a period when the Nation was buckling down to the biggest production job in its history and when wastage of human skills and energies in any sector of the economy could scarcely be tolerated."[30] The Administration also recognized the "prolonged idleness at the relocation centers would be exceedingly harmful to the evacuees themselves: it would, in all probability, sharpen the frustrations they were already feeling as a result of the evacuation and deepen their sense of isolation from the American scene."[31]

The Deputy Director said:

The entire future of the Japanese in America is dependent on their deeds during the emergency. If the Japanese assist in the war effort and prove, by constructive deeds, that they are loyal Americans, the public will recognize this fact. WRA does not desire the relocation center to have any more restrictions on it than is necessary, but whether or not Japanese can leave relocation centers during the emergency must depend on public opinion. Cooperation in the Food-for-Freedom Program and in other useful work by the Japanese is essential in the efforts of WRA to secure favorable public opinion for the Japanese.[32]

WRA's sensitivity to "public opinion" was clearly an overriding concern. The "necessary restrictions" upon work opportunities for the evacuees were defined by a Hearst press attack asserting that the evacuees "will be paid much more than the American soldiers fighting the country's battle overseas. . . . Whereas the base pay of the American private soldier is $21 a month, all of the employable Japanese men and women, alien and citizens alike, will be paid salaries ranging from $50 to $94 a month."[33] The Director's answer to this charge was that the Administration "had considered this scale, among others as gross wages, with deductions for room and board which would bring it into line with Army pay," and assurances were made that "the maximum rate of pay for evacuees working on public projects would not under any circumstances exceed the minimum rate of pay for the American soldier."[34] The plan which was finally devised provided for compensation for evacuee employment at the rate of $12, $16, or $19 per month. Employed evacuees and their dependents were given clothing allowances of from $2 to $3.75 per month. An employable evacuee who was out of work through no fault of his own received unemployment compensation payments of from $1.50 to $4.75 per month for himself and each of his dependents.

WRA's policy of providing work for all able-bodied adults led to overstaffing and "boondoggling." Evacuee productivity was low and work habits were lax. The Administration was faced with the

perennial problem of encouraging efficiency and conscientiousness among evacuee workers at the centers . . . many of whom . . . merely wished to "get by" with the least expenditure of time and effort ... and ... who were capable of good work performance but saw no reason to exert themselves unduly when the cash incentive was less than a dollar a day. Although WRA was greatly impressed in the beginning by the unquestioned reputation for energy and efficiency which the people of Japanese descent had built up as workers on the Pacific coast over a period of 25 years, it soon learned that these habits were not necessarily carried over into the economically constricted environment of government-operated centers.[35]

In an attempt to encourage the evacuees to relocate, WRA decided in the late spring of 1943 to revise its work policy. A 30 per cent reduction of the evacuee payrolls in all centers was ordered, and evacuee jobs were eliminated unless they could be classified as "essential" or "desirable."[36] The revised policy met with resistance and protest by the evacuees, but the Administration considered its action generally beneficial because it eliminated over-staffing, encouraged evacuees to consider relocation, and "drove home an effective and early warning that WRA was wholly sincere in its determination to close the centers at the earliest feasible date."[37]

The development of WRA's community self-government policy was characterized by a chronic lack of communication between the Administration and the center residents. An October, 1942, statement of the Solicitor of WRA read in part:

Community self-government among the evacuees is not being instituted as an end in itself, even though it is rich in intrinsic values, but is rather a means to the larger end of effective administration of the whole program of the War Relocation Authority.... Administrative Instruction No. 34 constitutes no Utopian's dream of an ideal government, but rather a practical administrator's attempt to preserve order in a somewhat special type of community.[38]

In summarizing the nature of community participation, the official WRA history states:

Community government became in actuality an adjunct of administration. Recreation and cultural activities were partly financed and almost entirely supervised and regulated by a non-evacuee staff. The other community services became an adjunct of a managerial hierarchy, with policy and supervision arising from outside the relocation community. It is true that many of the workers were drawn from the community, but the control rested in what came to be known as the "appointed staff." This managerial-administrative combination was established in practice and policy early in the history of actual center management and was never relaxed during the history of the Authority.[39]

The Issei were ineligible to hold elective offices in the center. This policy was actively protested by large segments of the evacuee population and provided much discussion on the administrative level. Nevertheless, the limitation was retained. On August 24, 1942, the Authority and its Solicitor's office maintained that

since the objective of WRA was to create a community as nearly American in its outlook and organization as possible, policy should conform with American practice, and only citizens should vote and hold office. Those concerned with the problem of public relations and possible criticism of the program maintained that it would be unwise to establish communities in which there was a likelihood that the governing council would be controlled by aliens. They pointed out that control might pass to those who were not in sympathy with the objectives of the Authority or with the war effort.

It was further pointed out that the evacuation of citizens from the West Coast was of doubtful constitutionality and had certainly created grave doubts in the minds of many Nisei as to their rights under the Constitution of the United States. Those taking this position argued that it was desirable to give some added recognition of the citizens beyond that extended to aliens to indicate to them that the Federal Government was cognizant of their status. . . . This point of view was advanced by representatives of the Japanese American Citizens League who were at that time in consultation with officials of the War Relocation Authority.[40]

There were, however, many protests against the exclusion of Issei from elective office. One petition stated that there was a

strong unity of purpose between citizens and non-citizens in all matters which are of vital concern to the people of this community . . . In view of this situation, to permit the citizens alone to hold elective positions would undermine seriously the harmony which so happily exists between the citizens and non-citizens.[41]

The Director of WRA replied that the Nisei deserved special recognition:

In addition to making elective offices open only to evacuees who are citizens of the United States, it is our intention to give them preference in considering application for leave from relocation centers, in assignment of work opportunities, and in other respects. . . . We are [also] of the opinion that if the Niseis [*sic*] alone are eligible for membership in the community council, the general character of the action taken by the community council will be more in keeping with American institutions and practices.[42]

In the light of the intergenerational problems reviewed above (see chap. i), the "harmony which so happily exists between citizens and non-citizens" was hardly an accurate estimate of the facts. The policy of excluding Issei from the council could serve only to widen the breach between the two generations. The policy which intended to strengthen the status of the Nisei bred conflict in the centers, such as the incident known as the "Manzanar Riot."[43]

The center environment tended to develop a culture unlike the ancestral Japanese culture, the composite culture of the ethnic enclaves, and the culture of the hakujin society. It emphasized prescribed official values, the importance of daily routine, orderly relations, the round of prepared activities, and responsiveness to announcements and directives. It contained unofficial elements emphasizing the contrast between administrative personnel and evacuees and specifying the conditions under which resistance to the Administration was approved. Clearly, much of this culture was so peculiar to the center environment that it had little or no transfer value to "outside" life.

The normal expectancies for the acculturation of the young Nisei to American forms were changed in several important ways. As we have already observed, they had to adjust to the unique properties of the center environment. More important, by being removed from the larger society, they lost contact with Caucasian youth and teachers at a critical time in the socialization process. Their lives and their learning were far more "Japanese" than they would have been. It is easy to recognize the consequences of this in the postwar period. Nisei who spent their early school years in the center are culturally more differentiated from the general population than are their older siblings whose early schooling and adolescent socialization occurred in the free society.

The older Issei were also strongly influenced by the different environment. Their association with other Issei reinforced conservative culture tendencies. It would be too simple to say that they were "reacculturated" to original Japanese forms, for most of them were too far away in point of time and experience from the sources of Japanese culture. Furthermore, the original forms had been modified in the process of acculturation in a host environment. In referring to this tendency, therefore, we should think of it as the reinforcement of the subculture of an immigrant enclave rather than of the authentic culture of Japan.

Although the older Nisei were not unaffected by these events, they were in general much less affected. Therefore, intergenerational stress was further increased by differences in the impact of the center environment on the different parts of the population. The older Nisei were more responsive to official policies and were earlier and more often eligible for relocation. As the relocation process proceeded the residue in the centers became more "Japanesy" and the regressive trend in acculturation was fostered.

MASS REGISTRATION AND BEGINNING OF RELOCATION PROGRAM:
FEBRUARY, 1943

What WRA attempted to give to the Nisei with its grant of political power it took away when it joined with the Army in a combined enlistment and loyalty registration program. On January 28, 1943, the Secretary of War announced plans for the formation of an all-Nisei combat team, and the Army sent recruiting officers to the centers. For the registration of all male Nisei above seventeen years of age, the Army had prepared a four-page questionnaire on the individual's past history and his loyalty." WRA required similar information for the implementation of its relocation program and consequently Army recruitment and leave-clearance registrations were combined.

We shall not analyze this particular questionnaire as a fact-finding instrument, although it may be arbitrarily asserted that it was a faulty device as questionnaires go. Assuming, however, that it was as good as possible, serious questions emerge about the wisdom and propriety of its use. Social scientists are well aware that questionnaires are defensible instruments only when administered to populations of known literacy, when the problems posed are simple, when the alternatives are clear, and when the setting for questionnaire administration is uniform and neutral. None of these conditions obtained in this case. Furthermore, it is ironic that a population not to be trusted with its freedom was trusted to give answers on which its freedom later depended.

The mass registration program came as a surprise to the center residents. In formulating the registration policy and in the conducting of the program, the Authority

ignored the existence of the councils, thus overlooking the possibility of utilizing the councils' influence and means of disseminating information among the residents. The plan agreed upon by WRA and the War Department provided that the initial announcement of the visit of the Army team should be made by the project director through the project newspaper.... It was not until considerable resistance to the registration had developed and the program was under way that appeal was made to the councils. By that time confusion was widespread.[45]

By not consulting the community councils at the outset, the Administration generated much resistance. By amalgamating its registration program with the Army's recruitment, the Authority created a confusion and anxiety that colored the attitudes of the population toward all future policies. As it was administered, the registration program destroyed the small security built up in the course of adjusting to center life. The demand for the affirmation of loyalty, the recruitment of the Nisei of military age, and the implied threat of forced relocation comprised the extreme instance of arbitrary manipulation and revived all the latent resentment and cynicism of the evacuees.

In each center the registration program produced high emotional tension, and in some centers a crisis situation. It raised issues of major importance in the lives of evacuees—equality of citizenship, the obligation of military service, and Issei status. In addition to the objection of many Nisei to the segregated nature of the proposed military service, many felt that they were being forced to volunteer for military service whereas other Americans normally were waiting to be drafted....

Prospective volunteers were concerned about what might happen to their Issei parents if they were killed in battle. They knew that their parents could not inherit real estate under the laws of the States in the evacuated area. They wondered if their enemy alien parents would be eligible for GI allotments.[46]

The anxiety aroused by the registration policy was still greater among the Issei, for it struck at the security provided in the Japanese family system. The prewar adjustment of the Japanese family to the dominant society was oriented primarily toward the future of the Nisei in America. Most Issei, handicapped by discriminatory laws as well as linguistic and cultural difficulties, could not fully realize the opportunities presented by American society. Within their ethnic enclaves they concentrated upon a narrow range of economic specialities, but they had greater ambitions for their American-born children. The Issei identified education as the major instrument for advancement, and their devotion to the task of providing educational opportunities resulted in the high educational level attained by the Nisei. In the few years immediately preceding the war, the older Nisei came of age, and the Issei were beginning to realize the product of their labor.

Old-age security among the Japanese is institutionalized in the practice of *inkyo* (in which aged parents are relieved of economic and social responsibilities by the eldest son). Although the evacuation had swept away their hard-won economic security, the security of the integral family unit had largely survived. In threatening to separate the Issei and Nisei, the registration also threatened to remove the essential condition for the postwar adjustment of the Issei. The registration program denied the Issei the secure present within which to adjust to a disrupted past and an uncertain future. In the face of these conditions, it is remarkable that it was possible for so many Issei to assert that their children were Americans who should serve their country loyally.

The administration of the program exacerbated the tensions. The registration questionnaire posed an impossibly confusing question. It read:

"Will you swear unqualified allegiance to the United States of America and for-swear any form of allegiance or obedience to the Japanese Emperor, or any other foreign government, power, or organization?"

To the great majority of the Issei . . . this question was not only unfair but almost impossible to answer in the affirmative. It called upon them to renounce the only nationality they had, in the face of the known fact that they could not possibly acquire citizenship in the United States. To answer it affirmatively, they claimed, would have made them "men without a country."

Within a few hours after the registration started, the Issei reaction to this question at the Manzanar center was so pronounced that the Assistant Project Director called the Washington office . . . and asked permission to use a substitute question in the registration of the Issei which could be more acceptable. . . . 4 days after the beginning of the registration, instructions were sent to all centers that the question for the Issei could be revised to read:

"Will you swear to abide by the laws of the United States and to take no action which would in any way interfere with the war effort of the United States?"[47]

The question in this form was acceptable to the majority of the Issei, but much damage had already been done. The protest against the wording of the "loyalty question," apparently a small thing in itself, was symptomatic of the extremity to which the population had been brought.

Considered in the perspective of 3 years of hindsight, the mass registration and Army Recruitment program still stands out as one of the most turbulent periods in the history of the War Relocation Authority. From the standpoint of Army recruitment, the program was a moderate success. Over 1,200 Nisei volunteered for Army service at the 10 centers and over 800 of these passed the loyalty tests as well as the physical examinations and eventually formed the original mainland nucleus of the 442nd Regimental Combat Team. From the standpoint of leave clearance, the program accomplished its main purpose of providing a backlog of application forms [*sic*] and thus speeding up the whole relocation process. Out of nearly 78,000 center residents who were eligible to register, almost 75,000 eventually filled out the forms. . . .[48]

SEGREGATION PROGRAM: AUGUST–OCTOBER, 1943

The evacuees assumed that WRA would select those who would be required to relocate on the basis of the loyalty question. "Rumors were current in many projects, during registration, that the Government would separate the 'disloyals' from the 'loyals,' and then would disperse the 'loyals' throughout the country."[49]

The evacuees viewed a positive reply to the question as expressing a willingness to be relocated, to be moved for the third time in a single year. This was an accurate estimate of WRA's intent. The relocation of the Japanese population to areas outside the West Coast had become the major policy, but pressures from politicians, from the press, and from the Army opposed the relocation of a population whose "loyalty" was assumed to be questionable. Within the Authority, administrators were calling for more effective methods of dealing with "disloyal" elements in the center. The registration program was designed to achieve the dual purpose of pacifying these external and internal demands and of implementing the relocation program. Assuming the validity of measuring "loyalty" by questionnaire methods, the segregation of the "disloyal" from the "loyal" population was an inevitable consequence. The project directors were unanimously in favor of the segregation program, and Dillon S. Myer, Director of WRA,

who still had rather substantial personal misgivings about the wisdom of segregation, felt that he had almost no alternative except to go along. Remarking that he still regarded relocation as "the only civilized way" of separating the two types of evacuees, he nevertheless made segregation the first order of business of the agency....[50]

The number of evacuees who answered the "loyalty" question in the negative and who requested repatriation was larger than WRA had expected. A belated analysis of the pressures on the evacuees and of the motivations underlying responses to the questionnaire led the Administration to reëxamine the "disloyal" respondents.

Under the policy finally adopted, all those who had requested the privilege of moving to Japan and who had not withdrawn their requests before July 1, 1943, were designated for segregation without further consideration. The second major group of potential segregants included those who had answered "no" to the loyalty questions during registration. In contrast to the repatriate group, these persons were given special hearings and an opportunity to reconsider and explain their original answers. Those who satisfied the hearing officers that their original answers were not motivated by actual feelings of disloyalty were recommended for clearance; those who stood by their original answers or failed to convince the hearing officers of the sincerity of their reconsideration were designated for segregation. The third group of segregants took in all those who were not included in the first two groups but who were denied leave clearance by the Director of WRA on the basis of some accumulation of adverse evidence in their records. The fourth group consisted of the immediate family members of the segregants who chose to remain with them.[51]

WRA's segregation policy permitted "loyal" members of a family to be segregated with "disloyal" respondents. Thus, a "no, no" response of one member was sufficient to qualify the whole family for segregation.

The family could therefore be maintained as a unit without forfeiting the loyalty status of the children.

The Tule Lake Relocation Center in northern California was chosen as the segregation center for about 18,800 people. By the end of October, 1943, the major reshuffling of the population was finished. The segregation movements having been completed, dossiers of the "loyal" population were subjected to an additional clearance check.

In all cases where the review committee felt, and the Director agreed, that further investigation was needed ... the applicant's docket was placed in a "stop" file at the center, and arrangements were made for a hearing to be held by a Board composed of several members of the center staff.... Out of over 11,000 cases in which hearings were held, approximately 8,600 were eventually granted leave clearance, over 1,400 were denied, and around 1,300 were not finally passed upon.[52]

The first six months of 1943 showed a sharp increase in the number of evacuees who were permanently relocated. As early as July, 1942, WRA policy had made it possible for citizen evacuees to leave the centers, but by the end of the year less than 900 had relocated. About 2,900 additional evacuees were outside the centers on seasonal and short-term leaves. By the end of June, 1943, over 9,000 citizens and aliens had left the centers, and by the end of 1943 more than 17,000.[53]

The great majority of those who left the centers in 1943 were Nisei between the ages of 18 and 30.[54] In a rather typical situation a Nisei son or daughter would go out on indefinite leave, leaving Issei parents and other family members behind in the center.[55] This movement tended to alter the composition of the center population rather gradually but quite distinctly.... It became inescapably apparent that the winnowing effects of the relocation program were going to make the relocation centers somewhat harder places to manage and that the relocation effort itself would become increasingly difficult as time went on....[56]

The Authority recognized that, so long as the West Coast continued to be closed to evacuees, it was impossible to achieve a complete depopulation of the centers. However, it was expected that many thousands would leave quickly under new relocation procedures.[57] When this expectation did not materialize, it was a considerable shock to many WRA officials to learn that, in spite of desirable economic opportunities, good public acceptance, and continued relaxation of security measures by the Army, many, if not most of the evacuees, preferred the familiar institutional life of a relocation center to the unexperienced conditions of life in an unfamiliar American community. The enigma of people choosing the security behind barbed wire and armed guards rather than the freedom of normal society was not easily understood. It was felt by many that a combination of pressure, salesmanship, and incentive would do the job.[58]

The Authority's approach to the problem of combining "pressure, salesmanship, and incentives" to promote relocation among the evacuees was presented to the center population in a memorandum issued on October 28, 1943. It stated: "A progressive relocation program can be achieved only through the full and complete participation and coöperation of the evacuee population; and there should be increased delegation of responsibility to the community council and other evacuee groups to make their participation possible."[59]

The Authority's invitation to the evacuees received a weak response which varied from center to center. Relocation continued disconcertingly slow until scheduled relocation was begun in June, 1945. (See below.)

In January, 1944, Selective Service, which had been discontinued for Nisei shortly after the outbreak of the war, was reinstituted. The action introduced another confusing element into the relocation program. Even before the war, the Issei had become increasingly dependent on the Nisei in coping with the dominant society. As WRA urged the evacuees to relocate, the draft removed the Nisei, the very ones who could be counted on to adjust to relocation most effectively. Consequently, "bitterness and resentment which had lain dormant for several months were expressed in violent emotional outbursts."[60] Petitions to the President, the Secretary of War, the Director of WRA, and other governmental agents were drafted by the community councils, protesting the reinstitution of Selective Service without the reinstitution of civil rights for the Nisei and their families. At the Heart Mountain Relocation Center, open and active resistance to the draft developed, and eighty-five Nisei were eventually convicted for failing to comply with the Selective Service Act. They contended that full restoration of civil rights must be a precondition to reinstitution of Selective Service.[61]

Although there was a certain amount of undeniable logic in this contention, WRA attempted to point out that this line of reasoning was likely to prove highly ineffective with a still-unconvinced American public and that it actually meant "putting the cart before the horse." After the initial upsurges of protest and bitterness had spent themselves, the community council leaders and the more stable element of the Issei population at most centers eventually came to accept the WRA position and began to urge that Army service by the Nisei offered the most practical opportunity for demonstrating loyalty and gradually winning back the full citizenship rights that were being sought.[62]

Throughout the summer of 1944, the Nisei units—the 442nd Regimental Combat Team and the 100th Infantry Battalion composed of Hawaiian Nisei—made an impressive military record, and WRA undertook to exploit this record in improving the popular image of Japanese Americans in general.

By 1944 WRA had increased the number of field offices, established administrative agreements with the Social Security Board for service and assistance to relocated evacuees, made arrangements with the National Housing Agency for advice and assistance in regard to housing, and stimulated civic organizations in problems of evacuee adjustment. Within the centers, the Authority instituted family counseling service, Japanese from relocated areas were sent to the centers to relate their experiences on the "outside," and representatives of potential employers were invited to visit centers for recruitment purposes. Although relocation increased during the early months of 1944, the number of persons absent from the centers was about 3,000 less in December than in September.[63]

No amount of successful relocation by families with similar problems seemed to convince them that they [the remaining residents] should do likewise. Center living was being accepted as a normal way of life by many people, and complacency in regard to it was common. Apathy marked the attitude of an increasing number, and it was apparent that continued center living was not only demoralizing, but was tending to disintegrate the fiber of a people who had, previous to evacuation, been unusually self-reliant, sturdy, and independent.

Children were being especially affected by the segregated nature of camp life, by lack of contact with other Americans. It was also apparent that the majority of the people remaining in the centers could neither continue living in them without great personal and social loss to themselves and to the Nation, nor could they be induced by voluntary methods to relocate. It was believed that most of the people would leave voluntarily if they could return to their former west coast homes.[64]

RESCISSION AND CENTER LIQUIDATION PROGRAM: DECEMBER, 1944

As early as March 11, 1943, the Director of WRA described problems of center morale and the evacuees' resistances to relocation to the Secretary of War, suggesting that the revocation of the Exclusion Order was a precondition to the successful reintegration of the population into American society.[65] However, it was not until December 17, 1944, that the War Department issued the rescission of the order. On December 18, 1944, WRA announced that all centers were to be closed within six months to a year after January 2, 1945, the date when the rescission became effective. At the time of WRA's announcement, 79,770 people remained in the centers. The Director cited the following reasons for adopting the liquidation policy:

1. For their own welfare, the evacuees need to get back into the life of the usual American community. Center living is generally destructive of good work habits, of the sense of responsibility on the part of family heads, and does not provide normal family living conditions.

2. The nation is in need of the manpower represented by the center population.

3. Appropriations for the maintenance of the centers would be difficult to obtain after the rescission.

4. The concentration of the Japanese in centers makes them more vulnerable to their enemies since the centers tend to heighten the impression that their loyalty is in question.

5. The wartime period of high employment presents favorable conditions for securing relocation opportunities.[66]

The Administration anticipated an immediate return of evacuees to the West Coast and the field offices were geared to slow down the movement.

However, a survey of the situation in April 1945 indicated that most evacuees still residing in the centers were in no hurry to return to the evacuated area. This made necessary the application of a vigorous program to stimulate resettlement to the West Coast States, similar to that which had been necessary to induce relocation eastward. It had been learned, also, that the relocation job locally on the west coast was essentially the same as in other parts of the country—that it consisted of finding jobs and housing for resettlers as well as securing favorable community acceptance.[67]

At first the evacuees did not believe that WRA would evict them from the centers or the Authority would be able to close the centers within a year. To counteract this attitude, the Director visited all the centers in order to state the policy publicly. Nevertheless, the belief persisted among evacuees that some centers would be maintained.

On February 16, 1945, at the suggestion of the Topaz, Utah community council, representatives of all the center councils except Manzanar and Tule Lake met at Salt Lake City to discuss problems raised by the WRA announcement.[68] The conference produced a list of twenty-one recommendations based on a "statement of facts" as perceived by the evacuees:

1. Mental suffering has been caused by the forced mass evacuation.

2. There has been an almost complete destruction of financial foundations built during over a half century.

3. Especially for the duration, the war has created fears of prejudices, persecution, etc., also fears of physical violence and fears of damage to property.

4. Many Issei (average age is between 60 and 65) were depending upon their sons for assistance and support, but these sons are serving in the United States armed forces. Now these Issei are reluctant to consider relocation.

5. Residents feel insecure and apprehensive towards the many changes and modifications of WRA policies.

6. The residents have prepared to remain for the duration because of many state-

ments made by the WRA that relocation centers will be maintained for the duration of the war.

7. Many residents were forced to dispose of their personal and real properties, business and agricultural equipment, etc., at a mere trifle of their cost; also they drew leases for the "duration," hence have nothing to return to.

8. Practically every Buddhist priest is now excluded from the west coast. Buddhism has a substantial following, and the members obviously prefer to remain where the religion centers.

9. There is an acute shortage of housing, which is obviously a basic need in re-settlement. The residents fear that adequate housing is not available.

10. Many persons of Japanese ancestry have difficulty in obtaining insurance coverage on life, against fire, on automobiles, on property, etc.[69]

The list of twenty-one recommendations included provisions for financial aid in the form of loans and grants to the evacuees, priorities for purchase of essential goods lost during the evacuation, financial aid to investigate relocation possibilities,[70] arrangements for reinstating civil service workers, police protection, and compensation for property lost during the period of internment.

WRA replied in a document which presented point by point comments.

In general this document stated that solutions to atypical situations and problems would have to be worked out on an individual basis and could be met only as examples came to the attention of the Authority. It explained how some of the suggestions were not feasible, while others were already an established part of WRA policy, sometimes in a form more generous than that requested. It pointed to plans already implemented for cooperation with existing Government and civic bodies, summarizing the definite progress which had been made in reintegrating evacuees into American communities.[71]

In the first six months of 1945, 17,485 people had relocated, but the movement fell off in June, leaving 62,558 still in the centers. In the latter group there were about 18,000 people who were considered "un-relocatable" owing to detention orders by the Department of Justice or the Army. The remaining 44,000 people were apparently planning to stay until the centers were closed.

In order to prevent a final residue as well as to adjust to transportation and housing problems, WRA initiated a series of steps calculated to effect terminal departure of all residents.

Announcement was made on June 22 that Units II and III at Colorado River (Poston) Relocation Center and the Canal Camp at Gila River were to be closed in September, and that the residents were not to be moved to another center or to the remaining camps at Poston and Gila River, but must relocate.[72]

On July 13 WRA announced the closing dates for all centers and emphasized the finality of this notice by the curtailment of operations and services. The standards on which services should be curtailed were based on the extent to which services affected relocation. All residents were required to set the place and date of their departure. Those who refused to do so were to be sent to the places from which they were evacuated.

This was followed by an administrative notice, dated August 1, which provided for scheduling the departure of all remaining center residents during the last 6 weeks of the centers' existence. In effect, this plan was a practical device for arranging an even flow of evacuees to the outside during the closing period. It was adopted only after careful consideration and weighing of many factors.[73]

The Director wrote to the project directors:

... we should not lose sight of the reason for scheduling terminal departures during the last weeks. This is in no sense a punitive measure. It is intended merely to enable us to do a good administrative job. We need a relatively even flow during the last few weeks so that we may continue to give individual assistance to center residents in completing their relocation plans and so that we may schedule the use of transportation facilities in such manner as to avoid last minute hardships.[74]

All centers were closed on or before the scheduled date. Thousands of evacuees who were forced to relocate on schedule were placed in temporary housing installations, most of them former Army camps, by joint arrangement with the War Department and the Federal Public Housing Authority. In December, 1945, the Director instructed district offices along the West Coast to conduct an intensive interview program among the evacuees to determine the kinds of problems they were encountering. Housing was the most pressing problem, and WRA attempted to help evacuees find permanent housing. WRA was to be liquidated by June 30, 1946, and the agency faced the problem of emptying its housing facilities by that date. Repeated attempts to remove evacuees from temporary housing to more adequate quarters failed in many instances, particularly in the Los Angeles area. WRA found it necessary to arrange for the Federal Public Housing Authority to take over the housing installations in order to meet the Authority's June 30 deadline.

Center closings were a Herculean task for the appointed staff and were not effected without confusion and some discomfort on the part of the evacuees. For some of the aged and for a small percentage of weaker individuals, the closing days were periods of real mental distress. However, for the greater majority of the people, the end of a long period of indecision came as a welcome relief, and most of those departing looked forward with interest and curiosity, and in general, with considerable assurance to returning home.[75]

We wish to remind the reader that the foregoing use of official records and historical reviews of the WCCA and WRA programs is not meant to imply an endorsement of the judgments and findings of the reports. We feel rather that the official record rarely needs further analysis or discussion. We have, however, occasionally succumbed to the temptation to underscore interpretations alternative to the official ones.

CHAPTER III

THE FRAMEWORK FOR DECISIONS

CENTER ORGANIZATION AND FAMILY CONTROLS

IN CONSIDERING the complexities of the family decision-making process, the intent of administrative policies must be distinguished from their consequences. As we shall see, the center environment profoundly affected group decisions and actions. The Administration's implicit assumption of pure rationality on the part of the evacuees with regard to the problems posed by its policies aggravated an already stressful situation. The confusion resulting from the wide disparity between the Administration's definitions of situations and those of the evacuees was further compounded by the sequence of "corrective" policies.

Among the decisions made at the outset of the evacuation program to "guide the evacuation along quite different lines than had been followed in the military evacuation of areas in European countries"[1] was the policy that the evacuation would not split family units or communities where this could be avoided. This policy was informed by the European experience of separating women and children from the adult male members of the family which

removes the normal economic support of the family and forces it to dissipate its resources. This in turn creates a community problem of dependency and disrupts the entire organization of the family. Only of slightly less significance than the decision to evacuate entire family units, was the decision to move communities together so far as this was possible under the pressure of the program. ... The basic principle of maintaining communities was adopted to maintain a natural community and economic balance and to preserve desirable institutions by moving each family with its relatives and friends.[2]

Although sociological and humanitarian considerations underlay these broad decisions, they were not further implemented. The evacuation of the family as a unit did not ensure its maintenance as an institution. (Even less did the evacuation of fragments of neighborhoods ensure the transfer to the centers of cohesive communities.) Indeed, the immediate impact of barracks housing with its fragmenting consequences for family organization would have suggested the need for important compensatory family activities if the group was to be sustained. In case 8, for example, the family unit was physically broken up and individual adjustment became determined in large part by associations outside the family.

[1] For notes to chap. iii, see p. 226.

Families were housed in one-room "apartments" (average size: 25 by 25 feet) in modified military barracks. In some cases two families, frequently strangers to each other, shared an apartment. The thin partitions, which separated an apartment from those adjoining, were meager protection of privacy. Family quarrels and celebrations alike were never free from the intrusions of visitors or neighbors, and the group was always constrained by the thought that the community was just outside the room.

The style of life was that of a modified barracks street. Community messhalls, lavatories, showers, and washrooms served the residents of a block of more than fifty families. The organization of the messhall did not explicitly provide for family dining, and the important mealtime socialization of children was hampered. The children often ate with their friends or left the messhall as their parents arrived. After meals, the children rushed in and out of the barracks on their separate ways. The limitation of space and the elimination of routine family activities restricted opportunities for interaction. If all members were in the barracks at the same time, it was more by accident than plan, and there was little occasion for the repair of a deteriorating group morale. In this setting the barracks served only as a place to rest and sleep. It was housing in the most physical sense of the word, and through the months of occupancy few residents could think of the barracks as home.

The contraction of family activities emancipated its members who channeled their new-found leisure into other associations. The Administration provided for increased leisure in a community recreation department, which established a recreation hall in each block, as well as an over-all program encouraging the development of hobbies, sports, and associations almost entirely differentiated along age, sex, and generational lines. Thus the family found few supports in a recreational program that emphasized individual rather than family participation. The administrative personnel who organized and directed recreational activities had a summer-camp notion of community participation, concentrating upon the integration of the individual into the larger peer group.

The concern of the Administration for the "normal economic support of the family" was not manifest in its employment policy. The standard pay rate of $12 to $19 per month hardly retarded the dissipation of meager economic resources. Most families had to maintain payments on fixed obligations such as insurance. Many felt the necessity of masking the starkness of the barracks, and in some cases spent considerable sums.

The monotonous and unappetizing messhall fare "costing no more than 45 cents per person per day"[3] was usually supplemented by purchases at the canteen. The clothing allowance was a mere token considering the extreme climatic conditions of the center locations. Families with young children were particularly affected since they usually received the earnings of only one member.

More mature families with older Nisei children were able to draw upon the earning power of several members and thus partly alleviate the drain upon family resources. However, in contrast to the prewar pattern, the economic activity of the family in the center was not an integrated enterprise. The Administration employed workers as individuals and, apart from clothing allowances, did not treat the family as a unit. With the minimum essentials of living provided by the government, the wages earned by children were spent for small luxuries.

In the center the Nisei experienced a degree of economic independence relatively rare in prewar families. In case 2 a large farm family, which had worked as an integrated productive unit, found itself scattered through a number of occupations. In the center the children were employed in unrelated jobs. Each individual dealt and was dealt with as a separate bargaining agent and received small wages for which he did not need to account to the rest of the family. The possibilities for the maintaining of any aspects of the family economy were therefore prejudiced. In case 10 the eldest son's strong reaction to his prewar economic and social dependence changed not only the economic unity of the family but also the pattern of parental authority. This independence of the Nisei undermined one of the supports for family organization. In the "economically constricted environment" of the center the Issei's traditional authority was overridden by Administration policies. The Issei received neither more nor less compensation than did his children. In effect, the center attenuated the Issei's control over his children by diminishing both the economic and social bases of his authority.

The maintenance of family solidarity and integration in the center increasingly depended upon the family's ability to draw upon the affectional resources of the group. The family's use of affection as a defense against deteriorative center influences was limited by its prewar character. Affectional bonds served to integrate families confronted with diverse situations in cases 4 and 7. In case 4—concerning a family with unusually strong ties of affection—the only child (a female) was among the first Nisei to leave her family in the center to relocate to the Middle West. This action was not only permitted by the parents but was actively encouraged by them and the family group maintained a high degree of solidarity through frequent correspondence. Case 7 presents an even more striking instance of affectional strength. The interned Issei father, having decided to repatriate his family to Japan, was able to draw upon the fund of familial sentiment for an acceptance of his decision. In rigidly authoritarian families the formal parent-child relationships were not conducive to the development of affectional bonds. Before the war institutional supports for the traditional Japanese family against the impact of the dominant society were imperfectly integrated and weak. In such families the socialization of the Nisei to their family roles was not clearly defined nor institutionally controlled. The arbitrary authority pattern imposed by the Issei lacked the compensation of reciprocal rights to the Nisei. For example, in cases 5, 8, and 10, the eldest sons carried major economic responsibilities for their families, but their parents withheld from them the authority to make independent decisions. In case 5, the son was expected to extricate the family business from the near-bankruptcy resulting from his father's management; yet the son was also expected to accept his father's power to veto his plans for reorganizing the business. Where the son in case 5 finally rejected his responsibility without authority, the sons in cases 8 and 10 were more acquiescent and complied with parental wishes. The major source of strength of formal authority lay in the economic dependency of the Nisei, and the ambiguities of such family structures induced serious strains and instabilities. The acculturation of the Nisei and their increasing participation in peer groups introduced alternative definitions of family roles and reduced the Nisei's emotional dependency.

The center environment encouraged the Nisei's emancipation from the family in two ways: by granting economic independence and by strengthening peer groups against family groups. As we have noted, one of the first administrative policies was to assign preferential status to the Nisei. The Administration systematically encouraged the emancipation of the Nisei from Issei control. Special recognition was accorded to the leadership of the JACL, which was committed to coöperation with the Administration. The preferential treatment toward the Nisei extended into all aspects of center life: community organization, employment, leisure, and relocation.

The declining functions of the family in the center were accompanied by the increasing significance of peer-group associations. Acculturation through peer-group associations was strengthened, and peer groups often governed decisions on such major issues as registration and relocation. In case 10 two Nisei brothers became involved through their center jobs and other associations with a pro-Japan Kibei group. Like their Kibei friends, they declared themselves disloyal and sought segregation. When their friends were segregated, thus removing the group support for their disloyal response, and their own segregation was not immediately ordered, the brothers changed their answers and made loyal responses. In case 8 the loyalty responses of the eldest son and daughter reflected the effects of their group affiliations. The son worked in the block messhall where Kibei and Issei predominated and where pro-Japanese sentiment was strongest. On the loyalty issue he complied with his mother's direction and answered negatively. On the other hand, his sister, who associated with Nisei favorably disposed to relocation, disregarded her mother and covertly gave loyal responses thereby becoming eligible for relocation. It seems clear that peer-group associations were the key to the formation of decisions in these cases. The extent of the acculturation of the peer group and the nature of its orientation to Japan, to the United States, and to the limbo of the center society tended to govern responses to administrative policies.

INSTITUTIONAL MANIPULATIONS AND THE LIMITATION OF ALTERNATIVES

The Administration's failure to formulate policies in the light of the evacuation experience and the conditions created by center organization left the policies open to gross misinterpretation by the evacuees. The Administration's assessment of community sentiment was clouded by the imputation of rationality to the behavior of a population under stress. With a sensitive attitude toward local and national "public opinion," the Administration formulated policies designed to "close the centers at the earliest feasible date."[4] The criteria of feasibility were never specified. The costs to family solidarity were apparently not assessed and this despite the stated policy to maintain the family unit.

We have discussed above the failure of the Administration to provide the prerequisites for family life in the facilities and organization of the centers and the unanticipated consequences of this failure. The family not only had experienced the crisis of the evacuation but was undergoing an equally serious erosion under the impact of center life. New policies were viewed against the bitter background of the evacuation and its sequels, and family interpretations of administrative policies and problems were not so rationalistic as the Administration apparently expected.

Given the high value of family unity in the Japanese culture, the conditions of community disorganization, the destruction of the family's economic base, and the acute uncertainty of the future, it is understandable that the maintenance of family unity should become a major concern, particularly of the Issei whose orientation toward the future was bound to their children. For them, only the family could provide security against the future. They therefore tested administrative policies against this rather narrow but primary concern. In case 9 a widower actively opposed his daughter's efforts to relocate, for relocation would reduce the ability of the family to act as a unit. Her reiterated requests were taken as insubordination and the family remained intact in the center until quite late in the relocation program. In case 1, aged parents who were dependent upon their Nisei son attempted to arrange for the repatriation of the whole family as a way to reunite the family with an Issei son in Japan. The Nisei son resisted, however, and the parents could not oppose him. Consequently, they acceded to his wishes and responded loyally to the registration.

Issei security had become dependent upon their ability to influence, directly or indirectly, their children's actions. With their increasing independence, however, the Nisei were not easily controlled. Although their future was as uncertain as their parents', they could face it with some confidence in their cultural competence and eventual employability. Furthermore, the cumulative effects of their peer-group associations led them away from the constraints of the family, and the more aggressive and acculturated Nisei initiated the movement toward relocation.

Issei definitions of issues were affected by their increasing awareness of their dependency, the Nisei's, by the conditions of independence fostered by the center environment. We suggest that the responses of families to the policies of the Administration must be interpreted within this framework of Issei and Nisei interests. In this light, our attention is directed to the resources available to the family to achieve unity in decision and action despite the pressures of often conflicting interests.

The first major crisis encountered by the family in the center was the registration program. Theoretically, this program was a means of expediting the relocation of eligible persons. The registration issue, however, precipitated a reaction derived partly from resentment against conditions within the center and partly from the unfortunate presentation and administration of the registration. The criteria which separated the eligible from the ineligible were the so-called "loyalty" questions. There was great confusion and concern about the implications that the answers would have for the conscription of Nisei and for the relocation of the family. The coördination of the Army and WRA registration programs inextricably linked the two issues. The population inferred that positive responses to the loyalty questions implied both a willingness to serve in the armed forces and a willingness to be relocated. This interpretation, which was in fact correct, aroused immediate and anxious concern in the family. A "loyal" response might make possible the drafting of the adult Nisei male and at the same time force the relocation of the rest of the family during his absence. In view of this, the mother in case 8 gave disloyal answers to forestall the drafting of her son.

The registration program presented two alternative courses of action for the family. It could record itself as loyal, in which case it would be obliged to leave the center in the near future and its sons would be subject to the draft. It could record itself as disloyal, thereby avoiding relocation and the draft, but at the cost of being further stigmatized or perhaps classified as an "enemy" of a country at war. The family's decision would affect both its wartime status and its postwar prospects. It was difficult for individuals or families who were against the registration but strongly oriented toward America to protest the loyalty questions as unfair. To endanger their futures in America was too great a risk to take. However, the loss of their prewar property, occupations, and communities made their future in America uncertain. The family could rely only upon the potential economic resources of its members, and, with the prospect of the draft, there was no assurance of even this source of family strength.

The inconsistencies implicit in the registration program were obvious; the evacuees commented bitterly that they had been denied the rights of citizenship during the evacuation but now were being asked to assume its obligations. Some asserted the government was not to be rid of them so simply, that having evacuated them, it could take care of them. The choice, nevertheless, had to be made, and the majority of the families registered affirmatively. However, it is clear from the Issei's general failure to plan for relocation that they had hedged their responses with the prevailing belief that WRA would maintain the centers for an indefinite period. In effect, the Issei created a third choice which involved neither relocation nor segregation. For example, the father in case 9 registered loyally and thus avoided segregation, but he did not intend to relocate.

Having presented the registration program in polar terms of loyalty, the Administration had to work out a policy of special treatment for the population responding negatively to the question that asked for "unqualified allegiance to the United States of America." The segregation policy was a consequence of the registration program, and it was a major factor in the family's deliberation of the loyalty questions. For the Issei concerned with the maintenance of family unity, segregation had its advantages. It made its members ineligible for the draft, it prevented the Nisei from leaving the family through relocation, and it ensured the family a relatively secure environment for the duration of the war. Case 8, to which we have just referred, was a clear instance of this.

For the Nisei, however, segregation publicized his disloyalty. Despite its ambiguity, disloyalty was stigmatized by the majority of his peers as well as by the society at large. It also committed him to remain in the center among the extreme pro-Japanese elements of the evacuated population. In case 10, two brothers strongly influenced by Kibei associates, registered disloyally in order to maintain group membership although they were not finally segregated. For the Nisei whose segregation was primarily in acquiescence to parental demands, the segregation center became an arena of intensive political activity in which he was the target of the pro-Japan group. Under threats of physical violence, the group coerced many Nisei to renounce their American citizenship.[5]

Families choosing the loyal alternative were no less harassed by administrative policies. Even while faced with the prospect of losing their Nisei sons to the Army, the families were subjected to increasing pressures to relocate. The relocation program was first directed at the Nisei, for in effecting their relocation the Administration assumed it would have a lever by which to relocate their parents. The effect of the Administration's policy, far from promoting concerted family action, encouraged individuated action by the Nisei. In case 2, a large family of Nisei, previously under the rigorous and formal control of the mother, cast off her authority. One son went on seasonal leave from the assembly center and never rejoined the family in the relocation center. The other children made independent plans and relocated from the center in rapid succession.

The residue, the "unrelocatables," who obstinately remained in the center despite the Administration's persuasion and warnings, were to plague WRA to the end of the relocation program.[6] The majority of the residue was comprised of families with young children and old Issei who presented dependency problems. For example, in case 6 the eldest son was drafted by the Army and a seventeen-year-old brother was almost eligible for military duty. The aged father's return to the center from the internment camp only increased the dependency of the family, and their meager resources were not sufficient to meet the problems of relocation. The family, therefore, made no plans for relocation and remained in the center until the closing of the centers was announced.

The Administration's encouragement of Nisei relocation was often utilized by the Nisei as a means of relieving themselves temporarily of responsibility for the Issei. Relief from familial responsibility was short-lived, however; the Administration closed the centers less than two years after the majority of the adult Nisei had relocated.

The announcement in December, 1944, that the centers would be closed within a year shifted the relocation program from a voluntary to a compulsory basis. The policy presumed that with rescission the evacuees would return to the areas from which they were evacuated and consequently no further rationale for the existence of WRA remained. Evacuation was to be undone by rescission. When the evacuees did not plan immediate relocation, the Administration presented them with the ultimatum, euphemistically termed "scheduled relocation." The foreclosure tactics were met by disbelief on the part of the residents. They thought it unlikely that they would be evicted. Grasping for security, they propagated rumors about inevitable residues of "unrelocatables" who would have to be cared for by the Administration. But as the January, 1946, deadline approached, pressure increased and the residents were aggressively advised, and finally impelled, to relocate. Contending that problems of housing, employment, dependency, and the like were individual and not group problems, the Administration systematically emptied the centers. Like the evacuation, scheduled relocation treated the population as a mass. The logistical theme once more was dominant. It was in response to this contrived urgency that children returned to the center to plan for relocating their families, sometimes taking upon themselves responsibilities they were unable to carry.

THE STRUCTURE OF FAMILY DECISIONS

The registration program required that each family assess its resources for future adjustments. Changes in policies, rumors, and interpretations of policy were scrutinized for effects on family interests and family resources. The demographic characteristics of each family were major determinants in defining the problems with which it had to deal and its ability to solve them. Problems of the number of minors and old-age dependents, occupational experience and employability, health, and draft status were objective considerations affecting the position of the family with respect to relocation or segregation.

The major consequences of decision on the registration issue were clear. Relocation demanded an immediate consideration of the problems of adjustment to the "outside" world; segregation would postpone such problems. Either course of action, however, involved risks that threatened the unity of the family. For the Issei to demand that his children commit themselves to the status of disloyal citizens and confinement in a segregation center for the duration of the war required a high degree of parental authority and power. As we have seen, such authority and power were difficult to maintain in the center except over the youngest and most acquiescent Nisei. Parental demands for segregation in the absence of effective control presented the danger of alienating the children. (See case 5, sec. ii.) On the other hand, if the Issei sanctioned his children's positive response to the registration, he might undermine his own security through removal of Nisei by the draft and individual relocation.

The issues raised by the registration struck at family unity and control. In facing these problems the family was thrown back upon its internal resources, and strong leadership became an essential condition for the maintenance of family cohesion. The family could not rely upon the community to reënforce its diminished strength. Evacuation had virtually eliminated the prewar community.

The prewar authority pattern imposed limits upon the means of mobilizing consent and control available to the Issei head. In the absence of the integrative function of economic and social activities within the family, group unity had little utilitarian value for the Nisei. It had few other advantages to offer them, whereas extrafamilial groups provided opportunities for new associations and activities. Group cohesion required the activation of latent familial sentiments that would make family unity a prime value.

The problems of leadership in traditional, authoritarian families were quite different from those of more acculturated families. The success of the leadership of the traditional family rested on its ability to counteract the individualistic tendencies fostered in the center. Nonconformance was interpreted as insubordination and lack of filial respect, and the full force of parental dominance was brought against it. (See case 9, sec. ii.)

Families whose formal roles were strengthened by well-developed affectional relations were less threatened by the individuative forces of the center. In such families, opportunities for individual members were thought to contribute to collective goals, and the Issei were not threatened by the prospect of emerging Nisei leadership. These Issei were more likely to review the registration issue as it affected the postwar chances of themselves and their children. To the degree that the Nisei had internalized the value of family unity, Issei interests were secure, and the risks of relocation were less threatening.

Although Issei interests emphasized security through family unity, the center environment directed the Nisei's interest toward peer-group associations and independence. Nisei who had been isolated and had lived in the shadow of parental domination learned from their peers different valuations of their family roles. Unquestioning submission to parental demands was viewed as a weakness, and the group often encouraged a break from familial controls. The peer group's emulation of American norms was supported by WRA's policy "to create a community as nearly American in its outlook and organization as possible."' In the peer group the Nisei debated the issues raised by the registration program. The level of acculturation and the different orientations of peer group and family posed the problem of registration for the Nisei. If the differential was great, the Nisei faced the alternatives of alienation from the peer group on the one hand and alienation from the family on the other. Submission to parental demands for segregation implied the denial of independence and the rejection of American society and culture. Opposition to the parents required the security of active peer-group support. Such action implied individualistic opportunism and denial of filial obligations. Although it also implied weak submission to administrative manipulation, relocation was supported by the Nisei peer group as a collective decision rejecting center life.

The conflict was much greater for Nisei males than females. The expectations of both peer group and family were less demanding for females. The male Nisei's actions were decisive for the family because he was the major resource upon which the Issei depended. Where parental insistence upon segregation was a means of disqualifying the Nisei from the draft, only the sons were made to answer the loyalty questions negatively. The acculturated peer group viewed the Nisei's compliance to such demands as disloyalty and cowardice. Females did not have these problems, and submission to parental demands coincided with their role expectations. Indeed a relatively greater degree of independence was necessary for the Nisei girl to oppose her parents. (See case 9, sec. ii.) It was much less probable that she would be able to withstand the weight of parental sanctions, and she was less able to depend upon the support of her peer group. In such circumstances the Administration provided her with the compromise solution of affirming her loyalty even though she was segregated with her "disloyal" family.

Although the registration was not defined by the evacuees primarily as a question of loyalty, they knew the Administration did so define it and would act on the basis of answers to the loyalty questions. Some answered the allegiance question (no. 28) affirmatively but the draft question (no. 27) negatively. As a declaration of loyalty, one answer canceled out the other, but taken together they expressed the dilemma posed by the question.[8]

Summary

We have presented the conditions under which the evacuated families faced the making of decisions. Under the stress of successive and sometimes contradictory manipulations some families were able to act decisively to achieve a highly integrated group adjustment, whereas others failed to act and comprised the large group of "unrelocatables." The cases presented show how variation in the structure, cohesiveness, and affectional and cultural characteristics of the family affected its adjustments to the demands imposed by administrative policies. In no instances are we able to say that the actions taken by any family were the only ones possible. The cases indicate that the families as individuals and as groups tended to be governed by their own relations and histories quite as much as by a rationalistic administrative policy. Of course, only an administration enabled to take each individual and family separately into account could have avoided a simple rationalism, and the mass character of the evacuation did not permit this. The Administration tried diligently to get the evacuees to interpret policies and problems as *it* did. But even when there was no meeting of minds, the Administration had to act *as if* there were.

In contrasting Issei and Nisei interests above, we are of course dealing with abstractions. The mere fact of generational membership did not determine an individual's position on the registration issue. Rather there was a complex of social factors that conditioned the individual's interests and his ability to act upon them. In any given family Issei and Nisei interests were mediated by unique factors, but such factors became meaningfully related to family decisions and actions when examined against Issei and Nisei interests. A family with a child in Japan may have been predisposed toward segregation and repatriation to achieve a reunion of the family. (See cases 1, sec. ii, and 9, sec. ii.) But the children in the center often resisted a move for the benefit of a sibling of whom they had little knowledge and for whom they had little affection. Even when affectional relations were strong between siblings in Japan and America, segregation and repatriation might have been rejected if they entailed the sacrifice of personal ambitions.

The detailed family histories, which follow, are intended to suggest the variety of individuals and families that passed through the experience of the evacuation, the resources with which problems were faced, the points of view from which the administrative acts were interpreted, and the bases on which decisions were made.

THE CASES

THE CASES

READING THE CASES

CERTAIN innovations have been introduced in order economically to retain significant data about the individuals. A notational scheme has been developed to release the reader from the obligation of remembering a large number of fictional names, some of which might unfortunately become identified with real persons, and to supply relevant information in lieu of meaningless fiction. The reader will need to learn the five items of the notational scheme and their order. Each parenthetical identification reports the immigrant status, sex, and generational status of the individual, and, when appropriate, his age and ordinal position in the family.

1. The first symbol identifies the individual as *I*ssei, *N*isei, *K*ibei, or *S*ansei by initial.
2. Age is recorded in the second position when useful in the account, and, of course, changes with time (unless it is directly relevant, it is not reported):
   (N *25*
3. Sex is noted by the conventional biological signs of ♂ for males and ♀ for females:
   (N 25 ♂
4. In the case of families with more than one child, each child's ordinal position is given after the sex symbol:
   (N 25 ♂ *1*
5. The generational designation, P for parental and F_1 for first filial, completes the notation (in two instances coresident siblings of parents are indicated as A):
   (N 25 ♂ 1 F_1) is a Nisei, twenty-five years old, male, the first-born child in the family.

Accompanying each case is a map depicting the geographic movements of the family. A bar ▬ indicates assembly center, a ▲ stands for the relocation center, and a hemisphere ◣ signifies an internment camp. The family constellation is represented by a circle containing the symbols for the parents with the children around the perimeter. F stands for a whole family.

Also accompanying each case is a chronological chart summarizing the family on December 7, 1941, that part of the family constellation in the center, and those members out of the center at each time interval. The chart employs the same symbols as the map for indicating the family constellation. Family members not living with the group are shown detached from it, except that children already married before the outbreak of war are not considered in the family and are not represented. A dotted-line rectangle indicates a living group. A small circle represents a new family unit formed by the marriage of a child. An arrow indicates no change.

Each case follows an identical outline, which makes explicit the way that the interview and interpretive materials have been structured. The outline follows:

    I. Prewar family
   II. Preëvacuation and center experience
 III. Relocation
 IV. Postwar family
  V. Interpretation
       a. Participation
       b. Family structure
       c. Wartime experience
       d. Character of adjustment

CASE 1

I. Prewar Family

(I ♂ P) was the eldest son of a farming family in Japan. Although he was expected in due course to take over the family farm, he determined to go to America. A disagreement ensued between him and his younger brother about responsibility for the farm and the parents. Over the younger brother's protests he arranged for a go-between to persuade his parents to consent to his emigration, and in 1905 (I 15 ♂ P) entered the United States. Upon arriving he went to work for the Union Pacific Railroad as a cook and waterboy for a gang of Japanese laborers. After a year and a half with the railroad, he migrated to Montana where he worked as a farm hand for three years. Then for two years he did odd jobs while attending public schools in Montana, Nebraska, and the Dakotas. In 1912 he went to Los Angeles for the first time and worked in a Japanese newspaper office for a year.

In December, 1913, (I 23 ♂ P) returned to Japan to visit his parents, and during his stay, his mother died. In 1914 a marriage was arranged by a go-between. (I ♀ P) came from a well-to-do farming family in a neighboring village. The marriage ceremony was a formal one and was performed at the high temple of the Higashi Hongwanji.

During his three years' stay in Japan (I ♂ P) spent most of the money he had saved while in America, and after paying for the expenses of the wedding, he did not have enough money for his wife's passage. Leaving her in Japan, (I 27 ♂ P) sailed again for America in 1917 and worked as a foreman on a fruit ranch in central California. (I ♂ 1 F₁) was born in Japan in 1917.

In 1921 (I 29 ♀ P) joined her husband in San Francisco. Her father had persuaded her to leave the child behind, because he might cause undue hardship for the couple while they were establishing themselves. It was decided that the child would be sent to America when he had completed his high school work in Japan.

A short time before (I ♀ P) arrived in the United States, (I 30 ♂ P) set up a dry-cleaning and hand-laundry shop in northern California. In 1922 (N ♀ 2 F₁) was born, and in December of that year the family moved to Los Angeles, where they established a dry-cleaning shop, which they operated until the outbreak of the war. In 1923 (N ♀ 3 F₁) was born, and (N ♂ 4 F₁), in 1926.

The family lived in quarters behind the cleaning shop located in a predominantly Caucasian neighborhood. One other Japanese family

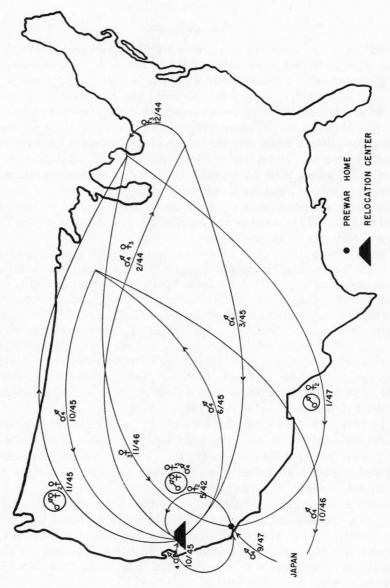

PREWAR HOME •
RELOCATION CENTER ◣

Map 1

Chart 1

resided in the immediate neighborhood, and another operated a small grocery store next to the cleaners. Within an area of a half-mile radius of these two shops there were twelve other Japanese families. There were no Negroes or Mexicans in the immediate vicinity. The Caucasian residents were white-collar office workers, and semiskilled and skilled workers. The children of the family mingled freely with other children in the neighborhood and established close relations in school and in play. They frequently visited in the homes of Caucasian friends. Most of the children's close friends were the children of old and regular customers of the shop. (I ♀ P) encouraged the children to make friends among all groups, and at school they had friends among the Negroes and Mexicans as well as Caucasians.

The parents' contacts with their neighbors were for the most part in the shop, and they achieved a respected status in the community. (I ♀ P) established cordial relations with a number of her customers, but she never learned English well enough to be able to converse freely, nor did she visit their homes except to deliver garments or to fit dresses. Occasionally when one of her customers was ill, she would call on him, taking one of the children along to act as her interpreter.

(I ♂ P), who drove a truck for a laundry, was able to speak English more fluently than his wife, and he associated with Caucasians as well as Japanese. He was occasionally invited into neighboring homes for dinner and learned some aspects of American culture through these contacts.

Despite the high rate of interaction with members of the dominant culture, the family retained many Japanese practices. The opportunities for rapid acculturation were not exploited by the parents. Their experiences in the neighborhood were generally pleasant, but their relations with Caucasians were conditioned by attitudes of subservience. The maintenance of their small shop depended heavily upon the good will of the neighborhood, and this fact, together with their relatively isolated position in the community, made for insecurity in relations with the dominant group. They reacted by withdrawal to form a culturally conservative and strongly knit family. For example, the number and detail of Japanese holiday observances were greater than in most families of this type, and family relations emphasized the role of the male. Relations between parents and children were informal, but the children were always taught to respect their father. They were indoctrinated in the principle of *oyakōkō* (filial piety and obligation), and out of respect, they spoke to their parents in Japanese as much as possible.

The daughters were closer to their mother than to their father, but (N ♂ 4 F_1) had access equally to both parents. He enjoyed more privileges than did the daughters, not only because of his status as the youngest in the family but also because he was considered the only son and accorded the preferential treatment of the *sōryō* (eldest son). The actual eldest son, (I ♂ 1 F_1), who was in Japan, had a history of tuberculosis, a stigmatizing disease to Japanese.

The affectional ties between the children were strong. They confided in each other and went to the movies together. They spoke English to each other in good-humored conspiracy against (I ♀ P). She was the disciplinarian, although on occasion (I ♂ P) lectured the children on good behavior and duty to one's siblings.

The relationship between the parents was more companionable than for most Issei couples. They often went to movies and visited friends together. Although authority rested with (I ♂ P), (I ♀ P) participated in decision-making. By the outbreak of the war the children had become less dependent upon their parents. Indeed, the latter were beginning to lean upon the children, economically as well as in mediating their relations with the community.

During the prewar years the family had a steady income from the dry-cleaning shop, which was supplemented by (I ♂ P)'s income from the laundry route. The average annual income ranged from $2,750 to $3,250. (I ♀ P) was in charge of the shop while (I ♂ P) worked the laundry route, with (N ♂ 4 F_1) helping him on Saturdays. The family lived comfortably on its collective labor even through the depression when shirts were laundered for eight cents and suits were cleaned and pressed for twenty-five cents.

In 1939 (I 49 ♂ P) suffered a cerebral hemorrhage that partly paralyzed him. He was unable to work, either with the laundry company or at the shop. (I 47 ♀ P) took over the family responsibilities, and her husband withdrew into partial retirement from family affairs. He was occasionally consulted when there were business decisions to be made, but the day-to-day activities were conducted by (I ♀ P) and the children.

The burden of the work fell upon (I ♀ P), who operated the shop with the part-time help of (N 17 ♀ 2 F_1). In November, 1939, (N 13 ♂ 4 F_1) found an after-school job at a window-display company at about $15 per week. On Sundays he worked at a nursery and was paid $3.50 for the day's work. In 1940 (N 17 ♀ 3 F₁) took a job as a "school girl" domestic in a doctor's home while she attended college. The job paid her $20 per month plus room and board.

The family adjusted to (I ♂ P)'s illness by pooling their resources and energies, and at the outbreak of the war, there was no financial distress. The loss of (I ♂ P)'s earning power, about $1,500 annually, was partly compensated by payments of $350 from an insurance policy. The total family expenses for an average month, including medical care for (I ♂ P), was about $300. Besides these household and business expenses, the family contributed perhaps $300 per year to the support of (I ♂ 1 F₁).

Before (I ♂ P)'s illness, the family was economically stable with a well-developed sense of coöperation among its members. They were relatively unacculturated as individuals and as a unit. The parents' tendency toward cultural conservatism hindered the rapid acculturation of the children. Although there were favorable conditions within the play groups and at school, the family was the major regulator of the rate of acculturation, and the children's adjustment tended to approximate Japanese patterns.

(I ♂ P)'s organizational activities were confined to groups within the Japanese community. During the three or four years before his illness, he was active in voluntary and community organizations. He was one of the organizing members of his *kenjinkai,* and he served as its second vice-president and treasurer. He worked in such welfare activities as the Japanese community campaigns for the Community Chest and Red Cross. He was also an officer of the Japanese Cleaner's association.

(I ♀ P) participated in the Women's Club of the language school and was elected its president for two successive terms. The daughters were members of a Nisei girls' club, an affiliate of the YWCA, whose purpose was mainly recreational. (N 17 ♀ 3 F₁) joined another Nisei social club when she was a student at college. (N ♂ 4 F₁) belonged to the Japanese Fencing Organization of Los Angeles, which he joined only at the insistence of his father. His reluctant attendance at fencing classes automatically made him a member of the group.

As in most families, regardless of their degree of acculturation, New Year's Day was the major holiday.* A few days before the New Year,

---

* In this case we have reviewed on p. 60 the relevant cultural and acculturation data for the general orientation of the reader. Other details are given on p. 74. In subsequent cases this information is relegated to an appended summary.

two or three families joined to make *omochi*. The men pounded the steamed rice with the help of the women, who then molded it into small cakes. These cakes of graduated sizes were pyramided three high, *osonae*, and placed before the household shrines. Beside the omochi was placed a decanter of *sake* and a small vase with pine, bamboo, and plum stems, called *shochikubai*, symbolic of good luck for the new year. On New Year's Eve the children celebrated in town while (I ♀ P) prepared holiday dishes.

On New Year's Day the family ate an early breakfast of *ozōni*, a soup with a piece of omochi in it. The meal was begun with a sip of sake served by (I ♀ P). Through the day the children went on house rounds, and (I ♀ P) remained at home to receive guests. The official New Year's celebration lasted ten days, during which all Japanese acquaintances were formally greeted. The careful attention given to form and detail in this family's celebration of the New Year is an example of an unusually strong carry-over of Japanese cultural patterns.

On January 15, the family celebrated the religious *koshōgatsu* (Small New Year), not usually observed in the United States. Although the shop was not closed for this occasion, (I ♀ P) prepared a special Japanese dinner of *osekihan* (rice with red beans), symbolic of good luck, and baked fish.

In March the family observed Girls' Day, *Hinamatsuri*, a Japanese religious and national holiday. Omochi was made for this occasion, and many Japanese dolls were displayed in front of the home shrine for about a week. A special meal was prepared for supper by (I ♀ P) with the assistance of (N ♀ 2 F₁). *Koimatsuri*, Boys' Day, on May 5 was commemorated by the flying of a paper carp fastened to a tall pole. Osekihan and baked carp were prepared for the evening meal. The shop was not closed for either of these holidays.

On *Hanamatsuri*, a Buddhist holiday, special Japanese confections were placed before the home shrine, incense was burned, and osekihan was prepared for supper. After the meal, the confection was eaten by the members of the family, and all went to Little Tokyo to see the Japanese street dance.

The family conformed to the observation of American holidays by closing the shop, but only Thanksgiving and Christmas were internalized as family activities.

In 1938 (I 46 ♀ P) went to Japan to look after (I 21 ♂ F₁) until he was well enough to come to the United States. However, when (I ♀ P) prepared to return after a year's stay, her son was refused a visa, and she returned alone.

(I ♀ P) continued to correspond with (I ♂ 1 F₁). She also wrote to her brother and mother regularly and undertook the obligation of corresponding with her husband's relatives. The children wrote occasionally to their brother in Japan, but only at the insistence of their mother. When (I ♂ 1 F₁) wrote to his mother, he would put in a note to his siblings, giving them advice about studying and caring for the parents. He clung to a hope that he might be able to meet them and study in an American university. (I ♀ P) brought back from Japan various souvenirs, such as photographs of the son, medals he had won in archery, and art objects. These mementos from the brother in Japan stimulated his siblings' interest in him. (I ♀ P)'s trip also awakened (I ♂ P)'s interest in the son he had never seen. He began to write to his son, but he never openly expressed a desire to see him.

The children in the United States attended a Japanese-language school for an hour or two every weekday after public school classes were dismissed. During the summer, classes were held each morning for three hours. There were about thirty students at the school and only one teacher. The teachers did not stay long with the school, and (N ♂ 4 F₁) remembers at least five different individuals during his eight years of attendance. The school was a coöperative effort of the Japanese neighborhood, and classes were held in one of the homes.

II. Preëvacuation and Center Experience

The Pearl Harbor attack made the parents afraid that violence might break out against the Japanese, and they warned their children to stay at home after dark. To placate them the children remained within a few blocks of the shop and they no longer visited the homes of Caucasian friends, although their friends came to the shop and would chat with them until late at night.

The kenjinkai was disbanded, and records in the possession of (I ♂ P) were destroyed on order of the officers of the organization. The home shrine was also destroyed, together with anything relevant to Japan: books, letters, Japanese dolls, and the like.

The following week a Justice Department agent searched the shop and house for contraband material. The parents' alien registration cards were examined and (I ♂ P) was questioned; (N 15 ♂ 4 F₁) acted as the interpreter. The agent found nothing in the house, but returned two days later to investigate (I ♂ P)'s participation in the kenjinkai. (I ♂ P) was not interned.

During the first few months of the war the family encountered no major acts of discrimination. The newer customers stopped patronizing the shop, and eventually only the older and regular customers remained, but this had little effect on the business. Many of the old acquaintances and some of the neighbors whom the family knew only casually expressed a friendly sympathy. When the news of the evacuation was published, the older customers offered their assistance.

The parents were confused and frightened. (I 50 ♀ P) felt incompetent to make the necessary arrangements and decisions, and she feared that if she handled the business affairs the family would suffer a great loss. The family responsibilities were thrust upon (N 15 ♂ 4 F₁). (I ♀ P) discussed the major problems with him and occasionally the daughters helped to decide certain issues. All savings were transferred to an account in (N ♂ 4 F₁)'s name. In addition to his new and burdensome responsibilities, (N 15 ♂ 4 F₁) continued his attendance at school and his work after hours at the display company. He adjusted with a remarkable energy and adaptability for a boy of fifteen. (N 19 ♀ 2 F₁), who managed the shop, assumed some responsibility, and (N 17 ♀ 3 F₁) kept her job in the doctor's home until March, 1942.

Early in March, when it was understood that the evacuation would take place, the shop was put up for sale. Again (I 50 ♀ P) turned over to (N 15 ♂ 4 F₁) the task of negotiating with prospective buyers. (N 20 ♀ 2 F₁) could not bring herself to make decisions of major importance. It was felt that (N ♂ 4 F₁) knew most about the value of the equipment, since he had gone with (I ♂ P) to make payments. He was also more willing to stand up to buyers who were trying to exploit the Japanese' disadvantageous position. Because of his illness (I ♂ P) was relieved of responsibility in the negotiations.

(N 15 ♂ 4 F₁) was instructed by the parents to sell at any price. The furniture in the house was put up for sale separately from the shop equipment, but many buyers insisted that everything go with the shop. (N ♂ 4 F₁) refused for five weeks to accept the poor offers and wanted to wait for a more nearly equitable price, but time was running short and friends of the family urged them to sell the shop and join them in town. Finally in April the shop and household equipment valued at $3,500 was sold for $300. Personal property was sold for small sums.

The following is a partial list of the items sold for a total of $300:

Shop Equipment	*Household Goods*
Pressing machine and boiler equipment	Washing machine
Electric sewing machine	Couch
Silk steam iron and equipment	Piano
Two glass-enclosed showcases	Electric refrigerator
Large work table	Dining table with four chairs
Cash register	Desk (executive type) with chair
Service counter	Laundry worktable
Two ironing boards	Cooking stove
Four metal clothes stands	Dresser
Three cast-iron flame irons	Bookcase
Several laundry shelves	Buffet

Other articles (books, art objects, dishes, and the like), stored in a friend's garage, were stolen during the war. The additional financial loss was small, for the possessions had little more than sentimental value.

For a month they had been the only Japanese family in the locality and had had an increasing sense of exposure. After the shop was sold, they left the neighborhood to join four other families in a hotel. The curfew regulations confined the group to the area immediately surrounding the hotel, and as a result the interaction between the families was intimate. The Issei found a sense of security in being together; they could even contrive a brighter view of the future. They spent most of the day talking about old times, the present crisis, and rumors concerning the camp under construction at Manzanar. It was said that the Japanese who had voluntarily evacuated to Manzanar were made sick by the food and water, the climate was extremely cold, no heat was provided, the evacuees were treated badly by the Caucasian personnel, etc.

During this period (N 15 δ 4 F$_1$) was relieved of the decision-making responsibilities. The Issei men acted for the whole group. In the council of males one of the Issei acted in the place of (I δ P) who, of course, was unable to represent his family. The ties within the family grew stronger through the common concern for the father's health, and the other families were protective of (I δ P) and his family.

Voluntary evacuation outside Military Area No. 1 of the Western Defense Command had not been considered by any of the families. While they waited for evacuation orders, the Nisei boys went to the homes of various friends to prepare them for evacuation. They hauled baggage, saw them to the assembly points, and bade them farewell. The

Issei, fearful of being harmed or robbed, left the hotel only when necessary. As each area was evacuated, it was closed to the Japanese; soon the Nisei had to get permits to shop or visit the bank. The group retained the use of automobiles that had been sold but were not transferred until the day of the evacuation.

Just before evacuation the curfew was more strictly enforced and the families stayed indoors after dark. As time passed, the members of the group became irritable and restless, but there was no dissension. They engaged in the characteristic overpreparation for center life and became reconciled to the idea of the evacuation.

On May 6, 1942, posters were placed about the neighborhood setting registration for May 9. At that time family identification numbers were issued, instructions were given, and the destination revealed. The families registered together to ensure being evacuated together. On May 16 they assembled and their destination was suddenly changed from the Pomona Assembly Center to Manzanar. Three families traveled by train, the other two by bus.

The initial adjustment to crowded and onerous center conditions was complicated by $(I \male P)$'s weak condition. After the trip to Manzanar he was confined to his bed for about three weeks. The food was unappetizing and the diet prescribed by his doctor was not available. The strangeness and insecurity of the center environment tended to draw the family together, and the children tried to facilitate $(I \female P)$'s adjustment through thoughtful help. In a center where some rooms were crowded with eight and nine people, this family's housing in a room 20 by 25 feet was relatively good.

Once more $(N 15 \male 4 F_1)$ became the leader of the family. Family leadership involved attending block meetings and reporting for the distribution of supplies. He arranged to have their excess baggage shipped from Los Angeles, made furniture for the room, and put up partitions. For three months the members of the family held no jobs, but they were kept busy fixing up the barracks. The women cleaned the barracks daily, did the laundry, and made draperies.

In September, 1942, a census office was opened. $(N 19 \female 3 F_1)$ went to work as a typist and $(N 16 \male 4 F_1)$ took a job as messenger boy. Their combined income was $32 per month. $(I \male P)$ continued to receive $30 per month from the insurance company. $(N 20 \female 2 F_1)$ remained at the barracks caring for the parents. $(I \female P)$, who was not well, required more and more care from $(N \female 2 F_1)$.

After $(N \male 4 F_1)$ went to work, his family responsibilities were distributed more evenly among the other members. The whole family, except (I ♂ P), entered into discussions, and decisions were arrived at jointly. (I ♂ P) puttered in the garden at the side of the barracks. The children had become economically independent of their parents, but the ties between them were strengthened by the reversal of roles.

During the first year the family expenses were heavy because (I ♂ P) needed food and medicine that could not be had in the center but were procured by mail order. Finally medical services were fully established, and the special diet and drugs were supplied by the center. When the center school was opened, (N 16 ♂ 4 F$_1$) attended classes and worked after school at the YMCA. The daughters continued at their respective jobs—(N ♀ 3 F$_1$) as a typist and (N ♀ 2 F$_1$) as a clerk in the center library, a job she secured late in 1942.

The announcement of the Army registration program in February, 1943, posed a problem the parents were not ready to face. (I ♂ P) wanted to go to Japan, for he had never seen (I 26 ♂ 1 F$_1$), and he wanted to return to Japan to die. (I ♀ P) also was concerned about (I ♂ 1 F$_1$), who might be drafted into the Japanese Army, and about her mother. The registration program presented the opportunity to satisfy these wishes.

The children had no desire to go to Japan. The daughters had little more interest in Japan than prospective tourists. They assumed that if they expatriated, they would not be able to return to the United States. (N 16 ♂ 4 F$_1$) argued that they knew nothing about current conditions in Japan, life would be miserable for the daughters who were accustomed to American ways, and the family should remain in the United States.

Although the discussion centered around expatriation, the major issue in this case, as in many others (see sec. ii of cases 5, 8, and 9, was the maintaining of family unity. After discussing the problem at length, the family agreed that all should answer the two loyalty questions "yes, no."* (See pp. 26–30 and 225) for a discussion of significance of loyalty answers.)

Because (N ♂ 4 F$_1$) was under seventeen, he was not required to answer the questionnaire, but his family's answers would seriously affect his position. If they had decided to answer negatively, he would have been obliged to be segregated with them or break away from the family. It is apparent, however, that his arguments dissuaded his parents.

---

* The terms "loyal" and "disloyal" throughout the cases indicate an arbitrary classification based on responses to the questionnaire, not an established attitude.

When he registered four months later, he too answered the questions according to the family agreement. (The parents were relieved later to learn that they had not renounced their Japanese citizenship.)

(N 17 ♂ 4 F₁) had conflicting feelings about voluntary enlistment. His father was ill and his mother's health was failing. The fate of (I ♂ 1 F₁) was unknown, and it was possible that (N ♂ 4 F₁) was an only son, thus increasing his responsibility to his family. Although he wanted to demonstrate his loyalty as an American citizen, he did not want to distress his parents by enlisting. In the balance, his concern for his parents outweighed his patriotic feelings.

III. RELOCATION

In June, 1943, (N 17 ♂ 4 F₁) left the center for three weeks as a delegate to a Christian youth movement conference. Late in 1943 his application to a Midwestern university was accepted. (I ♂ P) objected to (N ♂ 4 F₁)'s relocating, and he reiterated rumors that Japanese in eastern cities were being robbed and beaten and a Nisei girl had been found brutally murdered in Chicago. (N 20 ♀ 3 F₁) also wanted to relocate, and the children appealed to (I ♀ P), who at first opposed their plans but finally gave in to their determined efforts. To gain (I ♂ P)'s consent, (N ♂ 4 F₁) had Issei and Nisei friends in the Midwest write to (I ♂ P), who was finally won over.

In February, 1944, the children left the center. (N 18 ♂ 4 F₁) enrolled at the university, and (N 21 ♀ 3 F₁) found employment as an office clerk. (N ♀ 2 F₁) took full responsibility for the family and devoted herself to the care of the ailing parents. In order to be as close to the family barracks as possible, she quit her library job to work as assistant block manager.

At the time of rescission only the two children had relocated. Although all the members received the news as a favorable sign, the family was unsettled about returning to California. (I ♂ P) wanted to return to the benign climate of Los Angeles, where he was known and had Caucasian friends. (I ♀ P) emphasized the importance of keeping the family together. (N 21 ♀ 3 F₁) was satisfied to stay in the Midwest, but (N 18 ♂ 4 F₁) was willing to return to the West Coast. To (N 22 ♀ 2 F₁), her parents' health was the chief consideration. (I ♂ P) had not fully recovered from the stroke suffered five years before, and (I ♀ P)'s health was deteriorating. (N ♀ 2 F₁) alone could not take the responsibility of a decision. Consistent with her passive role, she waited for a plan to be worked out by the family as a whole.

After a year (N 19 ♂ 4 F₁) was drafted. In March, 1945, he returned to the center until he was called to active duty in June. (N 22 ♀ 3 F₁) moved to another Midwestern city where she found a job as a store manager-clerk with a large dairy company.

The news that the center would be closed at the end of November, 1945, found the family without plans for relocation. In October, (N 19 ♂ 4 F₁), who was stationed at Ft. Snelling, Minnesota, was granted an emergency furlough to return to the center. He spent three days in Los Angeles at his own expense but was unable to find housing for the family. (N ♀ 3 F₁) urged the family to join her, and (N ♂ 4 F₁) and (I ♀ P) agreed they should do so. Before returning to Minnesota (N ♂ 4 F₁) made the arrangements at the relocation office and left instructions with (N 23 ♀ 2 F₁). The haste with which these arrangements were made illustrates the coercive nature of the scheduled relocation.

In November, 1945, the parents and (N 23 ♀ 2 F₁) joined (N 22 ♀ 3 F₁) in the Midwest. Of the five families that had consolidated at the time of the evacuation, three had relocated to the same city, and this facilitated the adaptation of the Issei. Neither was able to work, and except for the $30 per month from (I ♂ P)'s insurance, they were totally dependent on their children. (N ♀ 2 F₁) found a job with a dry-cleaning shop doing alterations on a piece-work basis and earned about $75 per week. The other daughter continued to work at the dairy store. The girls paid the rent of $30 per month. The parents received dependency benefits of about $75 from the son. In all, the monthly income was about $500.

In March, 1946, (I 54 ♀ P) died following a cerebral hemorrhage complicated by pneumonia. She had been attended by a Nisei doctor. Funeral arrangements were made by (I 56 ♂ P) at a Buddhist temple that had been established in January of that year. The day after the wake the funeral was held at the Buddhist temple with friends from Chicago attending. The body was cremated and the ashes were placed in custody of the church.

In October, 1946, (N 20 ♂ 4 F₁) left the United States for occupation duty in Japan. Soon after his arrival he met (I 29 ♂ 1 F₁) for the first time. He was ill at ease in the presence of a brother who was a stranger, but the distance was bridged with family news and the community of grief over their mother's death. Together they went to see their relatives and exchanged news of family happenings during the war. After a brief period of uneasiness, (N ♂ 4 F₁) was able to talk quite freely with his relatives. He had taken part of (I ♀ P)'s ashes with him, and the brothers arranged a burial in the family plot. Funeral services were held at the ancestral home with the high priest of the Higashi Hongwanji Temple officiating. At the services (N δ 4 F_1) met relatives on both sides of the family.

He also visited a number of acquaintances in Tokyo and Fukuoka who had expatriated to Japan during the war. He found most of them ill-adjusted to Japan and eager to return to the United States. By the time he left Japan, he had come to know his brother well. After returning to the United States in September, 1947, he corresponded with his brother, who wrote frequently that he wished to bring his family to visit America.

IV. POSTWAR FAMILY*

In the winter of 1946–47, (N 23 $\female$ 3 F_1), concerned with (I δ P)'s health, moved to Los Angeles to seek a home. (N 24 $\female$ 2 F_1) and (I 56 δ P) followed soon after. By this time most of their savings were exhausted. Home furnishings to the amount of $1,000 were purchased on deferred-payment plan.

A few months after returning to Los Angeles, (N 25 $\female$ 2 F_1) married a Kibei who had spent twelve years in Japan. As a first daughter, her training had been conservatively Japanese, and this facilitated her adjustment to marriage with a Kibei. In the center she had a number of Kibei friends, and she shared many of their attitudes. Her husband is the recognized source of authority, and her relationship with him is harmonious although more permissive than the Japanese mode.

In 1949 the family paid $45 per month rent, and living expenses averaged about $150 monthly. These expenses were met by (N 26 $\female$ 3 F_1), who was working for the city as clerk-typist at $190 per month. (N 23 δ 4 F_1) earned about $25 per week for part-time work at a gasoline station. He also had a monthly subsistence under the G.I. Bill and attended a university in late afternoons and evenings.

(N δ 4 F_1) was considered the head of the family, and he made most of the decisions for the group. He discussed serious problems with (N $\female$ 3 F_1), and a mutually satisfactory decision was usually reached.

As of 1950 (I 59 δ P) is becoming senile and is almost totally dependent upon his children, who are concerned about his loneliness and his insistence on doing things that tax him. When the children are away, he cleans the house and visits (N $\female$ 2 F_1) to play with the grandchild.

* Information recorded at the time of the last interview is reported in the present tense.

Even short automobile rides tire him, but he often takes the streetcar into Little Tokyo.

Since the death of his wife, (I ♂ P) regularly attends the Higashi Hongwanji Temple, of which she was a member. Both (N ♀ 3 F₁) and (N ♂ 4 F₁) are rather inactive members of the Episcopal Church (Japanese).

(I ♂ P) corresponds with (I ♂ 1 F₁) and other relatives in Japan each month and sends packages regularly to his son and occasionally to the others. (N ♂ 4 F₁)'s stories of his visit in Japan have increased (I ♂ P)'s desire to see (I ♂ 1 F₁). The children have discussed the possibility of sending their father to Japan for a visit, but they fear his health will not permit it. Even after more than twenty-five years, (I ♂ P) has a persistent feeling of guilt for having left his son in Japan.

The wartime experiences of the families in both countries have drawn them closer together affectionally and economically. (N ♀ 2 F₁) also sends relief parcels to (I ♂ 1 F₁). Although she does not correspond with him, her Kibei husband does.

Organizational participation is much less than before the war. Although the kenjinkai has been reorganized, (I ♂ P) has not involved himself. (N ♂ 4 F₁) joined the JACL but has not been attending meetings. He has not joined the Nisei Veteran's Association, although he has been approached several times. (N 26 ♀ 3 F₁) has not affiliated with any group. Her job and work around the house more than account for her time.

The family lives in a polyethnic neighborhood and associates with Mexican, Caucasian, and Negro neighbors. Some of the prewar Caucasian neighbors are visited from time to time, and occasionally the visits are returned, but most of the prewar friends have died or moved away.

V. INTERPRETATION

Participation.—In this case we have documented the sequence of changes in an urban entrepreneurial family that operated a small shop. The shop provided work for (I ♀ P) as well as for the children, and (I ♂ P)'s outside employment supplemented the family income. The high degree of solidarity achieved by the family was securely tied to the daily routine of the family enterprise. Many years of coöperative effort had established a symbiotic relationship within the family with (I ♂ P) assuming the rights and obligations of leadership.

As we have noted, the family was not ecologically segregated, and all the members had a large volume of contact with American culture.

They nevertheless maintained within the home a strong cultural conservatism, for example, in the observance of Japanese holidays. More important was the parents', particularly (I ♀ P)'s, indoctrination of the children in the Japanese values of filial duty and piety, hard work, cleanliness, and sibling loyalty.

It seems probable that the strong affectional bond which is characteristic of this family but is not consistent with its cultural orientation, was an adaptation to their ecological isolation from the Japanese community. The pressures of the dominant culture were undoubtedly great, especially upon the children, and the strictly Japanese family with its formality and authoritarianism would probably develop strains which might threaten family unity. For the parents whose response to their cultural and spatial isolation was withdrawal, family unity was of primary importance. The modification of the traditional family structure in such circumstances was by no means universal, although it was distinctly successful in this case. Perhaps formalism in the Japanese family functionally requires community support and larger institutional contexts.

The resistance of the parents to the American culture despite favorable conditions for acculturation underlines the essential fact that this phenomenon is not merely additive. Rather, impact values are to be understood in terms of the factor of time and related to the interactive situations as defined by the ethnic group. For example, immediately before the evacuation the Issei of the family were extraordinarily fearful. Equivalent anxiety was not found in families relatively isolated in rural areas. This suggests that twenty years of frequent and friendly contact with Caucasians had not yielded security. Indeed, we suggest that there was a sense of exposure to a potentially hostile environment, and this may have affected their cultural conservatism. A more Japanese environment, therefore, might have moved the family further on the acculturation continuum. In the Caucasian neighborhood they were continually aware of racial visibility, and their relationships with their neighbors were in terms of this racial definition. The passive adjustments expected in their type of business minimized a manipulative attitude toward the social environment and contributed to the relative lack of acculturation.

The ecological separation of the family also had consequences for its relations with the ethnic community. Family participation in ethnic group affairs tended to be peripheral. However, the friends with whom the family frequently exchanged visits lived in ethnic enclaves, and it was predominantly through them that the family maintained its relationship to the ethnic group and expressed and reinforced its cultural identification.

Family structure.—We have noted that the patriarchal structure of this family was modified by its isolation. The father's observation of American family behavior in Caucasian homes may have provided a model for his attitudes toward his wife and children. The traditionally low status of the mother was ameliorated in this family—(I ♀ P) exercised much power—and there was little of the factionalism characteristic of cases 2 and 5. The informality of the affinal relations, as well as those between the parents and children, gave an affectional tone to instruction in filial duty. The promptness with which (N 17 ♀ 2 F_1) and (N 13 ♂ 4 F_1) assumed responsibilities at the time of (I ♂ P)'s illness is indicative of the degree of family integration.

The familial adjustment to new circumstances points to the traditional orientation of the group as well as the strong dependence of (I ♀ P) upon her children. The parents' attitude toward (N ♂ 4 F_1)'s status in the family was an expression of the rule of primogeniture observed in the traditional Japanese family. The son was expected to assume important responsibilities upon (I ♂ P)'s illness, and (I ♀ P) depended heavily upon him as well as upon her two daughters.

Wartime experience.—The crisis precipitated by the war demonstrated the uneasiness with which (I ♀ P) acted as family coördinator. Her fear for the family's vulnerability was so disorganzing that she relinquished her power and authority to her son, (N 15 ♂ 4 F_1). This coincided with the Japanese provision for a "strong father." (I ♀ P), who had for so long discharged with efficiency her responsibilities to the family, failed at this critical time. The rapidity with which her health deteriorated also may have been symptomatic of her inability to adjust to a disruptive situation in which she had no one to direct her. The war and the looming evacuation, combined with (I ♂ P)'s illness, comprised a highly stressful situation. But the completeness with which she turned over family affairs indicates that (I ♀ P)'s original adjustment to her husband's illness two years before was conceived as a temporary one and depended on the support of the children.

(I ♀ P)'s ability to coördinate the activity depended upon her familiarity with a very specialized situation. The familiar patterns were destroyed by the war, and the consequent insecurity disqualified her as the family coördinator. Had the evacuation not intervened (I ♀ P) might have maintained her role until (N ♂ 4 F₁)'s age and training enabled him more adequately to carry the responsibilities.

Despite his youth, (N 15 ♂ 4 F₁) was regarded more able to handle the demands of the new situation than either (I ♀ P) or (N ♀ 2 F₁). (N ♂ 4 F₁) did, in fact, show remarkable maturity and capability in the handling of affairs before the evacuation and in the center. Once leadership was given him, the parents were content to act upon his advice, further reflecting the basically Japanese definition of the situation. The informant's reference to retirement as inkyo expresses the parental obligation.

Since (N 19 ♀ 2 F₁) was four years older than (N ♂ 4 F₁), it would seem logical that she should have shared the burden with him. She did not do so because her Japanese training developed obedience at the expense of qualities of leadership. (N ♀ 2 F₁) was certainly capable, for in the crisis of (I ♂ P)'s illness and later in (I ♀ P)'s abdication the daughter discharged her duties well, but she could not lead.

The strong solidarity established during the prewar period did not deteriorate during the evacuation and their subsequent experiences. Even the registration issue, which precipitated conflicts for many families, was constructively worked out. Registration did confront the parents with a decision they had avoided since 1924 when they realized (I ♂ 1 F₁) would be unable to join the family in America. It opened the possibility of reuniting the family in Japan. Chiefly for this reason both parents favored repatriation. But the Nisei opposed repatriation, and the parents acceded to their wishes.

Note the disparity between the Administration's definitions of the loyalty registration and the considerations that affected the answers of this family.

Character of adjustment.—This family showed throughout its wartime experience strong integration, which had been early established. Its well-developed affectional bonds facilitated adaptability to the crises and manipulations of the evacuation. Had the family been rigidly structured on an authoritarian pattern with the attendant undercurrents of intergenerational conflicts, the rise to power of (N ♂ 4 F₁) at such an early age might have been impossible.

There were no serious disruptions of interpersonal relations chiefly because the family adjusted as one unit. The family had, even before the war, begun to take the form that was precipitated by the evacuation. Adjustments to (I ♂ P)'s illness indicated the role for which

(N ♂ 4 F₁) was being groomed. The shift of leadership and authority from Issei to Nisei had already begun, and the war catalyzed but did not change the direction of the process.

The success of this family's adjustment must be credited to (N ♂ 4 F₁)'s leadership and the ability of the family to maintain affectional solidarity. An effective functional division of responsibility sustained the group throughout the war in the face of financial disaster and the additional strain of invalided parents.

Cultural Data

PREWAR

POSTWAR

Religion:
(I ♂ P) had no religious affiliation in U.S. (I ♀ P) attended Buddhist temple. The children attended Episcopal (Japanese) church. Buddhist and family shrines in home; also Bible, Common Prayer Book, and book of Buddhist scriptures.

Religion:
Following (I ♀ P)'s death, (I ♂ P) became interested in Buddhism and attends (I ♀ P)'s prewar temple. Children's religious participation has diminished.

Holidays:
For Japanese holidays, see sec. i. American holidays were family occasions, and American customs observed.

Holidays:
Japanese New Year's Day observances simplified. Other Japanese holidays eliminated. Family attends (I ♀ P)'s Buddhist temple on Memorial Day. American holidays observed but much less family activity.

Diet:
Japanese food preferred. See sec. i.

Diet:
Fare is predominantly Western.

Reading matter:
The Book of Knowledge, Bible, Common Prayer Book, some classic Japanese novels, English and Japanese dictionaries, a home book of medicine in Japanese, and a directory of Japanese families in southern California.

Reading matter:
Most of the prewar library was salvaged from storage. (N ♂ 4 F₁) has added a few textbooks in the course of his attendance at the university.

CASE 2

I. Prewar Family

Little is known about (I ♂ P)'s background in Japan. His family were probably farmers. (I ♂ P) was the second of two sons. He attended high school and, in 1897, (I 18 ♂ P) emigrated to the United States where he first worked in a streetcar roundhouse in Los Angeles.

When he was about thirty-five years old, his relatives in Japan arranged his marriage to a picture bride. (I ♀ P)'s family engaged in fishing and farming. As a child she was frequently sick and was withdrawn from school, and for a time she worked as a seamstress. She was unable to write Japanese. (I 35 ♂ P) and (I 18 ♀ P) were married in 1914 at a Christian church in San Francisco. Although the marriage was arranged according to Japanese custom, the ceremony was performed in the American style.

(N ♂ 1 F$_1$) was born in 1915, followed by (N ♂ 2 F$_1$) in 1916 and (N ♀ 3 F$_1$) in 1918. In 1920 (I ♂ P) started a *meshiya* (Japanese restaurant) in Little Tokyo. After the birth of (N ♂ 4 F$_1$) in 1920, he moved the family to a small beach city about 25 miles from Los Angeles because he regarded the Japanese section unsuitable for rearing children. In this city (I ♂ P) worked as a janitor in a music store and (I ♀ P) worked in the fish canneries. (N ♀ 5 F$_1$) and (N ♀ 6 F$_1$) were born in 1923 and 1924, respectively.

In 1926 the family, hoping to be better able to support their six children on a farm, moved to a town a short distance from the beach city, leased a plot of from 15 to 20 acres in a Caucasian's name, and engaged in truck gardening. The last child, (N ♀ 7 F$_1$), was born in 1927.

The first few years on the farm were difficult; (I 48 ♂ P) worked hard to make it a profitable venture but was only moderately successful. He managed the work alone except for the harvest-season work crew and occasional help from (I ♀ P). As the children reached their early teens, they were given chores which increased with the years, and (I ♂ P) assumed the role of manager of the enterprise. (N ♂ 1 F$_1$) and (N ♂ 2 F$_1$) gradually took over the operation of the farm, and when (N ♂ 4 F$_1$) was eighteen he was given complete responsibility for taking the produce to the market. He acquired a reputation for shrewd trading and before long he was marketing the produce of neighboring farmers. This extra work enabled him to earn enough money to cover his first year's expenses at a university.

Although the sons were responsible for the farm and directed its

[75]

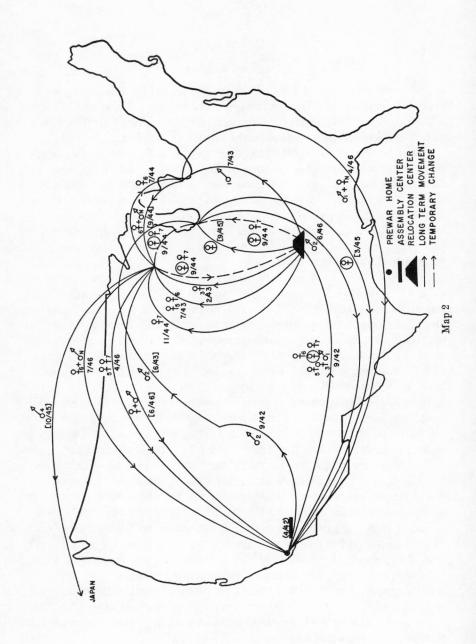

PREWAR HOME
ASSEMBLY CENTER
RELOCATION CENTER
LONG TERM MOVEMENT
TEMPORARY CHANGE

Map 2

Chart 2

actual operation with little assistance from (I ♂ P), the father retained the final authority in matters of the farm as well as in the family. The sons' labor increased (I ♂ P)'s leisure, and he spent much of it drinking. He could not be depended upon for responsible tasks, and in the several years preceding the war he played a minor economic role.

The family bought three small buildings, which together totaled about eight rooms. One building housed the kitchen, the second, the living room, and bedroom, and the third, the workers' quarters. These buildings were moved from farm to farm, a common practice among Japanese farmers.

During the depression of the 1930's the family in the name of (N 22 ♂ 1 F_1) leased a new farm of sixty acres. On 40 acres they grew strawberries, which were marketed in Los Angeles or sold to haulers from the beach city. During the harvest season as many as fifty Japanese workers were hired. By 1939 the produce situation had improved and in that year the farming operations netted about $20,000. With this profit the family bought a large new truck, a new tractor, a new Oldsmobile, a pump, household furniture, and equipment. (N 21 ♀ 3 F_1) was sent on a tour of Japan.

During the early years of the family, (I ♂ P) was the head and (I ♀ P) was not permitted to question his authority. The children feared him and he lectured them at great length when he was intoxicated. Ordinarily (I ♀ P) was in charge of their discipline. (I ♂ P) and (I ♀ P), who were separated by seventeen years, quarreled frequently and violently. (I ♂ P) looked down upon his wife for her lack of education, and she nagged him persistently for his irresponsible behavior. He would often return drunk from the market where he had sold a few crates of produce and gambled. (I ♀ P) bitterly reproached him and accused him of infidelity. The older children censured (I ♀ P) for aggravating (I ♂ P) but generally blamed him for their family troubles. There were some good moments, however. The girls could coax (I ♂ P) into giving them money for clothes by joking playfully with him.

The siblings were affectionally close to each other and jointly participated in recreational activities. The children had freedom in their choice of friends, but in the case of (N ♀ 6 F_1), the family as a whole disapproved of her companions. This daughter was relatively isolated, although the three younger children as a group did many things together.

The Nisei varied widely in their degree of acculturation. At one extreme was (N ♀ 3 F_1), who had the greatest facility in Japanese and was interested in Japanese flower arrangement and sewing. Her organizational activities were limited to the JACL and a girls' club, which was affiliated with the Japanese Baptist Church. At the other extreme was (N δ 4 F_1), who was very popular in high school and at the university. He often dated Caucasian girls and belonged to a Caucasian fraternity.

The other children were exposed to American culture at school but did not actively assimilate as did (N δ 4 F_1). They chose their own friends and occasionally brought them into the home, but Caucasian acquaintances were not entertained by the family but by the individual. There is no record of intimate friendships with Caucasians, with the exception of (N δ 4 F_1), who lived in a dormitory at the university. The parents had few contacts with Caucasians, although (I δ P) was on friendly terms with his neighbors. Discriminatory experiences, if any, were well repressed. The family did not test the rule that forbade the use of local public plunges to Japanese.

Most of the children were active in age-group organizations. (N δ 1 F_1), (N δ 2 F_1), (N $\female$ 3 F_1), and (N $\female$ 5 F_1) participated largely in ethnically delimited groups; however, (N δ 4 F_1), (N $\female$ 6 F_1), and (N $\female$ 7 F_1) were active members of predominantly Caucasian associations. (N δ 4 F_1) was president of the high school senior class, captain of the football team, and a member of several special interest and service clubs. Both (N δ 4 F_1) and (N $\female$ 7 F_1) did well in school, but the rest of the children did not. (I δ P) favored the good students and castigated the others.

(I δ P) was an officer and active member of the Nihonjinkai and kenjinkai, a member of a farmer's association (*nōgyōkumiai*), and made regular donations to the Japanese-language school and the church attended by his children. (I $\female$ P) was a member of but one organization, the Mothers' Club of the Japanese school.

Neither parent was an active agent of Japanese culture, and tradition played a minor role in family life. The children received little positive support for acculturation, but neither were they faced with parental opposition to American culture.

No family tradition bound the participation of members in religious activities. There was no Shinto shrine in the home. (I δ P) was from a Buddhist family in Japan and occasionally attended the temple when the family first moved to Los Angeles. After moving to a harbor city in 1937, he became interested in the *Seichyō no Iye* (a medicoreligious cult), and he subscribed to, and read, their publications but never attended the meetings. (I ♀ P) also had been a Buddhist in Japan. During her residence in Los Angeles she occasionally visited the Los Angeles Holiness Church upon the urging of friends, but she never gave up her Buddhist orientation.

The parents encouraged the children to attend Christian services. The three older children went to the Japanese Presbyterian Church Sunday School during their residence in the beach city (1921–1926). When they moved to the farm in 1926, the children attended a Sunday school conducted by a Nisei minister from the Los Angeles Holiness Church. All but (N ♀ 5 F_1) and (N ♀ 6 F_1) were baptized. When the family moved again in 1937, the children attended a Japanese Baptist church and joined its Young People's Union in a neighboring town.

All the children attended a Japanese-language school, which enrolled about a hundred students. During their first years of attendance the children studied diligently, but as they grew older, they regarded the language school as a place to meet friends.

Members of the family made trips to Japan on three occasions. In 1921 (I ♀ P) took her four children with her to Japan, where they stayed with her family for a year. Only (N 6 ♂ 1 F_1) attended school, and the effect of the visit on the children's acculturation was negligible. (N 22 ♀ 3 F_1)'s visit to Japan in 1940 was primarily an expression of the parents' cultural interest. The trip was a reward for (N ♀ 3 F_1)'s hard work in the family and the interest she had shown in Japanese culture. She was able to read Japanese novels with ease, and through her reading she held a romantic view of Japan. She visited the country with great pleasure and toured Japan for six months with a student group sponsored by a Los Angeles Japanese-language school. She found the differences of cultures interesting, and she got along nicely with her relatives although she never quite felt at home during her visit.

In May, 1941, (I ♂ P) went to Japan in retreat from his wife's incessant charges of infidelity. At the outbreak of the war, the family group consisted of (I ♀ P), two sons, and four daughters. (I ♂ P) was stranded in Japan. (N 21 ♂ 4 F_1) volunteered for U. S. Army service with the encouragement of his Caucasian friends at the university. Although his friends were made officers, he was not commissioned. (I ♂ P) and (N ♂ 4 F_1) did not experience the evacuation.

II. Preëvacuation and Center Experience

At the time of Pearl Harbor (N 26 ♂ 1 F_1) and (N 25 ♂ 2 F_1) operated the farm with the help of (I ♀ P) and (N 23 ♀ 3 F_1). The farm had been planted in strawberries, and the family continued to cultivate the plants throughout the winter and early spring. There were no major changes in the family. (I ♀ P) continued as the head of the family, and the war had no significant effect upon relations within the group. Curfew regulations kept the family at home in the evenings, but there were few activities to draw the members closer together. The language school was closed without notice after December 7, but the younger children continued at the high school until shortly before the evacuation.

Rumors of the evacuation increased through February but the family made no preparation. When it became clear late in March that evacuation would be ordered, (I ♀ P), over the protest of the older children, urged the selling of all the farm equipment and household furniture. The tractor, two trucks, and other equipment were sold for $1,000, an estimated loss of $10,000 to $13,000. The farm was taken over by the landowner, who leased it to a Mexican farmer, and the furniture valued at more than $1,000 was sold to various buyers for nominal sums.

Late in March, 1942, the family registered with the WCCA. (N 27 ♂ 1 F_1), as the legal head, directed the preparations, and the family was evacuated as a unit to Santa Anita Assembly Center. The move was accomplished with a minimum of difficulty. The group was housed in a small room and the family quickly fell into the center routine of hours of leisure punctuated by three mess calls and sleep. Several weeks after their arrival, the children applied for work. (N ♂ 1 F_1) was hired as a fireman, (N 26 ♂ 2 F_1) as a messhall timekeeper, and all the girls worked as waitresses.

In the six months before their transfer to the relocation center, the family members earned about $500, which they spent with an additional $500 for clothes and miscellaneous items. The children's earnings were considered their own, but the family fund was controlled by (I ♀ P). She approved or vetoed expenditures and coördinated the work of the girls in the few household tasks such as washing and cleaning.

Center life freed the children from economic obligations and relieved (I ♀ P) of the many responsibilities with which she had been burdened. For the first time since her marriage she was free of the demands of the farm and the numerous worries of the family enterprise. (I ♀ P) did not work in the center but devoted herself to her new leisure and visiting with Issei friends. She observed the independence enjoyed by the divorced and widowed women in the center, and she became more self-assertive and spent some money on clothes and cosmetics. The children were not so close to each other as they were before the war. Recrea-

tional activities were numerous, and the children found their own
interest groups.

In the fall of 1942 (N 26 ♂ 2 F₁) joined a group of volunteers for
seasonal farm work in the beet fields of the Rocky Mountain states. He
did not return to the center. In September, 1942, the family was ordered
to Jerome, Arkansas. The second move entailed dismantling the room,
repacking possessions, the confusion of directions and redirections, and
a long, weary trip. At Jerome, they were assigned two rooms, measuring
about 20 by 24 feet, a living arrangement superior to that in other
centers where a family of seven often occupied only one room. With
some scrap lumber and other material (N ♂ 1 F₁) furnished the barracks with tables, chairs, and a closet. The girls decorated the rooms
with curtains and draperies and made them as homelike as possible.

(I ♀ P) was not a strong leader, for her authority over the children
was more formal than it was affectional. She was aware of the disinte-
gration of her control over the family, but she attempted to maintain it.
The activities of the center and free movement of the children within
it encouraged individuation and undermined her authority.

In the center, each of the workers in the family [all but (N ♀ 7 F₁),
who was enrolled at the high school] received $16 per month. During
this period the family spent all of their monthly earnings plus about
$200 for clothing, food, and other items.

The registration did not precipitate in this family the conflict and
ambivalence that split many groups in the center. The Nisei passively
accepted the manipulations of the group. To them the registration was
only another administrative act, and the children were less concerned
about the implications of the program than about choosing the least
complicated decision. They had no attachment to Japan, nor was
(I ♂ P)'s presence in Japan a serious complication. Except for sending
the children to the language school, the parents had made few efforts
to transmit Japanese culture. Their acculturation and identification
with America was not countered by parental or nationalistic sentiments. Even in the evacuation crisis there was little questioning of the
allegiance of the children. The children interpreted the registration as
another opportunity to affirm their loyalty to the United States. They
accepted the proposal to separate the loyal from the disloyal by means
of the registration, and their major concern was that their decision
should not threaten their future status in America. For (I ♀ P) to go
to Japan would mean a reunion with (I ♂ P), and she was content to
abide by the children's decision. However, she cautioned (N 28 ♂ 1 F₁)

against volunteering for the Army. (N 25 ♀ 3 F_1) had happy memories of her visit to Japan, but she never considered expatriation. Indeed, she proposed relocating as soon as the family was transferred. However, (I ♀ P) refused to give her permission, but after six months of persistent pressure (I ♀ P) capitulated.

III. Relocation

(N 25 ♀ 3 F_1) left for a Midwestern city in February, 1943. She found work as a clerk-typist at an army camp, and there she met a Hawaiian-born Chinese whom she married after two weeks of courtship. When (I ♀ P) learned of (N ♀ 3 F_1)'s proposed marriage, she vainly urged the children to dissuade her.

In July, 1943, (N 28 ♂ 1 F_1), (N 20 ♀ 5 F_1), and (N 19 ♀ 6 F_1) left the center together. The girls joined (N ♀ 3 F_1), and (N ♂ 1 F_1) went north to work as a foreman in a soap factory. In August, 1943, he married a girl he had known in the center.

Both (N ♀ 5 F_1) and (N ♀ 6 F_1) found work as power-machine operators in clothing factories. (N ♀ 5 F_1) worked with one firm for most of her stay from July, 1943, to April, 1946. (N ♀ 6 F_1), on the other hand, changed jobs four times. This daughter (the member least integrated into the group) has had the most problems of job adjustment. Her occupational mobility may be symptomatic of other adjustmental problems during the initial period of relocation.

In July, 1944, (N 20 ♀ 6 F_1) was married to a friend of (N ♂ 1 F_1). The families of the bride and groom were acquainted and were evacuated to the same center. Shortly after their marriage the groom was inducted into the Army, and the couple found quarters near the camp.

(N ♀ 7 F_1) and (I ♀ P) were left behind in the center. When Jerome was closed in June, 1944, they were transferred to Rohwer, Arkansas. There was little correspondence between the relocated members and the two remaining in the center. (I ♀ P) was illiterate in Japanese, and she depended upon (N ♀ 7 F_1) for communication with the relocated children.

In September, 1944, (N ♀ 7 F_1) and (I ♀ P), at the former's urging, left the center on seasonal leave to visit (N ♂ 2 F_1) in Chicago and the sisters. The trip reminded the children of their responsibilities to (I ♀ P), and this tended to reëstablish a sense of solidarity within the group. The trip, which was financed by the center, also enabled (I ♀ P) and (N ♀ 7 F_1) to experience firsthand the conditions of relocation without the stress and strain of adjusting to its immediate problems.

From October, 1944, to June, 1946, while (N ♀ 3 F₁)'s husband was overseas, she continued to work at the camp. In 1946 (N ♀ 3 F₁) and her husband moved to California. In April, 1947, she gave birth to (S ♂ 1 F₂), and when her husband was sent to Japan in June, 1947, she and the child went to live with (I ♀ P) in Los Angeles.

(N ♀ 7 F₁) and (I ♀ P) returned to the center after a few weeks, and in November, 1944, (N ♀ 7 F₁) left again to live with (N ♀ 5 F₁). During the summer of 1945 she was employed in Chicago, and she attended a Midwestern university during the academic year 1945–46.

By the time of rescission all members of the family had been relocated to the Midwest with the exception of (I ♀ P). She wished to return to the West Coast immediately, but the children were reluctant to enter what they thought to be an insecure situation. However, none of them felt committed to remain in the Midwest, and they all intended eventually to return to California.

When (N ♂ 1 F₁) learned in 1945 that the Rohwer Relocation Center was to be closed, he moved (I ♀ P) to (N ♂ 2 F₁)'s apartment in Chicago. Early in 1946 (N 26 ♂ 4 F₁) returned to the United States after serving for a year and a half with the Army in the China-Burma-India theater as an interpreter. He was discharged shortly afterward, rented an apartment in southern California, and initiated the reorganization of the family in California. He had aggressively and overtly adapted himself to the larger society and assumed the leadership of the family during this period. As a first step he sent for (I ♀ P).

In June, 1946, he bought a grocery store and a war-surplus truck with the money he had saved while in the service. The venture was not promising, and after two weeks he sold the business at a loss of $500. He then leased space in a wholesale produce market, and (N 30 ♂ 2 F₁) came from Chicago to help him. By the end of August, 1946, (N ♂ 4 F₁) had sold a half interest in the enterprise (probably at a loss) to a Nisei and had given the other half to (N ♂ 2 F₁). (N ♂ 4 F₁) then returned to his prewar university for the fall semester.

In April, 1946, (N 31 ♂ 1 F₁) and his wife purchased a car and drove to Los Angeles. After settling in a small apartment-hotel operated by a Japanese, he worked as a tomato sharecropper with a Mexican partner and commuted daily to the farm. A few months later, they moved to a $35 per month apartment closer to the farm.

(N 23 ♀ 5 F₁) and (N 19 ♀ 7 F₁) also returned to California in April, 1946, and moved into (I ♀ P)'s apartment. (N ♀ 7 F₁) attended summer session that year at a local junior college and in September she enrolled at the state university, working for her board and room as a "school girl" in a Caucasian home.

When (N 22 ♀ 6 F$_1$)'s husband returned to the United States in July, 1946, after serving with the occupation forces in Japan, they lived with (N ♀ 6 F$_1$)'s family. (N ♀ 6 F$_1$) and her husband worked in a fish cannery until he enrolled as a sophomore at a local university in February, 1947. After a year he left the university and returned to work in the cannery with his wife.

In June, 1947, (N 27 ♂ 4 F$_1$) received a Bachelor of Arts degree. The family attended the commencement exercises where they met the Caucasian girl whom he had been dating. When he hinted of his intention to marry her, (I ♀ P) resisted, and the relationship was terminated. Shortly after graduation, (N ♂ 4 F$_1$) volunteered for military intelligence service and was reinducted into the Army. After a refresher course in Japanese, he left for Japan in September. His reënlistment was undoubtedly related to the unhappy resolution of his relationship with the Caucasian girl.

In Japan he saw (I ♂ P) occasionally and reported little beyond his drunkenness. (I ♂ P) had ¥10,000 worth of Japanese Manchurian bonds before he went to Japan. After the Japanese defeat, however, they were worthless. Penniless, he went to live with his younger brother. He applied to return to the United States, but the family made no effort to assist. His absence has relieved the home of constant tension, and his return would be disruptive both for the children and for (I ♀ P).

In June, 1947, the family were relieved of their crowded housing when they found a seven-room house which they leased at $70 per month, furnishing it at a cost of about $400. (N ♀ 7 F$_1$), who was until that time working for her board and room, moved into the house. When her husband went overseas, (N ♀ 3 F$_1$) joined them. (N ♂ 1 F$_1$) gave up his unprofitable farming venture and turned to contract gardening at which he earned about $300 per month. He and his wife also moved into the house. (N ♀ 5 F$_1$) and (I ♀ P) then joined the family so that only (N ♀ 6 F$_1$) and her husband were separated from the group.

During this period, (N ♂ 2 F$_1$) and (N ♀ 3 F$_1$) paid the rent. The food expenses were shared among all the members. Except for (N ♀ 7 F$_1$), who was in college, the children were financially independent. (I ♀ P) received the Army allotment of $60 per month provided by (N ♂ 4 F$_1$).

Although the housing situation necessitated a degree of economic coöperation, the family was not integrated as it was before the war.

Rather the economic resources of the group represented the contributions of three primary family units, which individually controlled their incomes. The children had become various kinds of workers—gardeners, restaurant cooks, power-machine operators, produce workers. (I ♀ P) had lost much of her authority and became increasingly dependent upon her children.

IV. POSTWAR FAMILY*

By the middle of 1949 all the children were married. As in the previous four marriages, each child made his own match, and for the most part the ceremonies were highly acculturated in form. (N 26 ♀ 5 F_1) eloped—but with (I ♀ P)'s foreknowledge—to avoid the prohibitive expense of a formal wedding. Only (N 33 ♂ 2 F_1) had a Buddhist wedding. (N 29 ♂ 4 F_1) was married in an Army chapel in Japan. Over the opposition of his family, he married a Japanese citizen, who, owing to immigration laws, would have difficulty entering the United States. As in the case of (N ♀ 3 F_1)'s marriage to the Chinese American, (I ♀ P) urged the other children to advise (N ♂ 4 F_1) against the marriage. The last child to marry was (N 22 ♀ 7 F_1), whose ceremony was held at a Caucasian church often used by Nisei couples.

None of the seven children were living together in 1950. The house they had occupied in 1947 was taken over by (N ♀ 5 F_1) and her husband, who shared it with relatives. (N 35 ♂ 1 F_1) and his wife were living with her parents in the outskirts of Los Angeles. (I ♀ P), (N 32 ♀ 3 F_1), and (S 2 ♂ 1 F_2) were temporarily in a housing project while (N ♀ 3 F_1)'s husband was stationed with the Army in Florida. (N 34 ♂ 2 F_1), was employed as a cook in a restaurant and his wife worked as a power-machine operator in a clothing factory.

(N 23 ♀ 7 F_1) was living in the Midwest where her husband was attending a university. All of the children except (N ♂ 4 F_1) in Japan and (N ♀ 7 F_1) were living in Los Angeles County. The relations between the children and their many in-laws are amicable. The fact that (N ♀ 3 F_1)'s husband is of Chinese extraction has created no stress between the siblings. Some of them believe that he does not treat his wife kindly and on this basis (I ♀ P) does not accept him fully.

(I ♀ P) is much attached to (N ♀ 3 F_1)'s child and she tries to teach him Japanese words and customs, but she has little control over him. She sees her other grandchild [the daughter of (N ♂ 1 F_1)] only rarely. She went to Japan in 1951 on the invitation of (N ♀ 4 F_1).

* Information recorded at the time of the last interview is reported in the present tense.

Allowing for the fact that the original family is divided into several separate units, (N 30 ♂ 4 F₁) is the leader of the family when it is called upon to act as a unit. The members of the family turn to him when help is needed or when some problem arises. They appreciate his looking after (I ♂ P) in Japan and respect (N ♂ 4 F₁) because he is capable and educated.

(N ♂ 1 F₁), who might have succeeded to the position of authority, is more concerned with his new family. His attitude toward the "re-united" family seems to be shared by the other children: the family facilitated the solution of relocation problems, but there is little effort to strengthen family solidarity as a value in itself.

V. Interpretation

Participation.—In 1941, after fifteen years of farming, this large family had begun to realize a moderate return from their enterprise. Over a period of years the Nisei sons gradually assumed the major responsibilities for the farm, and the father's role became more formal as his control over the farm gradually diminished.

After forty years of residence in the United States, (I ♂ P) showed little acculturation, particularly in his attitudes toward his wife and family. He had few contacts with the dominant society, either directly or indirectly, through the children. (I ♀ P) appears to have been equally unaffected by American culture, although her relations with the children were more informal. Like many Issei farm wives, she was thoroughly insulated from the dominant society.

The acculturation and interethnic participation of the children varied greatly. As might be expected, particularly in a farm family, the eldest daughter was the least acculturated. At the other extreme, (N ♂ 4 F₁) was actively assimilationist, utilizing both formal and informal associations within the school to enlarge his interethnic contacts. The popularity and success of this aggressive son made him the object of admiration for his siblings who informally accorded him the role of leader. The esteem in which he was held by both parents and children undoubtedly played an important part in the amelioration of the family's formalism.

The large number of children provided the conditions for the development of a congenial group. In their leisure-time association they found mutual support of their acculturation. All of them, with the exception of (N ♀ 3 F₁), had Caucasian friends, but these relationships did not draw the family as a group into the interethnic community.

The children's attendance at the language school and church related

the family actively to the Japanese community. The children participated in the activities of their peer groups whom they met in both
language school and church. They joined organizations sponsored by
the community institutions which provided them with frequent opportunities for participation in sports and other interests.

These participations were more individualistic than group-oriented.
Family participation in community affairs was rare, although (I ♂ P)
represented his family in various ethnic organizations. Activities involving the participation of the whole family appear to have been lacking in the ethnic as well as the dominant community.

Family structure.—Before the war this family was integrated by the
farming enterprise managed by (N ♂ 1 F$_1$). However, his influence in
the family was not commensurate with his role as the leader of the
economic activities of the group. In the absence of (I ♂ P), (I ♀ P) was
effectively the head, and she retained control of family affairs. Although
the children did not fear her authority as they did (I ♂ P)'s, they respected her parental status if not her leadership.

(I ♂ P) left his family few pleasant memories when he departed for
Japan. His leadership of the family was characterized by irresponsible
authoritarian power, frequently compounded in drunkenness. In spite
of the years of unhappy marital relations, (I ♀ P) failed to gain the
sympathetic support of her children. This may have been related to
her negative attitude toward their acculturational problems, which she
was apparently incapable of understanding. In this she allied herself
with the alienated father so that together they represented the restric-
tive image of Japanese culture. Had (I ♀ P) been more sympathetic
toward her children, she might have received their support in disputes
with (I ♂ P). As it was, the children disapproved of (I ♀ P)'s nagging
tactics, just as they disapproved of (I ♂ P)'s drinking and violence.

In exercising the authority assumed upon the departure of (I ♂ P),
(I ♀ P) drew more upon the strength of her formal status than upon
the meager fund of sentiment the children felt for her. She effectively
dominated (N 26 ♂ 1 F$_1$), who quietly discharged his filial obligations
in the management of the farm.

Wartime experience.—The close relationship between the farm and
(I ♀ P)'s control over her children is seen in the changing structure of
the family in the center. The center did not provide the conditions for
a meaningful restructuring of the group, for there were no major
problems in the center which demanded concerted family effort. Center
activities were not organized for family participation; work and recreational activities emphasized the importance of the peer group. Thus,

where the prewar family structure depended upon formal goals and the subordination of its members to them, the family in the center could offer few satisfactions that could not be more fully realized through membership in other, largely age-stratified, groups. The individual freedom afforded by center life undermined leadership based on formalistic controls, and (I ♀ P)'s power to maintain the integration of the family decreased with the loss of family function and the gradual deterioration of interaction among its members. (I ♀ P)'s efforts to retain control over her children were without avail, and her insistence upon treating them as small children only estranged them further.

The registration was not a serious problem for the children. They had little anti-American sentiment and certainly no pro-Japan attitudes. Segregation and expatriation would have entailed a commitment to the family as a group and also to a reunion with (I ♂ P).

(I ♂ P) was hardly missed by his children either before the war or later in the center. In fact, his absence tended to increase the possibility of greater group coöperation. The farm and family functioned more smoothly without the complication of the formal relationship introduced by him. Even after the end of the war the family remained disinterested in his return.

All the children were eager to leave the center, but they acted as individuals, not as a group. This break from the family was most notable in the unconventional marriage of (N ♀ 3 F$_1$), who had been a model Japanese daughter—passive, adaptive, and respectful. (N ♂ 1 F$_1$)'s independent action in arranging his marriage was also in sharp contrast to his earlier domination by (I ♀ P). However, the children's realization of their independent status cannot be interpreted as a rejection of their sense of obligation to their mother. On the contrary, their achieved independence made them aware of her dependence upon them. They easily rationalized her remaining alone in the relative security of the center, but when the closing of the centers was announced, the children efficiently adjusted to her relocation.

Character of adjustment.—The high degree of geographic and occupational mobility of this family illustrates the extent to which administrative policies provided the opportunities for the emancipation of the Nisei. The movement of the children represented a permanent family reorientation, which opened the possibility of relatively unhampered individual adjustments. In the absence of strong family bonds, the dispersion of the children had permanent fragmenting effects on the group during the postwar period.

The reunion of the family on the West Coast was unsuccessful because the economic enterprise which was the basis of the prewar family no longer existed. Without the farm not even the material symbol of the home remained. Nor did (I ♀ P) supply an integrating focus for the group. It is probable that only (N ♂ 4 F$_1$)'s return to the United States can provide the basis for familial union.

Had the war not intervened, the family would have dispersed in the course of separation through marriage, but the family would not have become so fragmented, for at least (N ♂ 1 F$_1$) would have provided continuity through maintaining the farm. (I ♂ P) would probably have returned to the United States, and, while his prestige would have been diminished, both he and (I ♀ P) would have been given security consonant with their age status.

Cultural Data

PREWAR

Religion:
(I ♂ P) and (I ♀ P) came from Buddhist families but were not religiously active in America. (I ♂ P) was interested in Seichyō no Iye cult. Children were encouraged to attend Christian churches.

Holidays:
Boys' Day (May 5), Girls' Day, and New Year's Day celebrated in traditional Japanese manner but not important family occasions. Family attended the annual *Tenchosetsu* (the Emperor's birthday rites) celebrated by community. American holidays observed as days of rest and recreation.

Diet:
Both Issei and Nisei enjoyed Japanese dishes, which dominated the family fare.

Reading Matter:
Subscriptions at various times to the Los Angeles *Times* and *Examiner*, and a local community newspaper, *Liberty*, *Farm Journal*, *Reader's Digest*, *True Story*, *Love Story*, *Romance*, and movie magazines. Parents subscribed to the magazines *Hinode* and *Fuji*. There were three sets of encyclopedias, an unabridged dictionary, children's story books, and mystery novels.

POSTWAR

Religion:
In center children attended Christian services but did not after return to West Coast.

Holidays:
No festive Japanese foods or holiday observances. Thanksgiving and Christmas passingly observed.

Diet:
Both Japanese and Western dishes. Frequently the style of cooking is mixed, and chopsticks and silver are set at the same time.

Reading Matter:
The collection of books reduced to a set of an encyclopedia, fairy tales, a set of Shakespeare, and some fiction and nonfiction books. Fewer magazines and papers; no Japanese magazines.

Language school:
Except for (N ♀ 3 F₁), language-school training was ineffective. Years of school attended, reader completed, and the level (corresponding to Japan) achieved:

(N ♂ 1 F₁) 12 yrs. Bk. 12 (6th gr.)
(N ♂ 2 F₁) 8 yrs. Bk. 12 (6th gr.)
(N ♀ 3 F₁) 10 yrs. Bk. of high school (12th gr.)
(N ♂ 4 F₁) 12 yrs. Bk. 12 (6th gr.)
(N ♀ 5 F₁) 10 yrs. Bk. 11 (5th gr.)
(N ♀ 6 F₁) 9 yrs. Bk. 8 (4th gr.)
(N ♀ 7 F₁) 9 yrs. Bk. 10 (5th gr.)

Language school:
None of the children has returned to language school.

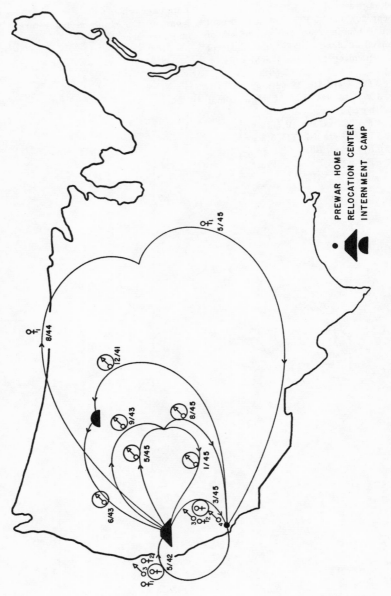

PREWAR HOME
RELOCATION CENTER
INTERNMENT CAMP

Map 3

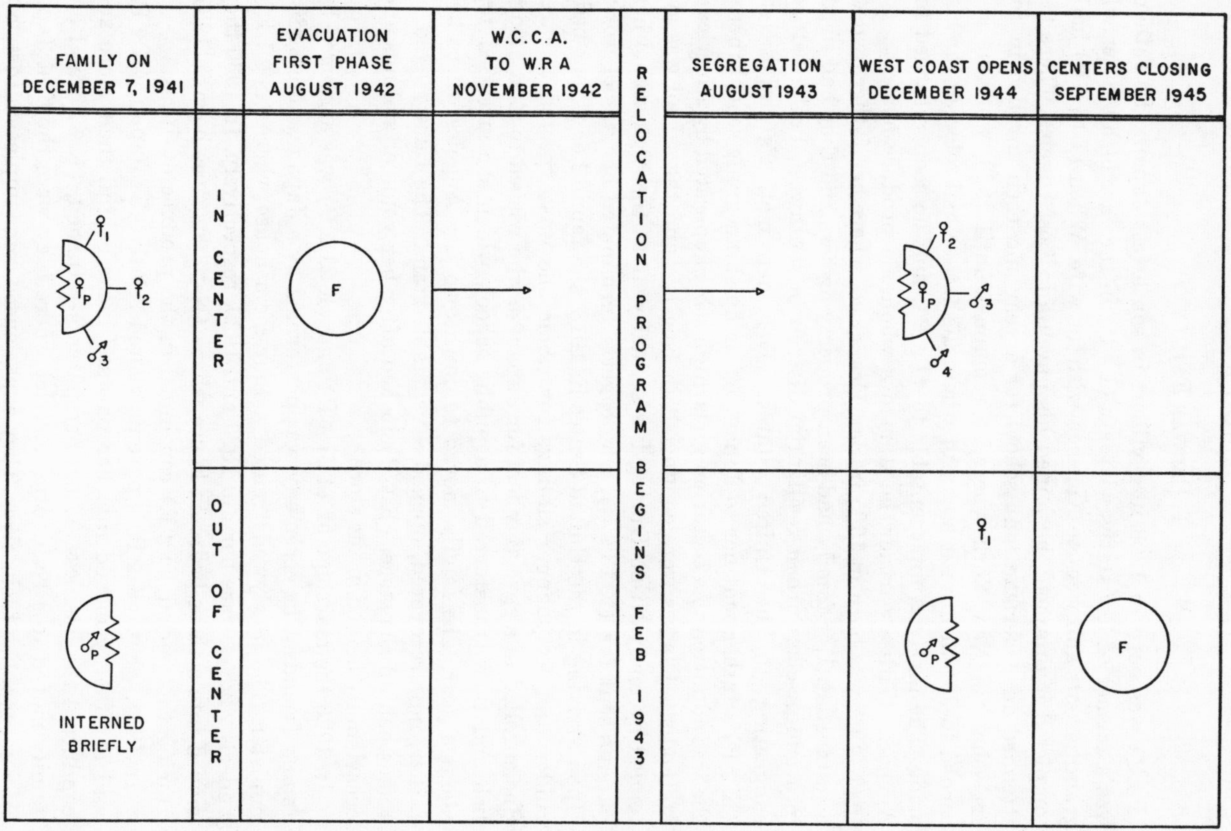

FAMILY ON
DECEMBER 7, 1941
EVACUATION
FIRST PHASE
AUGUST 1942
W.C.C.A.
TO W.R A
NOVEMBER 1942
RELOCATION PROGRAM BEGINS FEB 1943
SEGREGATION
AUGUST 1943
WEST COAST OPENS
DECEMBER 1944
CENTERS CLOSING
SEPTEMBER 1945
IN CENTER
OUT OF CENTER
INTERNED
BRIEFLY
F
F

Chart 3

CASE 3

I. Prewar Family

(I ♂ P) was born in 1899 in a village in southwest Japan. His father was a farmer of low status who left (I ♂ P) in the care of his paternal grandparents and went to America with his wife. When (I 18 ♂ P) had completed high school, he joined his parents in Los Angeles. There he attended an American high school for a year and then enrolled in an art school in New York where he remained until 1923, when he returned to Japan to visit a cousin whom his father had selected for his bride. The girl was unacceptable to (I ♂ P), and he soon returned to America. With a partner, he started a wholesale produce market.

(K ♀ P) was born in 1905 in San Francisco, where her father owned a restaurant. Her family had been property owners and they had lived in a middle-class urban residential district in southwest Japan before emigrating to the United States. Over her mother's opposition (K ♀ P)'s father sent her to Japan. After finishing grade school there, she was admitted to a sectarian girls' high school operated by American Methodists. Classes were conducted in English, and the school was attended by many Nisei. During her second year at the high school her parents sent for (K 13 ♀ P), who eagerly terminated her school work. Upon arriving in the United States in 1918, she found her father bedridden and six younger siblings for whom she was expected to care. She enrolled in a special school for Japanese who wished to study English and then transferred to a public school, which she attended for about a year. The family moved to downtown Los Angeles where her father, now recovered, opened a vegetable stand. The family lived in rooms behind the store. (K ♀ P) looked after her younger siblings and occasionally helped in the store.

In 1926 the marriage of (I 27 ♂ P) and (K 21 ♀ P) was arranged by family friends. The ceremony was performed by a Japanese Methodist minister. The newlyweds rented a four-room house where (N ♀ 1 F₁) and (N ♀ 2 F₁) were born in 1926 and 1929, respectively. In 1930 they moved into a three-bedroom house where (N ♂ 3 F₁) was born in 1931. During this period, (I ♂ P) continued in the produce business.

In 1934, when (K ♀ P)'s parents visited relatives in Japan, (K ♀ P) and her family moved into her parents' home behind their store and conducted the business. When her parents returned, (K ♀ P) and her family moved to a residential district where they were the first Japanese to establish themselves. They experienced some unpleasantness but soon gained a reputation for being dependable tenants and respectable neighbors. The landlord of a house nearby was favorably impressed and asked the family to find a Japanese tenant for him.

In 1933 (I 34 ♂ P) opened a service station with a Caucasian partner, and in the next few years they established a small chain of five stations.

In 1939 the family moved into a new stucco house in a middle-class residential section of Los Angeles. The house was purchased in the name of the Caucasian partner. There was another Japanese family in the immediate neighborhood, and the two families became the target for intermittent agitation of an unfriendly Caucasian. Most of the neighbors, however, were tolerant if not friendly.

(I ♂ P)'s leadership in the family was unquestioned. He made all important decisions affecting the family, and (K ♀ P) was told little about financial matters. From the beginning of their marriage, she was given $25 per week for household expenses, and although (I ♂ P)'s business improved, her household allowance remained unchanged until the outbreak of the war.

(I ♂ P) appears to have been the most highly acculturated member of the family. His partnership with a Caucasian gave him confidence in his dealings with other Caucasians. He tended to accept the more obvious characteristics of the culture (music, recreation, attitude toward social dancing), whereas (K ♀ P) was more strongly oriented toward the Japanese culture. She had learned to play the *koto* (Japanese harp), the *samisen* (Japanese lute), and *karuta* (Japanese cards). She did not take part in the social dancing enjoyed by her husband and was consequently either left at home or a spectator while he danced with other women. Both parents, however, encouraged social dancing by their children, and frequently the family went to see American movies, which suggests a positive orientation toward acculturation.

The formality of this patriarchal family was ameliorated by the affectional relations between the parents, and between the parents and children. The latter were between the ages of ten and fifteen in 1941 and were well within the control of their parents. (N 15 ♀ 1 F$_1$) tended toward passivity and tried at all times to please her parents. She played the big-sister role in her relations with the two younger children, arbitrating their disagreements and pacifying them whenever necessary.

Although both parents came from Buddhist families, they accepted the Christian faith and were baptized. (I 26 ♂ P) was baptized by a

Japanese Methodist minister in 1925 during the period of his engage-
ment, but he was not active in the church and after his marriage did
not attend services. When the family was living in Little Tokyo, (K ♀ P)
attended services at the Japanese Christian Church nearby, and in
1936 she was baptized. The children also attended Sunday school there
as well as the language school conducted in the church buildings. There
were Japanese and English Bibles in the home, but no Buddhist or
Shinto shrines.

Each child began Japanese-language school training when he was
about seven years old. When the family moved in 1939, they were more
conveniently located to a language school, where the children were enrolled. There, scholastic requirements were much higher than those of
the previous school, and they found the work difficult. After a half-
year at the school, an achievement test was required, and fearing a
poor showing and subsequent "shame," the children quit the school
before the examinations were given. They wanted to stop language
school entirely, but the parents arranged for them to return to their
former school, which they attended until the spring of 1941. (K ♀ P)
then undertook to teach the children, but although they completed
readers 9, 6, and 4, respectively, the attempt was a failure. The children could understand only the simplest Japanese, and their conversations with their parents were almost wholly in English.

Most of (I ♂ P)'s activities in organizations were related to his business interests. Before evacuation he was president of the California
Japanese Farmer's Association and the Japanese Garage Association.
He held nominal membership in the Nihonjinkai, kenjinkai, Japanese
Methodist Church, and the YMCA, making financial contributions
regularly. He made donations to many organizations and seldom refused when approached. He helped in the accounting committee of the
JACL and attended some of the organization's dances. (I ♂ P) believed that the Japanese should concentrate their efforts on such organizations as the JACL instead of the Nihonjinkai and kenjinkai.

(K ♀ P) was a member of the Mothers' Club of the Japanese Christian Church and was also active in the Women's League, an organization engaged in such work as collecting funds for the relief of Japanese
victims of leprosy. She contributed regularly to the financial support
of the Japanese YWCA and was a nominal member of the PTA. The
children were organizationally inactive before the war, except for
(N 15 ♀ 1 F₁) who was a member of a Nisei teen-age YWCA club.

The family had few relations with members of other races. (I ♂ P) played poker and golf with his Caucasian partner and sometimes went out to dinner with him. (I ♂ P)'s partner, however, was invited to dinner with the family only once. The children had Caucasian playmates but no close friends in their almost completely Caucasian residential neighborhood. Very rarely were friends brought into the home, and they were never entertained as guests.

II. Preëvacuation and Center Experience

The family had just returned home from a movie on December 7 when an FBI agent arrested (I 42 ♂ P). (I ♂ P) had once donated $20 to the *Kaigun Kyōkai* (Navy Society) for the entertainment of Japanese sailors visiting America. He was, presumably, imprisoned for that reason. (I ♂ P) was first detained at Lincoln Heights Jail, transferred to a CCC camp at Tujunga, and finally sent to the Missoula internment camp about December 25.

During December and January the business partner gave (K ♀ P) $100 per month for living expenses. Since (I ♂ P) had never discussed the business with her, there was little she could do to look after his interests. During the first few months of her husband's absence, (K ♀ P) often talked about her family problems with her Japanese neighbor.

After (I ♂ P) was interned, the business partner and his wife called on the family, and some of the children's classmates tried to express their sympathy. The children continued to attend school until the evacuation in the early part of May. Their church was one of the few Japanese organizations that did not close with the Pearl Harbor attack, and (K ♀ P) and the children attended its services and activities regularly.

In February (I ♂ P) decided to sell his interest in the service stations to his partner, who gave $500 in cash to (K ♀ P). This apparently represented a full and final settlement. As the date of evacuation approached, (K ♀ P) sold the family car, a 1940 Buick, for $650 and a Bendix washer for $85 (a loss of $65). Small household goods were stored in the basement of the Japanese neighbor's house. Another neighbor offered to store their refrigerator, but (K ♀ P) sold it for $110, a loss of about $50.

Although (K ♀ P)'s parents were considering voluntary evacuation, they did not invite her and her family to join them. (K ♀ P) could not believe evacuation would be ordered. In any event, she thought her family would not have to evacuate because she and the children were native born. She decided that the family should not take voluntary action pending the clarification of governmental policy. During this period of indecision, the family grew closer together, if only temporarily. Evacuation orders were received in April, and two weeks later the family was evacuated to Manzanar.

In June, 1942, (I ♂ P) was released from the internment camp to join his family in Manzanar. In August (K ♀ P) gave birth to (N ♂ 4 F₁). (I ♂ P) took a job in the center as a garage mechanic in order to learn more about automobiles. In September he assumed the responsibilities of block manager, a position he held until February, 1943. For several months afterward he worked as the manager of the canteen.

None of the children was active organizationally except in the church. (N 17 ♀ 1 F₁) was persuaded by some Catholic friends to attend services held in a barracks close to the family's apartment. The services appealed to her, and she persuaded her younger brother and sister to attend. Although the parents remained Protestant, they consented to the conversion of the three older children.

When confronted with registration, the parents decided their home was in America, and they did not wish to return to Japan. (I ♂ P), however, qualified his "yes, no" reply with a statement to the effect that since he was a Japanese citizen ineligible for American citizenship, he could not very well renounce allegiance to the Emperor. (K ♀ P) gave an unqualified affirmative reply. At the time of registration she was not certain about her citizenship status. Her friends told her that she had automatically lost her citizenship when she married an alien. Accepting the rumor as fact, she never sought reliable information on this matter. The children were too young to be required to answer the loyalty questionnaire.

III. Relocation

In September, 1943, (I ♂ P) went to Utah on terminal leave. He worked there as a greaser for a cab company until January, 1945.

(N 18 ♀ 1 F₁) was graduated from the center high school in June, 1944. In August, with the help of the Catholic priest, she secured a job as a laboratory technician apprentice at a hospital in the Midwest, and she left the center on indefinite leave.

Upon learning of rescission, (I ♂ P) returned to Manzanar in January, 1945, to take his wife and three younger children back to Los Angeles. Because of his answer in the loyalty registration of 1943, he was required to have a hearing before being permitted to return to the West Coast. In March the family learned from their prewar Japanese neighbor, who had returned to his home, that (I ♂ P)'s house was vacant. (K 40 ♀ P) immediately left Manzanar for Los Angeles with her three younger children, age sixteen, fourteen, and three years.

Meanwhile, (I ♂ P) waited for his hearing. In May he gave up hope that he could be cleared soon and applied for permission to return to Utah, where he was reëmployed by the cab company. In May, 1945, (N 19 ♀ 1 F₁) rejoined her family, and three months later (I ♂ P)'s return to Los Angeles completely reunited the group.

(K ♀ P) went to work at a factory whose owner was sympathetic toward the returning Japanese, and when (N ♀ 1 F₁) returned from the Midwest, she was employed as a bookkeeper with the same firm. (I 48 ♂ P)'s former partner refused to take him back into the service station on the grounds that it would hurt the business to associate with a Japanese. (I ♂ P) then purchased a service station in his wife's name. This enterprise has turned out satisfactorily, and (I ♂ P) is happy with his greater independence.

IV. Postwar Family*

Two years after the family's return to the West Coast, (I 48 ♂ P) maintains his patriarchal leadership of the family. (N 21 ♀ 1 F₁) is the only child who is economically independent, but she continues in her submissive filial role. Parental discipline is effectively maintained, and all the children help with domestic chores.

(N 18 ♀ 2 F₁) is less compliant to parental demands than (N ♀ 1 F₁) and tends to reject parental advice. However, she has been unable to oppose parental authority. When she graduated from high school in 1947, she wanted to attend college, but (K ♀ P) urged her to take a secretarial course at a business college. After arguing with her mother, (N ♀ 2 F₁) has complied. The parents have looked more favorably upon a college education for (N ♀ 1 F₁) who worked until December, 1946, as a bookkeeper. She then enrolled as a chemistry major at a state university; but after a semester's work, she is uncertain about continuing her education.

The family has replaced the household equipment they sold at the time of evacuation, and items stored with their neighbors were recov-

---

* Information recorded at the time of the last interview is reported in the present tense.

ered in good condition. The house is still being paid for at the rate of
$57 per month.

(I ♂ P)'s postwar business is more time-consuming than before the
war, and this added to the fact that the children are older and more
independent has led to decreased family participation.

The two girls' organizational activities are largely related to their
membership in the Catholic Church. While working as a bookeeper,
(N ♀ 1 F₁) attended an interethnic business girls' club at the downtown
YWCA. She has lately been an active member of a Nisei girls' organization of the Mission. (N ♀ 2 F₁) is a member of another Church club.
Although both (N 18 ♀ 2 F₁) and (N 16 ♂ 3 F₁) attend Catholic services regularly, they are impressed by (N 21 ♀ 1 F₁)'s serious practice
of Catholicism. She is active in the Church work, always wears a medal,
and has set up an altar in her room. The priest is a close consultant,
and on his advice she refused a job as camp counselor offered by the
nondenominational, polyethnic organization that conducts its school-
year activities at a Protestant church. (K 42 ♀ P) attends the Japanese
Christian Church, as before the war, and (I 48 ♂ P) is still an inactive
member of the Japanese Methodist Church.

(I ♂ P) has withdrawn from the many organizations that used to
keep him busy before the war. Now that he is running a station on his
own, he has little time for outside interests. (K ♀ P) has rejoined the
Women's League but has not renewed membership in the YWCA.

V. INTERPRETATION

Participation.—Before the war this family was a closely knit group
made up of (I 42 ♂ P), (K 36 ♀ P), two young teen-age daughters, and
(N 10 ♂ 3 F₁). The roles of both husband and wife were clearly defined
along patriarchal lines with the latter's duties confined to the household
and care of her children.

For twenty-four years (I ♂ P) adjusted to American society with
enterprising aggressiveness. After a year in an American high school,
and several years' experience in New York, he began his career in
small business, finally entering into a partnership with a Caucasian.
(I ♂ P) did not seek the security of the ethnic community. His instrumental approach to the dominant culture launched him upon a delib-
erate and purposeful attempt to acquire the attitudes and symbols
of the society. With facility he assumed the surface attitudes toward

economic standards, leisure, and the like, characteristic of American life, but he internalized the accompanying values to a relatively low degree.

In his relations with his family, (I ♂ P) was a dominant patriarch, and despite his own efforts toward acculturation, he did little actively to encourage the acculturation of his family. Indeed, his sink-or-swim approach to the society precipitated stresses for his less aggressive wife and children. This is illustrated by (I ♂ P)'s moving into an exclusively white neighborhood. The children were threatened rather than stimulated by their interethnic associations. They were exposed to interethnic problems for which they were expected to invent techniques of adjustment. (I ♂ P) either did not understand or care about the burden he had put on the children. His economic role required an aggressive adaptation, and his interethnic contacts were largely confined to business, where aggressiveness is legitimate. His foreign birth permitted a degree of cultural ineptness not permitted his native-born children.

It is not surprising that the children, unprepared for intensive interethnic contacts, advanced surprisingly little beyond the acculturation achieved by (I ♂ P). The family did not provide preparation, nor did the children have a fund of ethnic peer-group experience to inform them in their associations. The conservative influence of (K ♀ P) was a further obstacle to an active and positive orientation toward interethnic contacts, for she provided the alternative of withdrawal. Perhaps (I ♂ P)'s aggressive pattern of acculturation would have been more effectively transmitted to his children if the eldest child had been a male. The acculturation of the children would have been achieved with less stress had the process been experienced in association with other members of the ethnic group rather than in direct contact with the dominant society. Isolated from the ethnic community, they were exposed to the tensions of interethnic situations without ethnic-group support.

(I ♂ P)'s approach toward acculturation also affected his participation in the ethnic community. Most of his activities in formal organizations were prompted by his business interests. However, he affiliated with the Nisei-run JACL because he believed it was the correct organization to advance the interests of the community and its members. This was atypical of Issei attitudes toward the JACL and toward Nisei leadership in general. As a relatively acculturated Issei, (I ♂ P) viewed himself with reference to the Nisei group. In it he would act as a friendly mediator of intergenerational relations and gain prestige for his good offices. The Nisei were tolerant of his relatively low degree of acculturation (compared with themselves) because he was an Issei, and he was able to learn new cultural techniques in a favorable environment.

(I ♂ P) availed himself of organizational activities within the ethnic community, but his family was isolated from ethnic associations. (K ♀ P)'s organizational participation was confined largely to the activities of the church women's group where most of her associates were Issei. The children could not have found much encouragement or direction for their community activities in her generally passive attitude.

Family structure.—(I ♂ P)'s authority and leadership in the family were unquestioned, and he discharged the responsibilities of his role with unusual competence. Although his relations with (K ♀ P) and the children were affectional, he delegated few responsibilities which would have developed an attitude of initiative among others of his family. Instead, he tended to isolate his family by his aggressive mediation of the family's relations with the ethnic and dominant societies. (K ♀ P)'s passivity and adherence to the traditional role of the woman further increased the family's dependence upon (I ♂ P).

Wartime experience.—When the problems of evacuation confronted the family, (K ♀ P) had to handle the crisis. Seizing upon the fact that she and her children were American citizens, she unrealistically assumed that they would not be subject to evacuation. She relied on the formal fact of citizenship as a sufficient protection, and she had been so shielded by her husband that she was unaware of discrimination against minority groups and the vulnerability of her own group in time of war. She did not understand the imminent evacuation, nor did she know about (I ♂ P)'s business. She relied upon the advice of her Japanese neighbor and in other ways she showed her dependency upon strong male leadership. Her failure to rise to the situation suggests that she had thoroughly internalized the role of the Japanese wife who was not charged with responsibilities for making decisions.

She could not turn to her children for help. Unlike case 1, in which a fifteen-year-old son assumed leadership, none of the children had been given systematic training for leadership and responsibilities. Indeed, (N 15 ♀ 1 F₁) was much like her mother in passive withdrawal. During these months of insecurity (K ♀ P) was in early pregnancy, and this too may have contributed to her anxiety. Leadership consequently never passed into (K ♀ P)'s hands. Control over family finances went by default to (I ♂ P)'s Caucasian partner. When (I ♂ P) returned to the family six months later, they were waiting for him to resume leadership.

(I ♂ P)'s adaptive resourcefulness is notable. Faced with the registration issue, he had no doubt about remaining in the United States. His internment and economic loss did not dampen his spirit of enterprise and optimism. His "yes, no" answer to the loyalty question was clear and forceful. He rejected answers that would jeopardize either his position in the United States or his status as a citizen of Japan. Having made this decision, he characteristically proceeded to capitalize on the opportunities afforded by the center. His work in the center was no stopgap; rather he made it an instrument for his future plans. His position as the manager of the center coöperative, along with further training in automobile mechanics, developed the talents and skills for his prewar occupation. Upon his return to the West Coast, he immediately approached his farmer partner and found him unreceptive to reëstablishing the partnership; he therefore proceeded to buy and operate his own business. (I ♂ P)'s positive adjustment is what we might have expected from this aggressively enterprising individual.

Character of adjustment.—The major crisis faced by this family was the internment of (I ♂ P) which left the group leaderless and vulnerable. They were, however, among the more fortunate economically. Many families with dependent children were deprived of their sole source of income and faced anxious months before they were evacuated. It is questionable whether (K ♀ P) would have been able to adjust to the crisis at all if she had not received the small monthly income from (I ♂ P)'s business.

The evacuation must have been a relief for her. In the center her responsibilities were limited to the care of her children, and (I ♂ P)'s return relieved her of all decision-making responsibilities. She again withdrew into her passive role.

The continued stability of the family through the war underscores the importance of (I ♂ P)'s aggressive adaptability. The family adjustment was primarily (I ♂ P)'s adjustment. His leadership was always decisive and oriented toward the future, and he did not allow the past to hamper current plans. He assessed the situation as realistically as he could, expressed his objections to the registration, and proceeded to lay the basis for the relocation of his family. The flexibility of his leadership lay in his ability to work within what he considered the limits of the situation.

Cultural Data

Religion:

(I ♂ P) and (K ♀ P) were active Protestants. The children attended Sunday school and language classes affiliated with it. No Buddhist or Shinto home shrines to suggest religious origins.

Holidays:

Japanese New Year's Day observed in attenuated form. Other Japanese holidays not observed. American holidays traditionally celebated.

Diet:

(I ♂ P) preferred Japanese foods, but the children favored Western dishes. (K ♀ P) prepared two separate menus.

Reading matter:

Parents' reading largely confined to the Japanese-language papers. Subscriptions to *Life, Reader's Digest,* Los Angeles *Times,* and *Ladies Home Journal.* The family owned the *Encyclopedia Britannica,* a dictionary, a health book, and copies of Christian religious writings.

Language school:

(N ♀ 1 F₁) 7 yrs. Bk. 9 (4th gr.)
(N ♀ 2 F₁) 3 yrs. Bk. 6 (3rd gr.)
(N ♂ 3 F₁) 2 yrs. Bk. 4 (2nd gr.)

Religion:

(I ♂ P) and (K ♀ P) are less active. The three older children are members of the Catholic Church. (N ♂ 4 F₁) does not attend church school.

Holidays:

Family participation in holidays has decreased markedly.

Diet:

Predominantly Western.

Reading matter:

A few textbooks have been added. Periodicals are much the same, but Japanese magazines are no longer read. Subscriptions are fewer as a matter of economy.

Language school:

Older children have not returned to language school; (N ♂ 4 F₁) has had no formal training.

CASE 4

I. Prewar Family

(I ♂ P) was reared in Yokohama. His family owned a sizable tract of land, which he inherited. Upon graduating from a trade school, (I ♂ P) worked as a clerk for an export house. Both he and his only brother, who worked for the Japanese government, left Japan. In 1920 (I 30 ♂ P)'s firm sent him to a branch office in Mexico, but when he docked at Los Angeles he decided not to go on. He attended school to study English and auto mechanics, and in 1922 became the representative of a Caucasian company. His annual income at that time was between $4,000 and $5,000.

(I ♀ P)'s family lived in a small town in Japan where her father was employed by the Japanese Army. (I ♀ P) was educated at a Protestant college where she majored in English. After graduating from college, she taught in a high school and tutored American missionaries in Japanese. In 1921 (I 32 ♀ P) emigrated to the United States to work for a Japanese welfare agency in Los Angeles.

(I 33 ♂ P) met (I 34 ♀ P) through mutual friends in Los Angeles. Unlike the majority of Issei couples, they had a Western courtship for several months preceding their marriage. In 1923, when (I ♀ P) had fulfilled her job contract, they had a garden wedding, followed by a large reception. The ceremony was conducted by the Japanese minister of the bride's church.

In 1924 their only child, (N ♀ F$_1$), was born. The couple at first rented a house in Los Angeles, but four years after the birth of the child (only eight years after immigration) they built a house in a middle-class residential district for approximately $10,000. Some of the neighbors of this white section were opposed to Japanese, and when the family first moved into the neighborhood, they encountered veiled antagonism. One family on the block was openly hostile, and they are suspected of having put up a sign reading "No Japs Wanted" and of strewing nails on the driveway. The memory of this experience was softened when (I ♂ P)'s financial success was eventually recognized in the neighborhood.

(I ♂ P) was the leader of the family, but (I ♀ P) freely participated in the making of decisions. The affectional ties within this well-acculturated family were strong and freely expressed. The attraction which had culminated in marriage persisted and (N ♀ F$_1$) was a part of the permissive affectionate group. She was allowed to voice her

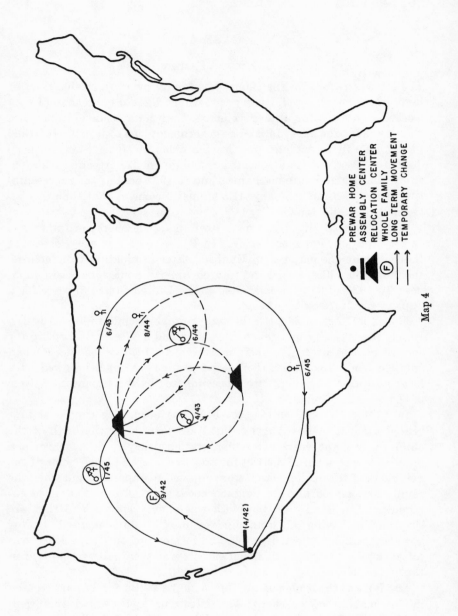

Map 4

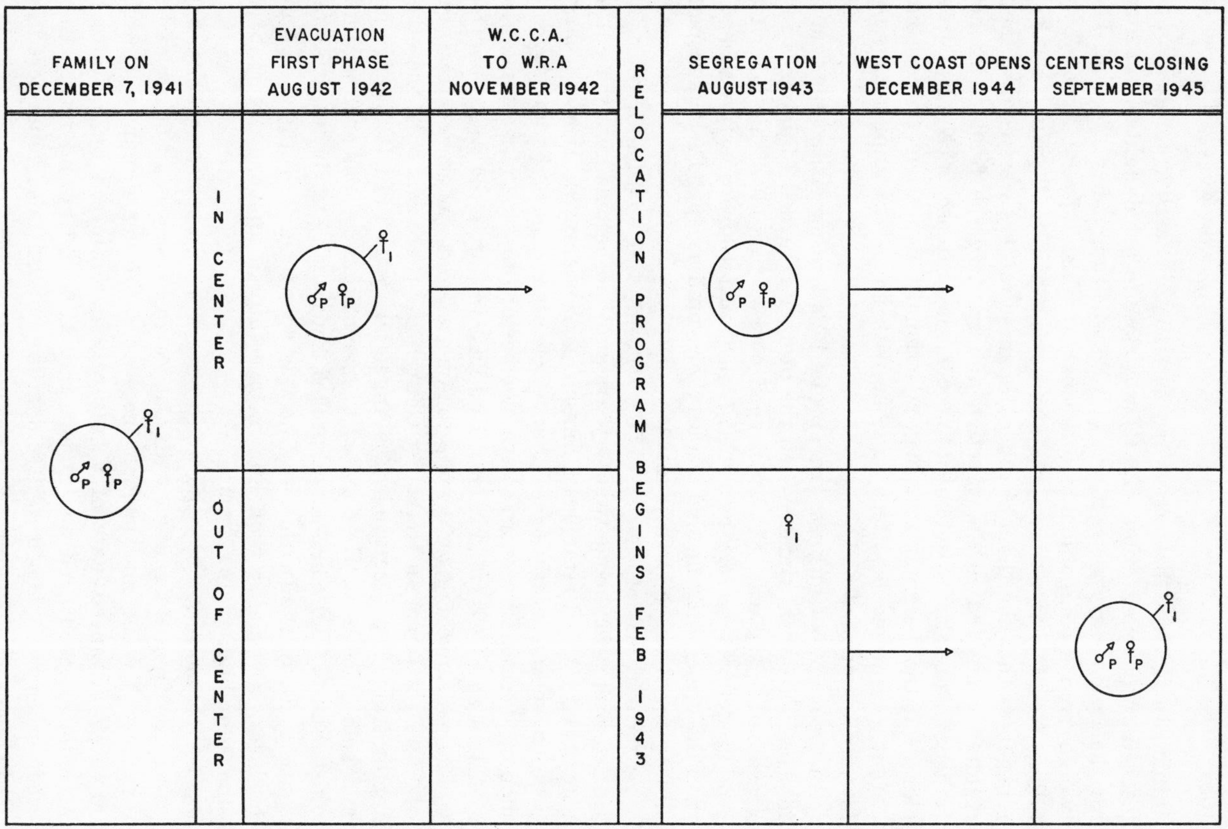

| FAMILY ON DECEMBER 7, 1941 | EVACUATION FIRST PHASE AUGUST 1942 | W.C.C.A. TO W.R.A NOVEMBER 1942 | SEGREGATION AUGUST 1943 | WEST COAST OPENS DECEMBER 1944 | CENTERS CLOSING SEPTEMBER 1945 |

IN CENTER

OUT OF CENTER

RELOCATION PROGRAM BEGINS FEB 1943

Chart 4

opinion in matters that concerned her. In this family, authority was leached away by affection. (I ♀ P) was close to her daughter, but during the child's early years it was (I ♂ P) who sought her affection. The two enjoyed a companionate relationship, which (I ♂ P) fostered by taking (N ♀ F₁) to amusements and buying her small gifts. (N ♀ F₁) remembers that she thought other Japanese fathers were cold to their children compared to the affection and security she found with her father. This relationship tended to become less intense as (N ♀ F₁) grew older, but the daughter remained affectionally dependent on both her parents, an atypical pattern and one with important implications for later adjustment.

In the course of business travel, (I ♂ P)'s brother visited the family in America several times. When the brother returned to Japan a few years before the war, (I ♂ P) turned over to him all of his inherited land as well as a factory he owned. This transfer of property was made with the understanding that the brother would accept (I ♂ P)'s responsibility for the care of their mother.

At the outbreak of the war (I 50 ♂ P) and (I 51 ♀ P) had lived in the United States for about twenty years and had become highly acculturated. (I ♂ P) had established himself as the representative of a large concern, selling mostly to a Japanese clientele, and he had achieved a modest success. He was an active member of the Japanese community. Although (I ♂ P) had been a Buddhist in Japan, he was converted to Methodism soon after coming to America and was elected treasurer of (I ♀ P)'s Japanese Methodist Church. As there was only one other family from his prefecture in Los Angeles, he joined (I ♀ P)'s kenjinkai and held office in it. He donated to many organizations such as Buddhist, Shinto, and Christian churches, kenjinkai, etc., in towns as far south as Brawley. In this way he was able to make contacts for his business. His success won him membership in an honorary club restricted to high-quota salesmen.

(I ♀ P) was active in social welfare work within her community, and came into frequent contact with Caucasians. She was an officer of the Japanese YWCA and one of the leaders of her Japanese church. (I ♀ P)'s advanced state of acculturation, reinforced by a desire to assimilate, encouraged her to join the PTA and attend its meetings when other Issei women were seldom present. She also volunteered for Red Cross and Community Chest work.

Both parents appreciated things American, but selected those values that best fitted their needs. They belonged to an intercultural organization whose membership was composed of Japanese and Americans interested in maintaining friendly relations between the two countries through cultural means. The organization did not survive the war. Both (I ♂ P) and (I ♀ P) are said to have "cultivated" American friends, but perhaps not consciously so. The nature of their work and activities brought them in contact with Caucasians in situations that encouraged friendships.

(I ♂ P) had one close Caucasian friend, the company doctor, whom he frequently invited to his home for dinner and with whom he went on fishing trips. He was also the family physician and was very much liked by both (I ♀ P) and (N ♀ F₁). (I ♂ P)'s other relationships with Caucasians were limited to those he met at the office and at conventions.

Although (I ♂ P) had joined (I ♀ P)'s church, after several years he became bored with the minister's sermons and attended a Caucasian church. (I ♀ P), however, continued to attend the Japanese church. (N ♀ F₁) attended a nondenominational Caucasian church in the neighborhood until she was ten years old. Then she transferred to a neighboring Japanese church and visited her mother's church from time to time. The religious literature in the home included several Bibles and works by Kagawa in Japanese.

In 1927, seven years after his arrival in America, (I ♂ P) visited Japan for two months to see his mother. About four years later the family took (N 6 ♀ F₁) on a pleasure trip to Japan for about a year. The parents compared the country with the Japan they had known and were impressed by the modernization of Tokyo, but (N ♀ F₁) was less impressed, especially with the plumbing facilities.

(I ♂ P) wrote frequently to his mother, each time enclosing money. He wrote to his friends as frequently. (I ♀ P)'s immediate family in Japan had died, but she wrote to one cousin and friends regularly. (N ♀ F₁) was required to write to her grandmother occasionally. Unable to compose Japanese letters, she would quarrel with her mother and compromise by copying a letter (I ♀ P) had written for her.

Until (N ♀ F₁) was nine, she had no formal training in Japanese. Parents and child usually spoke English, and English was occasionally used between the parents. However, (I ♂ P) insisted that only Japanese be spoken at the dinner table. Both (I ♀ P) and (N ♀ F₁) agreed to this rule but promptly set it aside when they found that the conversation suffered.

Many of (I ♂ P)'s Japanese friends encouraged him to send (N ♀ F₁) to a language school, but he did not think it wise for the child to attend

Japanese school after attending public school all day. (I ♀ P), who wanted to send the child to language school, gave in to her husband's argument that it might be detrimental to her health. When the child was nine, however, she was enrolled in a small school conducted by an Issei woman in her home.

Like many small Japanese-language classes, this one was short-lived, and after a year and half the school was closed. For the next two years, a private tutor was hired to come to the home. When her services were no longer available, (I ♀ P) took it upon herself to teach her daughter, but (N 14 ♀ F_1)'s lack of interest led to frequent arguments. (I ♀ P) attempted to induce greater coöperation by asking a neighborhood girl to take the lesson with (N ♀ F_1). This arrangement continued until (N ♀ F_1) was sixteen, at which time both teacher and student surrendered. By that time (N ♀ 1 F_1) had studied readers 1 through 12 (6th grade level), but she had little facility with the language.

Until (N ♀ F_1) was in high school, her Caucasian neighbor-classmates were quite friendly and there was a high degree of interaction in informal play groups, reciprocal birthday parties, and dinner invitations. She was a Campfire Girl at grammar school, and she joined the French Club in high school. The strength of her relationships with Caucasian friends declined as she became aware in junior high school of the status differences between herself and the others. When (N ♀ F_1) was about sixteen, the social interests of her friends turned increasingly outside the immediate neighborhood in which she was known and accepted. She attended social activities at school and at the Caucasian church, but she did not feel a part of the group. In high school she had a few dates with Caucasian boys. Although her experiences with Caucasians were positively valued, her feeling that she was not completely accepted turned her toward a closer identification with the Nisei group in high school. The principal of the school discouraged the organization of a Japanese students' club in an attempt to assimilate the Nisei into the school activities. However, on and off campus the Nisei tended to segregate themselves in their activities, organizing social clubs of which (N ♀ F_1) was an active member.

(N ♀ F_1) recounts an experience of discrimination when, as a junior high school student, she attended a class picnic at one of the local parks. When it came time to go swimming, the management would not allow her to enter the pool. This form of discrimination was not uncommon and is noted in cases 5 and 10. Another incident occurred one night soon after the outbreak of war. (N ♀ F_1) and her Nisei escort went to a

Hollywood dance hall and danced for an hour or more without incident, but when three other Nisei couples arrived and they congregated in one spot, the management tactfully asked them if they were of age, and with that, refunded their money. They drove to another place for more dancing, but the incident in Hollywood dampened the spirit of the evening.

II. PREËVACUATION AND CENTER EXPERIENCE

(I ♂ P) was particularly vulnerable to discrimination because the company he worked for ceased selling to Japanese after December 7. He was automatically dropped from the membership in the honorary club, and many business acquaintances rejected him. The general manager of the office told (I ♂ P) not to return after the war. Others who had remembered him at Christmas with greetings and gifts no longer did so, and this was a source of great disappointment. Several times a week (I ♂ P) had given a neighborhood girl who worked for his company a lift into town, but after Pearl Harbor she would not ride with a "Jap." These incidents contrasted sharply with his previous acceptance, and he found them difficult to rationalize. He became hypersensitive, negativistic, and bitter.

(I ♀ P) was better insulated against acts of discrimination and prejudice, for many of her friends were former missionaries, educators, and social-welfare workers. With some of them she enjoyed intimate friendships and exchanged visits. Not only did these friends stand by her after the outbreak of war; they were actively sympathetic. With this support to cushion her, the almost inescapable experiences of discrimination were less damaging and created less tension.

Several of (N 17 ♀ F₁)'s school teachers expressed sympathy for the Nisei students and offered to assist them, and as rumors of the evacuation grew, one of the family's Caucasian friends and a neighbor offered the family space to store their things, an offer the family was happy to accept. When the evacuation became imminent, the family received many telephone calls asking them whether they wanted to sell any of their property, but (I ♂ P) flatly refused. His refusal was probably prompted as much by his negative reaction to the discriminatory nature of the evacuation as it was by a belief that he would be returning to California.

Because (I ♂ P) had resolved not to sell anything, the completely furnished seven-room house was rented at $45 per month to a Caucasian family. Books and a few other personal objects were stored in the basement. With the tenant, who was a friend of (I ♂ P), the family left some garden tools and electrical equipment valued at $75. The tenant moved away during the war and entrusted the stored items to the neighbor who had opposed their moving into the neighborhood. The family automobile was stamped for identification, stored in an empty Japanese grocery store, and recovered when the family returned after the war.

When the time came for evacuating the area (I ♂ P) and (N 17 ♀ F₁) disagreed about which group they should leave with. (I ♂ P) wanted to go with friends who were located near his office, whereas (N ♀ F₁) wanted to register with her neighborhood friends. However, she could not continue to oppose her father when she realized how unhappy the wartime experiences had made him. In April the family received their notice to evacuate from the Little Tokyo section of Los Angeles to Santa Anita Assembly Center.

The common problems of adjustment to the center drew the family even closer together. The communal living encroached upon the daily family routine, but this well-integrated family resisted the impairment of functions by maximizing the opportunities for family life and strengthening affectional bonds. (N 17 ♀ F₁) was consulted more frequently in matters that were the concern of all.

Both parents and daughter felt bitter toward the government, but the family was not unified in its interpretation of the event. (I ♂ P) reacted sharply to the discriminatory nature of the evacuation, and he was strongly pro-Japanese during the first months in the center. His attitudes were reinforced by lengthy discussions with other Issei. (N ♀ F₁), however, considered the economic and social setback suffered by the Japanese as the most important consequence; but the center offered more exciting interests for young people than dwelling upon the miseries of evacuation.

(I ♂ P)'s grave view of life in the center created a conflict about (N 17 ♀ F₁)'s conduct. This conflict was brought to a head when (I ♂ P) asserted that with a war going on, and with the people in Japan undergoing hardships, it was not a time for dancing and gaiety. He forbade his daughter this recreation. (N ♀ F₁) rejected his argument, but after two weeks of unhappiness on both sides, (I ♂ P) changed his mind and agreed that perhaps young people had a real need for recreation.

(N 18 ♀ F₁) completed her senior year in high school through correspondence and received her diploma in June, 1942. Then she worked at one of the messhalls with her friends. (I ♂ P) was employed in the personnel office. In his leisure time he cultivated a small garden. (I ♀ P) taught knitting and in her spare time made clothes for her daughter.

In September, 1942, the family was transferred to another center, where (I ♂ P) became the manager of his block. One of his major interests was an abortive effort to establish a consumers' coöperative for the center. It failed, as rumor had it, because some of the appointed personnel (Caucasian) were making profits from the Community Enterprise which would have been replaced by a coöperative. It was rumored that those known to be working for the organization of the coöperative were sent to detention camps as agitators.

(I ♀ P) was a social case worker. It was her job to arrange for public assistance, marriages, funerals, divorces, distribution of clothing, etc. Both she and her husband received $19 per month.

In October, 1942, (N 18 ♀ F$_1$), through the help of the Student Relocation Council in Philadelphia, went on indefinite leave to a Midwestern college. She was among the first evacuees to leave the center. The parents strongly favored her relocation and did what they could to facilitate it, for they were anxious for her to complete her education. For themselves, the parents were content to wait until they could return to California.

(N 18 ♀ F$_1$) was apparently well adjusted to her new situation and enjoyed association with Caucasian students. In the summer of 1943 she returned to the center to visit her parents. She taught a vacation Bible-school class until she returned to college for the fall semester. For the summer of 1944 she took a camp counseling job. In August she again went to the center to visit her parents and then returned to the Midwest in September.

In the spring of 1943 (I ♂ P) visited friends in another center for about one month. He arranged to meet (N 19 ♀ F$_1$) in a nearby city, where he was attending a meeting of church laymen and ministers from the various centers, and together they had a happy holiday. In June, 1944, both parents visited outside the center. These trips made (I ♂ P) optimistic about readjustment to the life outside the centers.

At the time of the Army leave-clearance registration (N ♀ F$_1$) was already out of the center. The parents did not seriously consider repatriation and answered both loyalty questions positively. Although (I ♂ P) had investments in Japanese stocks and bonds, they did not represent the bulk of the family fortune, and they were not enough incentive for repatriation. Investments in Japan, which were common among the relatively well-to-do members of the Japanese community, were not necessarily indicative of either a patriotic or a sentimental attachment. Few Issei were able to cope with American investments, but investments in Japan were facilitated by Japanese agents in America. Not only did the Issei feel that more familiar Japanese investments afforded them greater security, but through their purchase they also acquired status in the community, as well as with families in Japan. The fact that (I ♂ P) had transferred his property in Japan to his brother several years before the war may indicate the extent of his commitment to residence in the United States. If the war had not occurred, however, he might well have gone to Japan for extended visits.

III. Relocation

When the opening of the West Coast was announced, the parents planned to return to their home as soon as possible. They had been waiting for the rescission, and with encouragement from Caucasian friends who offered to help them get settled again, they applied to return. The parents' previous experience of generally pleasant relations in a Caucasian neighborhood, reinforced by assurances of aid from their friends, made them less susceptible to rumors about the dangers of returning to the West Coast. The center restrained their individualistic attitudes, and they were more than willing to forfeit monotonous security to gain freedom and the opportunity for individual enterprise. Their individualism made these Issei most likely to respond to rescission. However, it was their extreme self-confidence and self-reliance that made adjustment so difficult, and finally impossible, for (I ♂ P).

Because their house was not yet vacant, the parents decided to visit friends en route to California. They traveled by bus, stopping at Granada and Poston (a relocation center in Arizona), and arrived in Los Angeles in February. They spent their first month with Caucasian friends and another two weeks with their Japanese neighbors.

Soon after their return, (I 55 ♂ P) began to seek a job. The company for which he had worked before the war refused to accept him. He considered employing some former center residents in a ceramics business, but he failed to carry out his plans. He ascribed his failure to discrimination rather than lack of ability and became embittered. He finally gave up the idea of going into business and began to look for work, but random job-hunting at his age was not rewarding.

During this period he contracted influenza. His illness destroyed his already weakened morale and left him despondent and personally disorganized. He found manual work in a factory but the demands of the job were too great for him, and, depressed, he committed suicide in August, 1945.

In June, 1945, after finishing her junior year at college, (N 21 ♀ F₁) joined the family in Los Angeles. Soon after her return she married a Nisei soldier whom she had met in the center. The ceremony was conducted by a Protestant minister in the home of one of the family's friends, but without the large number of friends of the parents which characterizes Japanese weddings. In the middle of 1945, six months after rescission, the Japanese population of Los Angeles was small, and traditional practices were not observed. Nonconformity was to be expected of this urban and acculturated family, and the force of tradition was further diffused by the fact that the groom's parents, who were living in Chicago, did not attend, and the bride's family was preoccupied with (I ♂ P)'s illness.

(N ♀ F₁)'s husband returned to his station shortly after the wedding, and she remained with her recently widowed mother. In September, 1945, she enrolled at a local college for her senior year. In January, 1946, (N ♀ F₁)'s husband was sent to Korea, but she awaited his return in Los Angeles, working in the mail-order department of a department store. In January, 1947, when her husband returned from Korea and was discharged from the Army, she quit her job and the couple lived with (I ♀ P) until the end of April. (N ♀ F₁) then worked at a community center until July when she left because of pregnancy. In June her husband became a real-estate broker.

IV. Postwar Family*

In June, 1947, (I 58 ♀ P) took a job as housemother of a residence for young Japanese women, leaving the house to (N 23 ♀ F₁), her husband, and a baby daughter. (I ♀ P) visited frequently with her daughter's family and was usually invited to spend the American holidays with them. Since their relocation to Los Angeles, they have not celebrated Japanese holidays. The death of (I ♂ P) and the displacement of the family by marriage has generally curtailed elaborate celebrations.

When the family returned to the West Coast, (I ♀ P) attended meetings of a religious interracial group. After several months she returned to her prewar Japanese Methodist Church. Here she found again a common body of interests with other Japanese of her age, and she was elected an officer of the women's club.

---

* Information recorded at the time of the last interview is reported in the present tense.

(N ♀ F₁) occasionally accompanied her mother, but she and her husband regularly attended a neighborhood Caucasian church to which they had been welcomed by the pastor. The couple were the only Nisei members of the church and were active in the young married group. They did not entertain any of the Caucasians in their home, however. The majority of their friends were Nisei, some of whom resented the fact that (N ♀ F₁) joined the Caucasian church and considered her a social climber. Organizationally, the young couple were not active. Most of their club activities were centered around the church, and socially they confined their activities to their relatives and Nisei friends.

The family's relations with the Caucasians in the neighborhood since their return has been generally pleasant. The family has been unable, however, to secure the return of the property stored with neighbors at the time of evacuation.

(I ♀ P) was made financially independent by (I ♂ P)'s death, but she is not content to devote herself to keeping house. The job as house-mother suits her need for new interests, and it enables her to become a part of a familiar group. She is able to leave the house to her daughter's family, an arrangement she prefers for herself as well as for them.

V. INTERPRETATION

Participation.—We have described a small, highly urbanized family of rather high socioeconomic status. The parental occupations brought them in frequent contact with Caucasian groups and individuals in many different contexts. Their community activities, unusually extensive for an Issei couple, included membership in community and occupational organizations. Organizational contacts often led to more informal associations which the parents cultivated; from these associations they learned the more subtle aspects of the dominant culture. Their membership in the Japan-American Society may be interpreted as an expression of self-conscious efforts toward acculturation and assimilation. In their interracial activities, they utilized their Japanese cultural background as an asset. Access to situations which facilitated acculturation was achieved in part through their identification with the "higher" forms of Japanese culture. This identification gave them status in the Japanese community as well as in interracial circles.

The family did not neglect its membership in the ethnic community. Although they lived in a nonethnic area the work of both parents was related to, and dependent upon, the Japanese community. As a matter of business practice, (I ♂ P) contributed to the charities and organizations of the community and was recognized as a leader, as was (I ♀ P).

Family structure.—The atypical affectional integration of this family deserves attention. In no other case is this aspect of family's life so highly developed. The one-child Japanese family itself was atypical, and it may well be that this is a major condition for the close integration. However, it does not seem probable that a less-acculturated family would have developed such an overtly expressed affectional pattern. The essential difference in this respect between the American and Japanese family is not, of course, that there is or is not affection, but in its forms of expression.

As might be expected in a family of such uniform acculturation, conflicts between parents and child were few, and when they did occur (e.g., with respect to the use of the Japanese language in the home), they were not defined as intergenerational and culture conflicts but merely as family problems. Nevertheless, (N ♀ F₁) did not wholly escape the problems of the second-generation child. Her parents' aggressive adjustment to the dominant society placed her in interracial situations in the neighborhood and schools where she experienced the subtle social discrimination of her peers. In the absence of an ethnic group to lend psychological support, such isolated Nisei often withdrew into passivity. Compare, for example, the adjustment of (N ♀ 1 F₁) in case 3. In the present case, (N ♀ F₁) sought the association of Nisei when she began to encounter discrimination. Her acculturated and affectionate parents were undoubtedly an important source of support for her, and their high status within the Japanese community provided her with ready opportunities for Nisei peer-group associations.

Wartime experience.—Their relatively advanced state of acculturation was an outstanding characteristic in the adjustment of this small family to the evacuation and the events that followed. There was little if any underlying familial dissension, and the disagreements which arose were a direct product of the evacuation and not a manifestation of preëxisting strains in the family. Such differences as the disagreement over the group with which the family should evacuate and (N ♀ F₁)'s insistence upon her right to participate in the social activities of the center were settled by drawing upon the strength of the existing familial relations.

A family of such solidarity might be expected to be less vulnerable to the disruptive effects of the manipulations to which it was subjected. This expectation is borne out by the fact that following (I ♂ P)'s initial reaction to the center, the family closed ranks and functioned as a unit in meeting the events with which they were faced. Both parents adjusted quickly to the work situation, applying themselves to work in which they were interested and could use their previous training. This was generally true of those with high occupational skills.

The parents encouraged (N ♀ F$_1$)'s prompt relocation. After she relocated, frequent correspondence and periodic visits sustained the family bonds. The common pattern of the parent joining the children at the time of relocation did not occur, however. This was congruent with the fact that although the family was closely knit, the usual correlate of strict interdependence of parents and child was lacking. The parents' familiarity with American culture made them independent of Nisei interpretation. Thus they could confidently await the opening of the West Coast, and their desire and intention to return to their home was kept alive through active correspondence with Caucasian friends.

Before the war they had enjoyed associations with Caucasians as well as Japanese, and their prematurely advanced assimilation placed them outside ethnic ghetto life, which was exaggerated in the center. The center returned them to a way of life they had outgrown and could no longer accept. On the other hand, they enjoyed high status in the Japanese community, and because of their work, they could not reject this even if they would. The parents adjusted to this ambivalent situation by capitalizing on the status accorded them by the Japanese, and at the same time maintaining and even advancing their acculturation. They accepted positions (block leader and social-welfare worker) that enabled them to function as liaison between the Administration and the Japanese.

It may well be, however, that their advanced state of acculturation underlay (I ♂ P)'s suicide. He was an ambitious and capable man and his successful prewar experience assured him that he could rebuild his business. This confidence was reinforced by his temporary leaves from the center which in themselves differentiated him from the majority of Issei who were "prisonized" and who viewed the prospect of relocation with alarm. He was unprepared for the strong resistance he met when he tried to reëstablish himself. The acts of discrimination together with the loss of occupational status were too great a burden for him. The last resort to manual labor undoubtedly symbolized the defeat that led to his suicide; in fact, the acceptance of such labor may have been a preparation for suicide, expressing as it did the magnitude of his defeat. Had he been less conscious of the symbols of status or had he been less eager to return to a status-valued job on the West Coast, he might not have failed.

Character of adjustment.—If evacuation had not intervened, this family would have achieved a high degree of Americanization and success. If the Japanese had been allowed to remain on the West Coast and take part in the war effort, this family would have made a useful contribution and would have met the crises of war without serious changes. Even after being uprooted from the environment to which it had so successfully adjusted, the group maintained a remarkable degree of integration and stability.

The most serious consequences of the institutional manipulations came as a result of the sudden rescission. Given the parents' strong orientation toward American society, their socioeconomic status, their ambitiousness, and their enterprising spirit, it was perhaps inevitable that they would be among the first evacuees to return to the area. Yet it was just such a couple who would experience the unsettled conditions of the West Coast as inhospitably hostile. They were in a real sense pioneers, but their prewar experience had led them to expect too much too soon. They were ill-prepared for a transitional period of declining tension and expanding opportunity. Perhaps they had internalized the American way too well.

Cultural Data

PREWAR

POSTWAR

Religion:
All members of family were Protestants. (I ♂ P) converted to Methodism upon marriage. (I ♀ P) educated at a Methodist college in Japan. (N ♀ F₁) attended Caucasian church as a child, later transferring to Japanese church.

Religion:
After return to the West Coast, (I ♀ P) rejoined prewar church and has been an active member. (N ♀ F₁) and her husband joined a Caucasian church.

Holidays:
Did not observe Japanese national holidays, but dolls displayed on Girls' Day, and festive rice cakes (*omanjū*) served. American holidays observed.

Holidays:
Since the death of (I ♂ P) and (I ♀ P)'s employment as a housemother, holidays have become of minor importance. (I ♀ P) is usually invited to spend American holidays with (N ♀ F₁) and her family.

Diet:
Both Japanese and American. Silver or chopsticks used with the appropriate meals.

Diet:
Growing predominance of Western-style meals.

Reading matter:
(I ♂ P) read widely. Collection included three encyclopedias, the Harvard Classics, Japanese novels, and many Japanese and English biographies and technical books. Subscriptions to *Reader's Digest*, New York *Times*, *Wall Street Journal*, *National Underwriter*, *Forbes*, *Kashu Mainichi*, *Rafu Shimpo*, Los Angeles *Times*, *Saturday Evening Post*, *Ladies Home Journal*, and two Japanese women's magazines.

Language school:
(N ♀ F₁)'s attendance at Japanese-language classes was irregular and after completing the 12th reader her facility with the language was poor.

Reading matter:
In the center (I ♂ P) joined a book club. Most of the prewar library was lost. Subscriptions have been eliminated except for a local newspaper.

CASE 5

I. PREWAR FAMILY

(I ♂ P) was born in 1880 in a rural area of southwest Japan where his family were landowners. The land was rented to local farmers, and the family itself did not engage in farming. (I ♂ P) was a third son, a half-brother to the older boys, and ineligible for inheritance. His brothers had some higher education, but (I ♂ P) completed only high school.

(I 22 ♂ P) landed in San Francisco in 1902 and took his first job in a fruit orchard in San Jose. For the next two years he worked in a Caucasian home as a "school boy" while attending a grammar school. He entered the fifth grade and continued for several years until he was able to speak understandable but broken English. He then worked as gang boss with the Southern Pacific Railroad, traveling through the west for eight years.

In 1911 he returned to Japan to seek a wife. His betrothal was arranged through a common relative. (I ♀ P) was born in 1891 in Tokyo where her family was of minor nobility. Her grandfather had been given a title for his service as a tutor to the crown prince. During the *Meiji* reformation the grandfather was a leading liberal, and to demonstrate his belief in egalitarianism, he is said to have renounced his title. Nevertheless, he and the descendant first sons for two generations were provided for under the pension system. The bride's father, therefore, received this pension, and her family lived a comfortable middle-class existence. The father was a fencing teacher, an occupation which marked him as of samurai descent.

When the couple was married, the bride was twenty-one and the groom was thirty-one. They came to the United States in 1912, and (I ♂ P) bought a nursery with his savings of $3,000. (K ♂ 1 F₁) and (N ♂ 2 F₁) were born in 1913 and 1915.

In 1916 (I 25 ♀ P) took her two sons to Japan intending to leave the elder with his maternal grandparents. She had planned to return immediately with (N ♂ 2 F₁), but (K ♂ 1 F₁) became ill and she was delayed. Six months after their arrival in Japan (I ♀ 3 F₁) was born, and about a year later (I ♀ P) returned to the United States with only one child—(N ♂ 2 F₁).

(K ♂ 1 F₁) lived in Kyoto with his maternal grandparents, and with them he had strong affectional bonds. Funds for his care were provided by his parents in the United States and his maternal uncle, who managed a department store in Shanghai. Because the grandparents' house-

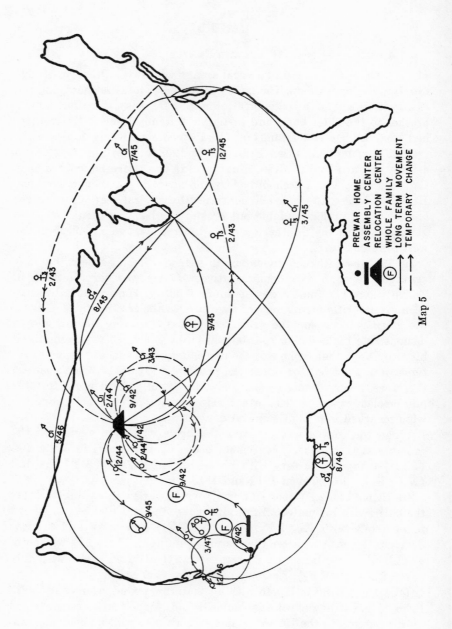

Map 5

Chart 5

hold already had five members—the grandparents, a grand uncle, (K ♂ 1 F₁), and a cousin—the elderly couple did not feel they could care for another small child, so a maternal aunt took (I ♀ 3 F₁). The families lived only about a mile apart, however, and the brother and sister frequently saw each other. The cousin, with whom the boy shared his grandparents' home, was an orphan, and theirs was a sibling relationship. (K ♂ 1 F₁) had no difficulty adjusting to Japan, having lived only the first three years of his life in America. His grandparents were of high social status, and with the help of servants they lived comfortably.

(K ♂ 1 F₁) attended school in Kyoto and often played on the palace grounds. He remembers that his playmates were intolerant of children of the lower classes who also came to play on the grounds. Group fighting aligned the children according to class, and if only a few of the lower-class children appeared, they were often abused physically and verbally. The children of the *eta* (outcast) caste were subject to contempt and were stoned and mistreated. This cruelty impressed the boy deeply, and he is now much opposed to the perpetuation of this subgroup in the United States.

During the period 1916–1923 when the two children were living in Japan, the parents wrote frequently to the uncle and sent packages and photographs to the children. The children did not correspond with their parents, however, and (K ♂ 1 F₁) soon forgot what they looked like and had no strong feelings about them. In 1923 the uncle who contributed to (K 10 ♂ 1 F₁)'s support died. The parents then decided the boy should return, and a friend of the family brought him back to the United States. Soon after he returned, (I ♀ P) went to Japan for (I 6 ♀ 3 F₁), who was one of the last Japanese to be admitted to the United States before the Oriental exclusion policy went into effect in 1924. (K ♂ 1 F₁) regarded his parents as strangers. He had been fond of his grandparents, and for a time he was homesick for Japan. For several years his parents would not allow the boy to speak to them in Japanese, and all Japanese literature was taken from him; when the family moved to an outlying area, one of the high school teachers was hired to tutor him in English. The parents used English, for they wanted him to learn the language as quickly as possible. The other children were not sent to the Japanese-language school until the eldest was about seventeen years old. The parents' interest in (K ♂ 1 F₁)'s English was not motivated by a wish to accelerate his acculturation but rather was an indication of their valuation of education. As we shall

see, the parents were grooming (K ♂ 1 F₁) to assume the role of family
leader upon the retirement of (I ♂ P). The parents were well aware of
the advantages of an American education for business success, and by
encouraging (K ♂ 1 F₁)'s learning of English they proposed to enable
him to maximize the value of his education.

In 1926 (N ♂ 4 F₁) was born. By this time the family enterprise had
prospered, and they had saved enough money to seek new business opportunities. (I ♂ P) was able to arrange for the lease of a new and
larger nursery, which entailed an investment of about $28,000. How-
ever, initiated in a period of high prices, the business was precariously
close to bankruptcy for several years. While the children were young,
the whole family joined in the work, but as school took up more of the
children's time, the business depended increasingly upon the work of
hired help. There were three or four permanent laborers, and during
the holiday seasons (Christmas and Easter) when the nursery was
especially busy, as many as twenty workers were employed.

One of the major crises in the family occurred during the depression when the business was operating at a loss. In 1933 (K 20 ♂ 1 F₁)
was in junior college and two other children were in private colleges
where the tuition and other expenses were relatively large. Because the
financial condition of the famliy was critical, (K ♂ 1 F₁) volunteered
to withdraw from school and asked the other two siblings to do the
same until the family was able to recoup. (I ♀ P), however, insisted
that (N 18 ♂ 2 F₁) and (I 16 ♀ 3 F₁) continue with their education
uninterrupted. (K ♂ 1 F₁) felt that this was unfair and argued that
all should help to bring the family through the depression, but (I ♀ P)
prevailed. Later the son became reconciled to the decision to keep his
siblings in school.

This family was relatively close-knit, perhaps more out of obedience
than affection. The children were taught the Japanese attitudes with
emphasis upon family honor and duty, and for (K ♂ 1 F₁) these values
were inculcated by his nine years in Japan. (I ♂ P) was obeyed by the
children almost without question, but he received little overt affection
from them.

Although (I ♀ P)'s role was subordinate, she was not without power.
It appears, in fact, that she wielded greater power over her children
than did (I ♂ P). This is particularly true of her relationship with
(K ♂ 1 F₁), whose judgment on business matters she supported against
(I ♂ P). She did not oppose (I ♂ P)'s methods of discipline, but she did
take a stand on issues she considered to be important to the future of

the family such as education, marriage, and the business. In business affairs mother and son agreed that (I ♂ P) had unrealistic and grandiose notions about expanding the business. They also felt that he made ostentatious and irresponsible large donations to the numerous demands of the Japanese community. In such disagreements (I ♂ P) would stubbornly maintain his position, finally wielding his authority to terminate discussion.

The nursery business did not improve, however, and in 1936 (I ♂ P) decided to change the greenhouse crop from flowers to vegetable bedding plants. The plants were sold successfully but only by carrying the farmers on credit. By 1939 (I ♂ P)'s business policy had created a situation in which there were $7,000 to $8,000 in accounts receivable, but very little cash to keep the family going from day to day. (K 26 ♂ 1 F₁), who had been working for (I ♂ P) since 1933 without regular remuneration, became impatient with this state of affairs. Because (I 59 ♂ P) would not let him manage the business, (K ♂ 1 F₁) took a job with a garage in Los Angeles (at about $75 per month) to provide money for immediate family expenses. The independent action on the part of (K ♂ 1 F₁) was within the context of family solidarity, and (I ♂ P) assisted him in finding the garage job.

A few months after (K ♂ 1 F₁) had left the business, (I ♂ P) asked him to take it over. (K ♂ 1 F₁) assumed responsibility for $4,000 in charges against the enterprise as well as $3,000 of (I ♂ P)'s personal debts. The lease was formally recorded in the name of (K 26 ♂ 1 F₁), and the ownership of the property (valued at $20,000) was signed over to him. (K ♂ 1 F₁) turned from the production of nursery plants to hothouse cucumbers because the latter could be marketed directly. The farmers who had purchased the plants were deeply in debt and were no longer regarded as good risks. The cucumber crop also required less labor, and this was advantageous because some of the acreage could be used for truck gardening. The first year of the change showed a small loss, the second year they broke even, and the third showed a profit. At the outbreak of the war, the debt had been reduced to about $3,000.

In classical Japanese form, the strongest affectional ties were between (I ♀ P) and the children, whereas (I ♂ P)'s relations with the children were formal in character. The mother often spoke to her children about the status of her family in Japan, and she wanted her children to have a higher education in order to encourage their broadest development. (I ♂ P), on the other hand, tended to think of education as a symbol of status. (K ♂ 1 F$_1$), who contributed much to the education of the other children, evaluates his siblings' education more nearly from (I ♂ P)'s point of view, despite the fact that he identifies more closely with his mother.

The family usually worked together, with (K ♂ 1 F$_1$) functioning as the most adaptive member. He made sacrifices when the others were unwilling to adjust to changing situations. He quit school and took a job to help the family, and this pattern persisted in the later familial adjustment. The Japanese culture gives approval to the eldest son who sacrifices (*gisei*) for the benefit of his family. There, however, was a higher degree of dependence of the younger children upon the parents and (K ♂ 1 F$_1$) than might be expected of postadolescent Nisei.

Until 1939 (I ♂ P) was the important decision-maker in the family. He handled business affairs and exercised strict control over the children. He opposed social activities where mixed groups were involved such as social dancing and movies and took pains to choose the right friends for his boys. His formal relations with the children tended to discourage discussion of their interests with him. Problems arising in school were discussed among themselves and did not have the counsel of the parents.

(K ♂ 1 F$_1$) had few contacts with girls until he discontinued his studies at junior college and joined (I ♂ P) to work on a full-time basis. Even then the work left him little time for social activities. He felt the consequences of this lack of training later when he was able to take part in social activities. For a long time he was inadequate and insecure in social situations, especially when women were present. Although (N ♂ 2 F$_1$) and (I ♀ 3 F$_1$) were dominated by (I ♂ P), they were able to enter into activities with students at the colleges they attended. (K ♂ 1 F$_1$), however, was always under the direct control of (I ♂ P) and consequently his freedom was circumscribed.

(I ♀ 3 F$_1$) was not so closely controlled by (I ♂ P). After graduating from the university in 1939, she looked for a stenographic position. She ascribed her failure to find a job to racial discrimination, although she could cite no specific experience. She became a tutor for the children of a Japanese consular official, and subsequently, a receptionist in a Japanese consulate in the east. There was some family discussion about (I 23 ♀ 3 F$_1$)'s working so far from home, but (I ♂ P) decided that she was old enough to go. She was happy in the east and felt much less discriminatory pressure.

In 1939 (N ♂ 2 F$_1$) was married as a yōshi (one who takes the wife's family name).* Although the couple had a courtship period of more than a year, their meeting and marriage arrangements were made through family friends. It was agreed between the parents of the couple, without the knowledge of (N ♂ 2 F₁), that in consideration for the sacrifice of his family name, his wife's family should finance his education, an opportunity his parents could not afford for him.

There was a strong and sustained persistence of Japanese cultural patterns in this family compared with others of similar residence in the United States. (I ♂ P) maintained almost absolute control over all phases of the family's activities until the three eldest children were out of high school. This control retarded the acculturation of the children. (I ♂ P)'s authority was not effectively challenged until 1939, when (K ♂ 1 F₁) was twenty-six. Until then the children had shown remarkably few overt signs of acculturation. They had few dates, did not join age-graded social organizations except for a strictly supervised membership in the Boy Scouts, and were not involved in adolescent gangs. The participation of (K ♂ 1 F₁) was especially limited. There was a differential rate of acculturation between (K ♂ 1 F₁) and his next two younger siblings. (K ♂ 1 F₁) was reared and educated in Japan until he was nine, had no opportunity to live away from home after his return to the United States, and was less exposed to American culture. The more Americanized younger siblings left home at the very period when they might have made their influence felt in the family, and although it accelerated their acculturation, it delayed the process for (K ♂ 1 F₁). His lack of experience in turn diminished the degree of interaction between himself, as the agent of the dominant culture, and his parents. The Issei were unfamiliar with the forms of social intercourse which might have made the family a more effective group in their dealings with more acculturated Japanese.

(I ♂ P) was active and held offices in various organizations in the rural community area, such as the farmers' or flower-growers' associations. He did not join his prefectural organization and there was no Nihonjinkai in the immediate area. Although he had an interest in the wholesale flower market in downtown Los Angeles, he was not active in urban organizations. He participated freely in special functions such as organizing the Japanese community for an immunization program.

Limited by her command of English and her rural residence, (I ♀ P) took very little part in community affairs. She did have an interest in the Parent Teachers' Association, and she was a member of the Japanese

---

* This new family unit is not considered a part of the primary family and does not appear on the family chart or map.

school mothers' club. Characteristically her organizational activities concerned her children.

(I ♀ 3 F$_1$) had some musical ability. She learned to play the piano, violin, and koto, and her interest in the violin continued throughout her college years. (I ♀ P) always fulfilled the children's requests for instruments or lessons that might allow them to develop their talents. The policy was (I ♀ P)'s, but was endorsed by (I ♂ P), who was proud of the high culture attained by (I ♀ P)'s side of the family.

The three older children attended language school for about two and a half years. They were older than their classmates, and they progressed rapidly, completing Book 12 (6th grade). (N 7 ♂ 4 F$_1$) enrolled at the language school in 1933 and continued for about four years, by which time he had completed the 6th-grade reader. The three older children were withdrawn when (I ♂ P) suffered business reverses in 1933. Attendance at the language school restricted the children's extracurricular activities at high school. For example, (K ♂ 1 F$_1$), who was interested in athletics, had to drop out of track. The high school coaches opposed the Japanese boys' failure to participate in sports, but even an aggressive reprimand by one of the coaches for (K ♂ 1 F$_1$)'s refusal to participate in a track meet could not move him to miss his language class.

While at college, (N ♂ 2 F$_1$) worked part time and joined no college organizations. (I ♀ 3 F$_1$) was an honor student at the university she attended. She did not join the Nisei sorority, although she was a popular girl and attended many of their parties. She played with the string section of the university orchestra as well as a junior philharmonic orchestra.

Strict family training and poor health contributed to (N ♂ 4 F$_1$)'s lack of participation in social activities. He did not join age-group organizations and occupied himself with his solitary hobbies. As the youngest child, he enjoyed the affection of all the other members.

The discrimination against Orientals in California was experienced through general awareness of practices rather than through personal incidents. References by the parents to *haiseki* (discrimination) and news items in the Japanese-American press were the chief sources of information. The children remember that at the local swimming pool minority groups were not allowed to use the pool when the water had been newly changed. At other pools the policy required doctor's permits of these minority groups. The two Caucasian friends with whom (K ♂ 1 F$_1$) and (N ♂ 2 F$_1$) went swimming refused to patronize such pools and instead went with their Japanese friends to the beach.

Having relinquished the management of the business to $(K \, \male \, 1 \, F_1)$, $(I \, 60 \, \male \, P)$ went to Japan in 1940 to visit relatives and to investigate the possible production of a machine he had invented for fabricating interlocking bricks. For seven months he traveled in China and Manchuria, and there he was impressed by Japanese industrial activity. In rural Japan, however, he found conditions much as he had left them twenty-five years before.

In mid-1941 $(I \, \male \, P)$ received a letter from a brother urging him to return to Japan with his family because war seemed imminent. Although $(I \, \male \, P)$ was skeptical of the prophecy, he was sufficiently impressed to instruct his daughter to quit her job and return to Los Angeles. His judgment turned out to be correct, for her job with the consulate later raised questions about her loyalty.

II. Preëvacuation and Center Experience

Although $(I \, \male \, P)$ had seen preparations for war in his visit to Japan in 1940, the family did not believe that a war would be precipitated. After the outbreak of hostilities, $(K \, 28 \, \male \, 1 \, F_1)$ thought Japan might win the war and that she had a moral right to begin it. $(N \, 26 \, \male \, 2 \, F_1)$ thought it impossible for Japan to win a war against the United States. $(I \, \male \, P)$ was pro-Japan. $(I \, \female \, P)$ was primarily concerned with the immediate effect the war would have on the family. She was reluctant to define the situation as a choice between Japan and the United States, and the thought of a victory for either country was distressing. $(I \, 24 \, \female \, 3 \, F_1)$'s sentiments were more clearly defined and pro-American. She was ambitious to use her talents and education in the United States.

At the outset the war affected the business little, for much of the trade was with Japanese farmers. Nor did the pattern of family life change under curfew restrictions, for the family ordinarily remained at home in the evenings. Relations with members of other racial groups were unaltered except for one incident—on the second day of the war a woman spat at $(K \, \male \, 1 \, F_1)$ as he walked into a bank.

In February, 1942, a government agent visited the house to search for evidence of illegal activity. He dumped all the papers from the desk and had $(K \, \male \, 1 \, F_1)$ clean them up. $(K \, \male \, 1 \, F_1)$ was worried because his sister had been told by federal authorities that she was under surveillance. The local police searched the house from time to time and once asked $(K \, \male \, 1 \, F_1)$ to go with them to see a federal agent. Late in February the government agents searched $(I \, \female \, 3 \, F_1)$'s room, and several weeks later (I ♂ P)'s belongings were searched. Although these investigations were distressing to the family, they were regarded as a normal consequence of (I ♀ 3 F₁)'s working at the Japanese consulate. Both (I ♀ P) and (I 25 ♀ 3 F₁) were composed when the agents took (I ♀ 3 F₁) to the Terminal Island jail, where a number of Japanese women were detained. She was detained only a few days but was placed under surveillance and required to report regularly to the pastor of a church.

After the "Battle of Los Angeles" on February 25, 1942, (K ♂ 1 F₁) decided to sell the business because he feared the incident would precipitate the much-talked-about evacuation of the Japanese. The outstanding debts and the perishable nature of the property (nursery stock and glasshouses) counseled the sale. A number of prospective buyers visited the nursery and many offered what (K ♂ 1 F₁) considered to be ridiculously low prices (as low as $3,000). One of the people sent by the Farm Security Administration offered $5,000 for the whole business, including three greenhouses, a pick-up truck, a passenger car, a tractor, equipment amounting to about $150, two houses, and part of their furnishings. The FSA agent explained to (K ♂ 1 F₁) that he was required to sign a statement that the sale had been made at a "fair price," and under the pressure of circumstances he did so. If he had been able to rent the nursery equipment, he might have made more favorable arrangements, but he was unable to find a reliable tenant. With the $5,000 the outstanding debts against the business were settled, and the family found itself without financial resources.

The terms of the sale required (K ♂ 1 F₁) to stay at the nursery until the day before his actual evacuation, and the family moved to a boarding house in Los Angeles. Some personal property was sold. Other articles, such as Japanese antiques, paintings, cooking utensils, and books, were stored with a Mexican who had worked for the family for a number of years. Only bedding, clothing, and personal effects were taken to the boarding house.

The evacuation notice was received in May, and after spending four weeks in the boarding house, the family was anxious to get the move over with. When their truck was tagged for identification, it joined the caravan to the Pomona Assembly Center. There the truck was unloaded and driven to a parking lot where the owners of motor vehicles were required to surrender their records of ownership so that the government could make a settlement. (K ♂ 1 F₁) rebelled at this, removed the certificate of ownership, and walked off into the crowd. Thus, the government could not sell the truck even though it had possession of it, and it was used at the center.

The family of five were given a barracks room to themselves; this afforded them a degree of privacy, but the construction was very poor and ordinary conversations could be heard from the adjoining apartments. The "bed count," conducted in a cavalier manner by the internal police (Japanese personnel), was much resented. Throughout the pre-evacuation and evacuation experience (I ♀ P) was controlled, but she wept when she entered the barracks for the first time.

(I 62 ♂ P) and (N 27 ♂ 2 F₁) were employed as carpenters in the center; (K 29 ♂ 1 F₁) worked as a mechanic and (I 25 ♀ 3 F₁), as a warehouse secretary. (I 51 ♀ P) did not work but knitted and read a great deal from Japanese books.

In the assembly center (I ♂ P) began to talk about repatriation. (I ♂ P) first approached (K ♂ 1 F₁), who rejected the proposal. When the others also reflected this opinion, (I ♂ P) was angered and refused to discuss the matter further. He was determined to go to Japan even if the rest were not, and he hounded the offices of the administration buildings to try to expedite the transfer. He believed his brick-making patent would make a comfortable living for the family in Japan. If he had succeeded in convincing his family, he would have regained leadership and recouped his lost status. (I ♂ P) was encouraged by the rumor circulated among the pro-Japan element that the Japanese government would send for loyal nationals in the first contingent of exchanges between Japan and the United States. The family did not resist (I ♂ P)'s plans, however, because they did not believe that the Japanese government would send for him as he expected.

The family was not compatible during the assembly-center period. The narrow confines of the room restricted their freedom; one could not rest, read, or listen to the radio without being disturbed or disturbing. The prewar pattern of integration was formal with clearly defined roles, and the family was ill-prepared for the forced intimacy of center life. (I ♂ P)'s preoccupation with repatriation was a constant source of tension. Although the children felt uncomfortable about their negative response to (I ♂ P), his actions further isolated him from the rest of the amily. Employment in the center, particularly for the Nisei, helped to alleviate the tensions by providing a routine apart from the family.

Possibly in response to (I ♂ P)'s plan for repatriation, the rest of the family decided to relocate as soon as possible. (I ♀ 3 F_1) was concerned about the effects of the center on young people. (K ♂ 1 F_1) was preoccupied with the economic status of the family. At the time of the evacuation, the family had only $2,300. (I ♀ P), who had invested much time and effort in preparing (K ♂ 1 F_1) for family leadership, supported his relocation plan with particular concern for the health and education of (N 16 ♂ 4 F_1). She rejected (I ♂ P) for his stubborn adherence to a plan which was not in the best interest of the family.

When the family moved to the Heart Mountain Relocation Center in September, 1942, it was still split by (I ♂ P)'s determination to repatriate. (I ♀ 3 F_1) tended to tolerate his arbitrariness even though she did not agree with him. (K ♂ 1 F_1), however, became increasingly resentful of (I ♂ P). The plan for relocation gained new impetus when (K ♂ 1 F_1) and (I ♀ 3 F_1) saw the danger of passive acceptance of center life.

Two weeks after the family was moved to the relocation center, (K ♂ 1 F_1) joined the first contingent of seasonal workers to go into the beet fields. (K ♂ 1 F_1) looked upon the work as an excursion, and (I ♀ P) did not discourage him, for she feared that if he remained in the center he would become involved with some girl and marry her. Returning for the winter months, he worked as a mechanic in the center motor pool.

The schism between (I ♂ P) and the rest of the family was partly healed as a result of the registration program. The family's indifference to (I ♂ P)'s repatriation plans left him with the alternatives of repatriating alone or relocating with the family. His answer to the loyalty questions are not known, for he did not discuss this decision with the family.

(K 30 ♂ 1 F_1) answered the loyalty question "no, yes." He was willing to serve in the armed forces on condition that the evacuation be terminated. Although he did not strongly protest the evacuation of the Japanese aliens, he regarded the forceable evacuation of the Nisei as a flagrant discrimination. He thought that many of the Nisei might have gone to the centers with their parents anyway had only Issei been ordered to evacuate.

(N 28 ♂ 2 F_1) answered "yes, yes." (I 26 ♀ 3 F_1), an alien, also answered "yes, yes." She was strongly pro-American and despite the evacuation she retained her confidence in American civil liberties as well as economic opportunities. (I ♀ P) also answered "yes, yes." (N 17 ♂ 4 F_1) was influenced by (K ♂ 1 F_1) and answered "no, yes."

In April, 1943, (K ♂ 1 F₁) left the center once more to work in a fruit orchard in Utah, where he remained until February, 1944. Like many other Nisei, he chose the Mountain States in order to be near the West Coast in the event that the Coast was reopened to the Japanese.

In the fall of 1943 (I ♂ P) became ill with an intestinal disorder and was advised to undergo surgery, which could not be performed at the center hospital. He was sent to a hospital in Montana where he remained for one month. During the critical period (I ♀ P) and (I ♀ 3 F₁) visited him several times. Each trip involved nearly 400 miles of travel, the expenses of which were borne by the family. Several blood transfusions were supplied by (N ♂ 2 F₁) and (I ♀ P). Although surgery and basic hospital expenses were paid by the government, other expenses of the hospitalization cost the family about $400. During his convalescence (I ♂ P) was visited by a Seventh Day Adventist who converted him. Such Adventist practices as abstention from meats, alcohol, and tobacco were compatible with the restrictions imposed by his ailment.

While working in the orchard in Utah, (K ♂ 1 F₁) received an Army induction notice, and he returned to the center in February, 1944, to take his physical examination. In the center he was asked to join a group being organized predominantly to resist the draft. (K ♂ 1 F₁) refused to participate, although he admitted that there might be a moral basis for such a protest. The parents left to (K ♂ 1 F₁) his decision on the induction notice, but they favored all legal means to avoid being drafted.

The draft-protest group exerted increasing pressure on (K ♂ 1 F₁). Its members aggressively urged him to resist the draft order and publicly abused him when he did not agree to do so. Parents whose sons did not resist the draft were the objects of gossip which accused them of sending their sons to die. (I ♀ P) became concerned for (K ♂ 1 F₁)'s safety and counseled him not to make public his opinions. To extricate himself from this situation, (K ♂ 1 F₁) took work as a mechanic on a Colorado farm. In September, 1944, he was instructed to report to Ft. Logan for his physical examination, and there he was rejected for a physical disability.

At the time of rescission, all five members of the primary family were in the center. The news was greeted with unanimous favor, but as was the case in many families, it did not evoke immediate action. Indeed, (I ♀ 3 F₁) and (K ♂ 1 F₁) held to their plans to relocate to the East Coast. (I ♀ 3 F₁) maintained that the Nisei could have no future in California, and she easily enlisted the agreement of (K ♂ 1 F₁), who was eager to see the country, although he expected eventually to return to California. (N 18 ♂ 4 F_1), who was to graduate from high school in the summer, planned to join them and enroll at one of the eastern colleges in the fall. The parents thought wistfully of returning to California, but return to the West Coast was then a pioneer venture which they could not undertake alone, and they agreed to follow their children.

III. RELOCATION

In March, 1945, (K ♂ 1 F_1) left the center to seek work in an East Coast city. After two weeks his sister joined him, and they took jobs with a machine-parts concern, (K 32 ♂ 1 F_1) as a machinist and (I 28 ♀ 3 F_1) as a time-and-motion-study technician. They were unable to find an apartment to which they could bring the rest of the family. (K ♂ 1 F_1) soon became discouraged with his job, for his wages of $1.35 per hour brought him about $75 per week, and he knew he could not support the family and put (N ♂ 4 F_1) through college. The general dissatisfaction was precipitated when (I ♀ 3 F_1) told him that she had learned that the company was hiring Japanese to exploit their poor bargaining position. They both quit their jobs but made no issue of their reason for doing so.

(K ♂ 1 F_1) favored returning to the West Coast, where he believed he would get more remunerative work. (I ♀ 3 F_1), however, found another job in the city. She wished to remain in the east, where she did not feel that she was being discriminated against on racial grounds. (K ♂ 1 F_1) decided he would stop in Chicago on the way back, and (I ♀ 3 F_1) agreed to join him there as soon as he had a place for her and the rest of the family. In July, 1945, he went to Chicago and quickly found a job as an automobile mechanic at $80 per week. He called (N 19 ♂ 4 F_1) out of the center in August and enrolled him at one of the junior colleges in Chicago.

After three months, (K ♂ 1 F_1) took an apartment large enough for his family. A few days before the parents were to join him, (I ♂ P) refused to go to a city he had heard was so cold. Instead, through the Seventh Day Adventists, he made arrangements to go to the San Francisco Bay Area in California. Although (I ♀ P) also preferred California, she felt obliged to join her sons in Chicago, especially since (K ♂ 1 F_1) had troubled to make arrangements for (N ♂ 4 F_1)'s schooling and to find an apartment.

Six months after (K ♂ 1 F_1) left for Chicago, (I ♀ 3 F_1) joined her family and took a secretarial job. The family remained in Chicago until

May, 1946, when (K ♂ 1 F₁) went to California where (I ♂ P), after living in a hostel for almost a year, had found a house for the family. During that period, (K ♂ 1 F₁) had sent him money, which was supplemented by (I 65 ♂ P)'s earnings at odd jobs as a carpenter. The two of them fixed the house as well as they could and then sent for the rest of the family. (N 20 ♂ 4 F₁) enrolled at a state university in the fall of 1946. (K ♂ 1 F₁) began work as a contract gardener and built up a route that brought him an income of $400 per month. (I ♀ 3 F₁) found employment as a secretary at a salary of about $230 per month. Neither of the parents was employed.

(K ♂ 1 F₁), however, was not satisfied with his opportunities in the Bay area. His prewar experience led him to inquire about establishing a nursery in southern California. He went to Los Angeles intending to buy a house, but inflated real-estate prices discouraged him. Instead he looked for a house to rent and after about three months found quarters on an estate where he could bring his family to live in exchange for gardening services. After preparing the living quarters, he sent for his family in March, 1947. During the period of looking for a house, (K ♂ 1 F₁) was building up a gardening route and lived at a boarding house.

In 1950 the gardening route was yielding an income of about $450 net per month. The general family expenses ran about $210 per month. (K 37 ♂ 1 F₁) was the chief financial contributor to the family, (I 33 ♀ 3 F₁) was employed as a legal stenographer at $245 per month, and (N 24 ♂ 4 F₁) worked at a nursery following his graduation from the state university and earned $160 per month. (I 70 ♂ P) was working around the estate and helping in this way to pay for the rent.

IV. POSTWAR FAMILY*

Since the family's return to southern California, their housing has been inadequate, and the estate on which they live is isolated from Japanese communities. The parents see few people outside the immediate family, and (I ♀ P) goes out only occasionally for household supplies. The family rarely has guests because of their small quarters. This is especially regretted by (K 37 ♂ 1 F₁), who has become active in the social life of the older Nisei. The family hopes to buy a house.

The patriarchal structure of the family has deteriorated and the family has become more democratic in its decision-making. (K ♂ 1 F₁),

---

* Information recorded at the time of the last interview is reported in the present tense.

upon whom the parents depend economically, is the major power in the home, and he is strongly influenced by (I 59 ♀ P). (I 70 ♂ P)'s declining health and prestige have left him with little influence, although the family is considerate of him. At the same time he has become more tolerant, and there is less tension between him and (K ♂ 1 F₁). Although he is the head of the family, (K ♂ 1 F₁) is considerate of his father's advanced years.

Major issues such as buying a house are freely discussed in the family, all opinions are heard, and decisions are informally arrived at. This procedure has tended to draw the family together, giving them a strong sense of security but at the same time committing them to a dependence upon each other. (K ♂ 1 F₁) is burdened by family responsibilities, and this limits his opportunity to find a wife.

(I ♂ P) attends a Seventh Day Adventist church in downtown Los Angeles. The other members of the family belong to no church and rarely attend services. The three children often carry their working associations outside work hours. (I ♀ 3 F₁) and (N ♂ 4 F₁) meet Caucasians socially. (K ♂ 1 F₁)'s friends are mostly Nisei, and he is the only one who has joined an organization, the JACL, of which he is an active member.

V. Interpretation

Participation.—The apparent socioeconomic status of this family was deceptively higher than the objective facts. Large capital investment during a period of inflation and indiscriminate extension of credit by (I ♂ P) had brought the enterprise close to bankruptcy. The wholesale business transactions required frequent contact with Caucasian buyers and sellers, but these rarely extended beyond business dealings. The family enterprise was dependent upon the patronage of other Japanese, and (I ♂ P) was active in various farmers' associations in the Japanese community in which he was a recognized leader. (I ♀ P)'s strongly developed sense of social status, reinforced by frequent reference to her ancestral family, magnified the importance of maintaining the family's position in the community. Her attitute toward (K ♂ 1 F₁)'s future role in the family strongly emphasized the Japanese rule of primogeniture which would ensure the continuity of the family's status in the community.

Compared with urban families the children participated in few age-graded associations. Informal activities (e.g., social gatherings, clubs, gangs), through which much of the Nisei culture was mediated, were restricted. The children's opportunities for peer-group associations were further limited by (I ♂ P)'s strong control over their activities.

The rate and degree of acculturation were not uniform among the children. Their direct participation in American society was largely confined to their school experiences, and (K ♂ 1 F₁) had fewer educational opportunities than his siblings. Both (N ♂ 2 F₁) and (I ♀ 3 F₁) had the benefits of college education and association with hakujin offered by boarding away from home. They were not under direct parental supervision while coming of age, nor were they burdened with the day-to-day expectations of their culturally conservative parents.

Family structure.—Although the strength of the family was in its integrated formal structure, its adaptability lay in the informality of (I ♀ P)'s relations with her children. The heavy demands she made upon (K ♂ 1 F₁) and indirectly on the other children were mediated by a strong identification with them. However, her sympathies were withdrawn when the children's individualism threatened her plans. None of the children, however, questioned the legitimacy of the plan or of (I ♀ P)'s right to implement it. She had trained them well, cementing the group through affection rather than coercion.

Within a strong patriarchal pattern, mediated by a matriarchal agent, filial duty was made a fundamental value in (K ♂ 1 F₁)'s training. It was expected that he would carry the main burden of perpetuating the name, and the family tradition and honor. As a young child, he was closely supervised in play, in his associations, and in his work in the family enterprise. Obedience was emphasized and subordination came to be accepted by him. (K ♂ 1 F₁) was trained to mediate the relations between the family and the dominant society, and the future of the group was entrusted to him. However, the parents attempted to prepare him for his role by socializing him to traditional Japanese forms, which were no longer functional for his adaptation as the future leader of the family in America. His lack of access to the influences of the environment limited him to the archaic instrumental forms of the Japanese culture. He was trained to be submissive and subordinate for a role that required aggressive and manipulative attitudes. To the child who needed to be most aware of changing economic and social conditions the parents denied the invaluable experience of peer-group associations and a college education. (K ♂ 1 F₁) was expected to manage the family enterprise in a rapidly changing economy while respecting (I ♂ P)'s authority to undo or countermand his efforts. Thus, the parents built conflicts into (K ♂ 1 F₁)'s socialization which later had unanticipated and dysfunctional consequences for the family group. The socialization of (K ♂ 1 F$_1$) within this traditional and isolated setting placed the major burden of acculturation on the family. In an urban environment, the socialization process probably would not have been so insulated against the dominant culture nor would the family's authority pattern have been retained for so long.

The family enterprise provided a focus for the integration of the group. All its members, even the younger children, were intimately involved in the business. The younger children were relieved of economic responsibilities by (I ♀ P), but she did not regard them as free of family obligations. Rather she conceived their obligations according to the Japanese tradition in which the eldest son insures the continuity of the family, and the remaining children carry the family name and tradition into the community at large. One feels in this case that (I ♂ P)'s ambitions were strongly ego motivated, whereas (I ♀ P) expressed her ambitions through the children. Her indirect resistance to her husband's activities may have been strengthened by the relative superiority of her family background.

The members of this group shared many common interests and sentiments, but they did not effectively act together. (I ♀ P), the central figure, was ambivalent about giving unqualified support to her children lest they become uncontrollable. However, the children were not well organized to assert their individuality, perhaps because of their uneven acculturation.

The suppression of intergenerational conflicts could be rationalized by both parents and children as being in the interest of the family. As we have suggested, however, the conflicts were latent, particularly in (K ♂ 1 F$_1$)'s role, and they found expression in the issue of the management of the business. (K ♂ 1 F$_1$)'s proposal in 1933 for a concerted family effort to save the business was rejected in spite of the family's critical economic circumstances. The rejection of his leadership again in 1939 led (K ♂ 1 F$_1$) to protest (I ♂ P)'s mismanagement by withdrawing from the family enterprise and taking a job in the city, but even then the move was made out of concern for the family welfare.

(I ♂ P) undoubtedly saw in 1939 that the time had come for him to abdicate, but he did not do so by capitulating to (K ♂ 1 F$_1$). Rather he rejected (K ♂ 1 F$_1$)'s leadership even when (I ♀ P) allied herself with the son. Three months later he consented to transfer authority to (K ♂ 1 F$_1$), an abdication without loss of face. The abdication was further attenuated by (I ♂ P)'s taking a trip to Japan; this relieved ill-feelings that might have damaged his own interest. Upon his return, little tension was left to mar the maturity with which (K ♂ 1 F₁) faced his new responsibilities. This diplomatic handling of what might have been a damaging situation firmly secured for (I ♂ P)'s old age the good will of his son.

The ability of this family to maintain its solidarity in the face of the conflict between (I ♂ P) and (K ♂ 1 F₁) may be attributed to the latter's profound commitment to the formal prescription of filial duty. The scope and breadth of this valuation allowed attacks on the authority figure in the name of family welfare. But a legitimate attack required the demonstration of a threat to the system and a recognition of the threat by the authority figures. (K ♂ 1 F₁)'s action in leaving the family enterprise in 1939 provided such a threat, and (I ♀ P) responded to it by giving the weight of her informal power to him. (I ♂ P)'s resistance to his loss of power and responsibility was contrary to the Japanese cultural provision of inkyo. A change of leadership in this family entailed (I ♂ P)'s loss of status as well as his release from responsibility. With a weaker leadership role in a less culturally conservative family, (I ♂ P) might have been able to maintain his status without responsibility. (K ♂ 1 F₁)'s refusal to accept responsibility without authority may be interpreted as a demand for the full recognition of his leadership. (Cf. case 8, sec. i.)

Wartime experience.—By December, 1941, (K ♂ 1 F₁) had securely assumed the leadership of the family and had reëstablished the stability of the family enterprise. His responses to the wartime crisis were directed toward the maintenance of the solidarity of the family. Each member considered his actions as a member of the group. Thus, when (I ♀ 3 F₁) was interned, certainly a stressful situation, neither she nor (I ♀ P) showed the strain under which they labored. The cumulative tensions of the preëvacuation and evacuation experiences were absorbed in the accommodative responses of the members to the crisis situations.

The familial reaction to (I ♂ P)'s repatriation plans revealed a strong solidarity between (I ♀ P) and her children. When (I ♂ P) threatened the interests of the group, he was dealt with harshly and was isolated from the rest of the family. This suggests that had they been capable of concerted action, the children could have changed the cultural orientation and family pattern long before. It is perhaps more significant that (I ♀ P) held the balance of power. Although her systematic attempts to indoctrinate her children with the sense of familial obligations blinded her to the strains she imposed upon the family, her primary identification was with the family as a unit and secondarily with her children. She recognized the leader by his ability to maintain the integrity of the group. (I ♂ P)'s unpopular plan and the schism it created demonstrated his inability to lead, and she joined the children in rejecting his plan and leadership.

The children's relocation plans offered a more hopeful prospect for the future of the family than (I ♂ P)'s proposal. Recognizing that a prolonged stay in the center would not only seriously reduce financial resources but also erode the basis of family life, (I ♀ P) encouraged seasonal work and relocation as realistic means of building reserves and reorienting the family to the resumption of more normal life on the "outside." Each step after the initial relocation of (K ♂ 1 F₁) and (I ♀ 3 F₁) moved toward reëstablishing the family unity. As the leader of the family, (K ♂ 1 F₁) assumed the responsibility of moving to an area which was satisfactory to the parents and provided opportunities for (N ♂ 4 F₁)'s education. Later to accommodate (I ♂ P)'s sudden refusal to relocate with the family to the east, (K ♂ 1 F₁) returned to the West Coast to secure a house to reunite the family.

This family history also indicates the costs of achieving a high degree of solidarity. Its strong economic and affectional interdependence is difficult to break. As late as 1950 both (K 36 ♂ 1 F₁) and (I 32 ♀ 3 F₁) were unmarried. They were unable to find mates suitable to themselves and to the rest of the family. As time goes on, the interdependence increases, particularly that of the parents upon the children, and the mutual involvement of family members defines marriage as a family concern.

Character of adjustment.—This family survived the evacuation and wartime experiences intact and essentially unchanged. The internal power problems which had threatened to disrupt the unity of the family had been resolved and stabilized before the war, so that the group met the wartime crises with a high degree of integration. Under a young and capable leader, the family drew upon its strong affectional bonds in a concerted effort to maintain its unity in an environment of unpredictable change.

But the price of integration was a loss of individuation and mobility, and the action of its members was conditioned at all times by considerations for family unity. The solidarity of this group proved to be highly resistant to changes in its internal structure while facilitating the maximum degree of group adjustment to institutional manipulations.

Cultural Data

Religion:
No established pattern of religious participation. (I ♂ P) converted to Christianity in Japan. (I ♀ P) from a Buddhist family but was of the Shinto faith. She discontinued practice of Shinto. Children had little interest in religion.

Holidays:
Family business did not permit suspension of work on Japanese holidays. Emperor's birthday celebrated at language school. Japanese New Year celebrated elaborately. American holiday celebrations informally observed.

Diet:
Menu both Japanese and Western.

Reading matter:
English, American, Japanese, and Russian literature as well as three sets of encyclopedias. Subscriptions to a vernacular newspaper, Los Angeles *Times*, *Saturday Evening Post*, *Collier's*, *Reader's Digest*, and popular science magazines.

Language school:
Attendance and level of achievement:
(K ♂ 1 F₁) 2½ yrs. Bk. 12 (6th gr.)
(N ♂ 2 F₁) 2½ yrs. Bk. 12 (6th gr.)
(I ♀ 3 F₁) 2½ yrs. Bk. 12 (6th gr.)
(N ♂ 4 F₁) 4 yrs. Bk. 12 (6th gr.)

Religion:
(I ♂ P) converted in the center to Seventh Day Adventist. Others have no religious affiliations.

Holidays:
New Year's Day modestly celebrated with Japanese foods. Other Japanese holidays are ignored. Secularized Christmas, Easter, and Thanksgiving holidays are observed.

Diet:
Two meals, one meatless in accordance with (I ♂ P)'s religion, are prepared. Western fare is slightly more frequent.

Reading matter:
Collection lost in storage. Few books other than textbooks. Subscriptions to a vernacular newspaper, the JACL *Pacific Citizen*, *Life*, *Reader's Digest*, *New Yorker*, *Collier's*, and *Saturday Evening Post*.

CASE 6

I. Prewar Family

(I ♂ P) came from a comfortable farming family. Although his eldest brother wished to go to the United States, family obligations did not permit this. However, he encouraged (I 18 ♂ P), who emigrated in 1902, and was followed by a younger brother several years later. (I ♂ P) found work first on a railroad in Washington, and then as a cook. Later he went into the hotel business in Oregon. In 1915 he left the hotel in the management of his younger brother and went to Japan to seek a bride.

(I ♀ P) was born to a relatively successful fishing family. An adventurous spirit, she accepted the offer of marriage arranged through a *baishakunin* and became the only girl in her neighborhood to go to America. The bride and groom were thirty-two and thirty-one years old, respectively, at the time of their marriage.

Upon reaching the United States in 1916, they discovered that the brother's poor management had bankrupted the hotel, and (I 32 ♂ P) once more took a job as a cook. In the same year, the couple moved to southern California where they worked in a citrus packing house. (K ♀ 1 F_1) was born in 1917, and in order to free (I ♀ P) for work, the child was taken to Japan and placed in the care of the maternal grandmother. During this visit to Japan, (I ♀ 2 F_1) was born, and in 1918 (I ♀ P) left the children and returned to the United States.

In 1920 the couple moved to Los Angeles, where (I 36 ♂ P) leased four stalls in a large retail fruit-and-vegetable market. (I ♀ P) helped him operate this enterprise until (N ♀ 3 F_1) was born in 1922, followed by (N ♂ 4 F_1) in 1924.

(I ♂ P)'s business was so successful that in 1926 the family was able to visit Japan for two years. After visiting their ancestral home, (I ♂ P) had a house built in southwest Japan where they lived for about a year. They seriously considered residing there permanently because (I 8 ♀ 2 F_1), who was born in Japan, was unable under immigration laws to go to the United States. Because of their business in the United States, however, they left the child in the care of (I ♂ P)'s brother and returned to Los Angeles with the other children, including (K 11 ♀ 1 F_1). The decision to leave the child in Japan gave rise to feelings of guilt which were repeatedly expressed by (I ♀ P). Having lived with her family for two years and then having been left behind, (I 10 ♀ 2 F_1)

[143]

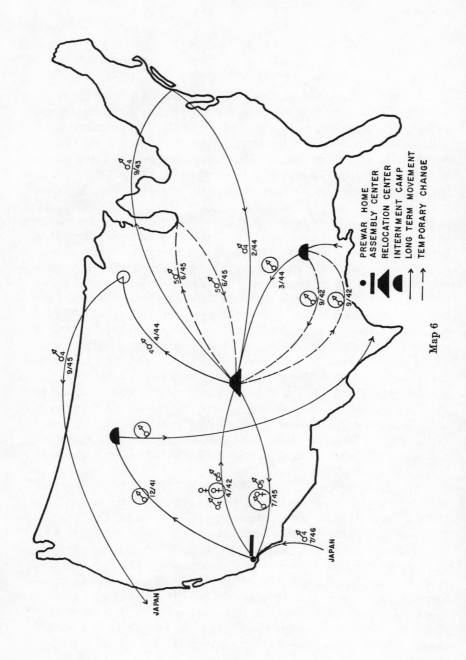

PREWAR HOME
ASSEMBLY CENTER
RELOCATION CENTER
INTERNMENT CAMP
LONG TERM MOVEMENT
TEMPORARY CHANGE

Map 6

Chart 6

felt unwanted and was resentful and bitter toward her parents for a long time.

(K 11 ♀ 1 F₁) had difficulty adjusting to life in America. Her relations with the rest of the family were formal and distant. She was not considered one of them by her siblings, owing partly to the age difference but more importantly because of cultural differences and lack of common interests. Being left out of the activities of the other children was a lonely experience for (K ♀ 1 F₁), and this accentuated the loss of her companionship with (I ♀ 2 F₁). (I ♀ P) was aware of (K ♀ 1 F₁)'s difficulties and tried to encourage her toward Americanization. Although (K ♀ 1 F₁)'s cultural background was more like her own than that of her Nisei children, she was never able to overcome the estranging effects of the discontinuity in the parent-child relationship. (K ♀ 1 F₁) eventually made friends with Kibei she met in a special language class in the public school. When they visited the house they spoke in Japanese and played Japanese records.

About 1930, (I ♂ P) sold all but one of his retail stands and in partnership leased space in the wholesale produce market in Los Angeles. This venture proved financially successful. During their early days in Los Angeles, the family lived in a rented house, but in 1936 (I ♂ P) bought a large, partly furnished frame house for $8000 and spent $5,000 more for improvements and furnishings. When the family moved into the neighborhood, it was not covenanted, but when they were followed by another Japanese family, the Caucasian neighbors agreed not to rent or sell to other nonwhites. There is, however, no record of unfriendliness. The neighborhood was occupied by a disproportionate number of old people and few children, so the children often returned to their old neighborhood to visit and play. Although (I ♀ P) did not speak English with facility, she got along well with the two immediate neighbors, a German couple and a retired minister and his wife.

(I ♂ P) was regarded as the leader of the family, but major decisions and problems such as the purchase of the house were discussed freely. (I ♀ P), who was atypically outspoken for an Issei woman, was the chief day-to-day decision-maker and enforcer of discipline. (I ♂ P) went to work before dawn in the morning, and the children had little contact with him until supper, which they ate together. The children were well disciplined and obedient, but the parents were not harsh in their disciplinary action.

(I ♂ P) urged the children to speak Japanese when they spoke English too rapidly for the parents to understand. The parents, particularly (I ♀ P), impressed Japanese cultural values upon their children. Before adolescence the children were affectionately close to their parents. (I ♀ P) would recount tales about Japanese feudal heroes, glorifying their bravery and endurance. But by the time the children entered junior high school, there was a growing breach between the parents and children. This developing cleavage in the parent-child relationship was symptomatic of the growing importance of extrafamilial associations for the Nisei.

The parents' attitude toward the acculturation of their children was permissive in general despite conflicts over specifics. Academic achievement was highly valued, but extracurricular activities such as sports and work on the school paper were discouraged. (I ♀ P) was ambitious for her children, and (I ♂ P) supported her attitudes toward schooling. He was proud of his sons' participation in sports even when he endorsed his wife's opposition to it. Although extracurricular activities at the public school were discouraged, (I ♂ P) encouraged (N ♂ 4 F$_1$) to practice Japanese fencing. At first (N ♂ 4 F$_1$) attended fencing classes under duress, but he eventually grew to enjoy its curious compound of aggressiveness and obedience.

The relationship between the parents was relatively informal, perhaps in part because (I ♀ P) was an outgoing woman. Both parents had favorites among the children. (N ♀ 3 F$_1$), as (I ♂ P)'s favorite, was the object of much affection and concern because as a young child she had been seriously ill. The youngest, (N ♂ 5 F$_1$), born in 1929, was (I ♀ P)'s favorite. The parental favoritism may have diminished affectional bonds among the children. Each of the three younger children had his own circle of friends, and, as has been noted, (K ♀ 1 F$_1$) was isolated from her siblings.

At the outbreak of war the three younger children were well on their way toward a complete acceptance of American culture. Like most Nisei, their associations were largely restricted to the relatively segregated Nisei society. Neither parent was notably acculturated. They were content to let the Nisei actively learn the new culture while they themselves learned more passively. The family was atypical in that they had visited Japan on three occasions after (I ♂ P)'s arrival in the United States. These pilgrimages to Japan may have strengthened parental involvement in their native culture, but this did not influence their attitudes toward the acculturation of the children.

(I ♀ P) corresponded regularly with relatives and in-laws in Japan as well as with (I ♀ 2 F₁). After the latter's marriage to a businessman in 1936, letters between the two were less frequent. The children, especially (K ♀ 1 F₁) who was proficient in Japanese, also wrote to their sister and relatives, the younger children using the more simple *kana* (alphabet).

For about a year the children attended a large Japanese-language school in southern California and then transferred to a small private school in their neighborhood. The children found it more pleasant to attend classes with their friends, but the school was no less a drudgery, and the Nisei continually complained about it. After several years of attendance they had learned little more than elementary Japanese.

The family was divided in their religious affiliations, but there was no conflict. The parents, who were members of a Buddhist sect, had the generally permissive Japanese attitude toward religion. Although they did not attend services regularly, they were officers in the organization. Influenced by friends, (N ♀ 3 F₁) and (N ♂ 5 F₁) regularly attended the neighborhood Japanese Methodist church. (N ♂ 4 F₁) was not interested in any church; (K ♀ 1 F₁), however, practiced Buddhism as she had in Japan.

(I ♂ P) was active in various Japanese organizations and served as an official of several. He was twice president of the Buddhist temple, an officer of the prefectural association, held offices in the Nihonjinkai, the Business Association, was a member of the Boy Scouts Parent Council, and also the organizations for *jūdo* and *kendō* (Japanese fencing). He made contributions to the Japanese Navy Association (Kaigun Kyōkai), because, as he said, "one of the solicitors was a good friend of (I ♀ P)." (I ♀ P) enjoyed organizational work and held offices in the women's branch of the prefectural association and the Buddhist temple.

(K ♀ 1 F₁) was the least active of the children. In high school she was a member of the Art Club and the Japanese students' club. (N ♀ 3 F₁) was popular in high school and belonged to several clubs in which she held various offices. She was elected a class officer on one occasion. She was also a member of a Nisei girls' club in an ethnic neighborhood where she met her friends. When she entered the university in September, 1941, she drew away from her friends in the neighborhood and was pledged to the all-Nisei sorority. (N ♂ 4 F₁) was the editor of his junior high school paper, and in high school, he was the sports editor. He was also a varsity football player and active in the honorary service organization and self-governing student body.

The family's relations with Caucasians were not extensive. (I ♂ P)'s few business associates did not visit his home except perhaps for New Year's Day. When the children were young, they played with their Caucasian neighbors, but these playmates did not become intimate friends. There was little continuity in the interethnic relations of the Nisei children. They hesitated to invite Caucasian school friends into their home because of the foreign language and customs. There were very few Nisei enrolled in $(N \male 4 F_1)$'s junior high school and high school, and he had several Caucasian friends.

In 1937 $(K 20 \female 1 F_1)$ married a twenty-six-year-old Issei accountant who had been educated in Hawaii and California. He worked in the retail produce business. In 1938 the couple had a son, followed by a daughter in 1942. Because this new family unit is not considered a part of the primary family, it does not appear on the family chart or map.

II. Preëvacuation and Center Experience

On December 7 an FBI agent arrested $(I 57 \male P)$. The family felt certain that $(I \male P)$ would be returned soon, for they knew that he had done nothing wrong. After two weeks they were notified to report to the Federal Building with $(I \male P)$'s warm clothing, but they were not permitted to see him before he was sent to an internment center at Missoula, Montana. His letters were limited to one a week, but the family was able to write to him more frequently. $(I \male P)$ worried fretfully about the family, the business, and his internment.

When $(I \male P)$ was arrested, his personal bank account amounting to several thousand dollars was frozen. Although the two senior members of $(I \male P)$'s produce company were also interned, the other partners were allowed to carry on the business until the time of evacuation. At the end, they were forced to give up their long-term lease on the stall in the fruit and vegetable market for a little over $1,000, a lease valued at $30,000 in 1950.

$(I \female P)$ assumed the leadership of the family, but her leadership was qualified by her limited knowledge of English, and she was thus dependent upon her children and drawn closer to them. She corresponded frequently with her husband for advice and talked with friends who faced similar problems. The children remained in school until two weeks before the evacuation, but they found it difficult to apply themselves, and their scholarship suffered.

The family discussed the possibility of voluntarily evacuating the area, but because their funds were frozen, they decided that it would be unwise. They were allowed to withdraw only $180 per month from

(I ♂ P)'s account, and this was supplemented by withdrawals from (N 19 ♀ 3 F₁)'s account. Even though they had nearly a month of grace before evacuation, some business was left unfinished. (I ♀ P) did not discuss business matters with (N 17 ♂ 4 F₁) at the time, but she told him later that she regretted it because she was victimized.

After seeking a tenant, the family arranged with a real-estate agent to rent their furnished house for $60 on a month-to-month basis. All art objects and other personal belongings were stored in a locked room. On April 30, clothing and a few personal belongings were loaded into the car and (K ♀ 1 F₁)'s husband drove it to the point of departure. There the car was unloaded and taken to a commercial storage company. (K ♀ 1 F₁) and her family were evacuated on the same day. The family took $400 in cash with them to the center.

(I 57 ♀ P) found the adjustment to center life difficult. Her concern for (I ♂ P) and the responsibilities of the family combined with the physical hardships of the center environment may have contributed to the condition which shortly necessitated a major operation. The children were usually considerate of (I ♀ P)'s difficulties and respected her efforts to maintain family unity.

The center school was opened shortly after the family's arrival. (N 18 ♂ 4 F₁) attended for only a few days. He then took a job with the center paper as sports editor and worked long hours at it. (N 13 ♂ 5 F₁) attended the summer school but was otherwise free to play and run about with his friends. Children of his age looked upon the evacuation and center life as a camping trip. The children corresponded a few times with some of their Caucasian friends. A friend of (N ♂ 4 F₁) visited him, and the other children were also visited by a former school teacher from the high school.

(N 20 ♀ 3 F₁) worked first as a messhall waitress, and later as an assistant in teaching first and second grade children. She was, however, a fragile girl and suffered a recurrence of a heart ailment. She was hospitalized early in September, 1942, and her heart condition was found to be incurable. (I 57 ♀ P) was also hospitalized for major surgery and the two were brought together in the same ward. (N 20 ♀ 3 F₁) inadvertently learned of her imminent death when the doctor, unaware that mother and daughter occupied adjacent beds, told (I ♀ P) that her daughter would soon die. (I ♀ P) suffered remorse for many months that (N ♀ 3 F₁) should learn of her fate in that fashion.

The family was transferred to the Colorado Relocation Center in September, 1942, and (N 20 ♀ 3 F₁) was left behind in a Los Angeles hospital, where she died three weeks later. Christian funeral services were arranged by one of her teachers in Los Angeles and were attended by former neighbors and teachers. This kindness is remembered with gratitude by the parents. A second funeral was held in the center. (I 58 ♂ P), who was then in a Louisiana internment center, was permitted to attend. (I ♀ P) reacted strongly to the death of her daughter, and she adjusted slowly to the bereavement. Her grief was complicated by her guilt for leaving the girl alone in Los Angeles even though the decision was made after a careful assessment of the advantages of hospital care. In the months following the funeral (I ♀ P) talked about the hardships of the evacuation as a major contributing factor to the death.

(N ♂ 4 F₁) felt much the same indignation as his mother about the events that surrounded the tragedy. He thought that the trying conditions of the assembly center in midsummer was a major factor in the deterioration of his sister's health, and he was angry that the doctor had let her know that death was imminent. (N ♂ 4 F₁) apparently did not generalize his resentment of the conditions of his sister's death to the evacuation as a whole.

In the relocation center (I ♀ P) and the two boys were assigned to a room superior to the assembly-center barracks. Their new room gave them a sense of privacy, and (N ♂ 4 F₁) furnished the room with tables, chairs, benches, and a cupboard, and curtains and scatter rugs were bought.

The family had just borne the tragedy of (N ♀ 3 F₁)'s death when it was faced with the Army registration and the question of segregation. (I ♂ P) was still interned; (N 18 ♂ 4 F₁) was eligible for military duty, and if he were drafted, (I 57 ♀ P) would be left with (N 13 ♂ 5 F₁), who would himself be subject to the draft in a few years. The length of the war could not be foretold, nor did the family know whether (I ♂ P) would be released. These factors had to be considered in responding to the loyalty issue. Where unknown factors were too numerous for rational and deliberative judgment, decisions had to be made on the assumption that the members of the family would survive the war. On this assumption the parents strove to keep the family together both during and after the war. The parents knew that neither (N 18 ♂ 4 F₁) nor (N 13 ♂ 5 F₁) was willing to go to Japan. The former was strongly loyal to the United States. (N 13 ♂ 5 F₁) was not yet seventeen and was thus exempt from the registration. The parents themselves did not want to be separated from their children, and they decided against repatriation. However, (I ♀ P) was bitter about her war-time experiences and answered the loyalty questions negatively as a protest. Apparently the Administration made allowances for the pro-test nature of her answer, and she was never scheduled for segregation.

In the relocation center (I ♀ P) worked as a kitchen helper. During her leisure she attended an English class organized by the Issei in the block, but soon gave it up. (N 18 ♂ 4 F₁) was enrolled in the center high school and in January, 1943, he graduated as a member of a national honor society. During the semester he held an editorial position on the high school paper. For a short time after graduating from high school he worked as an accountant and was paid $19 per month. He then quit the job to join the staff of the center newspaper and arranged to leave the center to attend college. He was encouraged to do so by his parents, and in mid-September, 1943, he left the center on student relocation leave for an East Coast university.

(I ♂ P) was interned for more than two years, being transferred from Missoula, Montana to Ft. Sill, Oklahoma, then to Livingston, Louisiana, and finally to Santa Fe, New Mexico. He felt that the internment was unjust. The government held him, he assumed, because he had donated money to the Kaigun Kyōkai (Navy Association) and he did not be-lieve that such a donation constituted an attack on the United States. The internment did not embitter him, however, and he was paroled in March, 1944, and joined his family in the relocation center where he became a steward in the block messhall. In his leisure time he played *go* (a Japanese board game) and cultivated a little garden.

In February, 1944, after a semester at a university, (N 20 ♂ 4 F₁) was ordered to report for his induction physical examination, and be-cause he had registered for the draft in the center, he returned there to see his family and friends. There he saw his father for the first time since his sister's funeral. In April he was inducted and sent to Florida for basic training. In September, 1944, he was sent to the Military Intelligence Japanese Language School and was graduated in August, 1945. He then went to Manila as an interpreter-translator and was transferred to Japan in 1946.

III. Relocation

Late in 1944 (I ♂ P) and (I ♀ P) visited friends in Denver; shortly after their return, rescission was announced. The parents had eagerly awaited the day when they would be able to return to their home, but when the West Coast was opened, they cautiously decided to wait. With

(N 21 ♂ 4 F₁) in the Army and (N 16 ♂ 5 F₁) still a youth, there was no dependable source of strength with which to face the problems of relocation and resettlement.

However, by June, 1945, conditions on the West Coast appeared reassuring, and the parents made plans to return to Los Angeles. Their relocation was delayed until July when their house in Los Angeles was to be vacated. Early in the summer of 1945 (N 16 ♂ 5 F₁) took temporary leave to visit friends in Chicago. While there, he worked for about a month in a rubber factory and then returned to the center.

In the meantime, (K ♀ 1 F₁) and her family were also planning to return to Los Angeles. In August her husband returned from Chicago, where he had relocated early in 1945. They were unable to find a house in the city, and they moved in with her parents' family.

Instead of returning to the produce business, (I 61 ♂ P) and one of his former partners bought a 1934 coupé and tools and began work as contract gardeners. His income from this work was about $175 per month which was totally consumed by living expenses. These earnings were far less than the prewar income. Had evacuation not intervened, (I ♂ P) could have looked forward to five or ten years of highly productive work. The evacuation disqualified him occupationally, and instead of reaping the rewards of years of successful work, he had to find a job compatible with his depleted physical and psychological resources. (I ♂ P) had often talked about the aggressiveness required for success in business, but he no longer spoke of that. If either of the sons had wanted to start a business, (I ♂ P) would have been willing to try again, but they were not interested. Shortly after their return to Los Angeles (I 60 ♀ P) found work to supplement the family income. Her salary of $38 per week from work in a dress shop was put away as savings.

After six months in Japan, (N 22 ♂ 4 F₁) returned to the United States and was discharged from the Army in July, 1946. During his brief stay in Japan he was able to visit his friends and relatives. He visited his sister (I 28 ♀ 2 F₁), whose marriage to a businessman had been a happy one.

In September, 1946, (N 22 ♂ 4 F₁) enrolled at a university as a sophomore. Part-time work, together with the benefits from the G.I. Bill, enabled him to contribute to the support of the family.

For four years after the family's return to Los Angeles, they shared the house with (K ♀ 1 F₁), her husband, and their family of four children. During this period, the increased number strained the capacity of the house, but there were apparently no conflicts. In November, 1949, (K ♀ 1 F₁) and her family moved into their own house in a Japanese neighborhood, and the two families visited each other frequently.

In the summer of 1949 (N 25 ♂ 4 F₁) married a Nisei who was also a student at the university. Several weeks after the wedding, the couple left for the Midwest where (N ♂ 4 F₁) enrolled in a graduate school.

IV. Postwar Family*

In the fall of 1949 when the last interview was conducted, the coresident group consisted of the parents and (N 20 ♂ 5 F₁), who was attending a university. The parents go to the temple more rarely than they did before the war, but (I ♂ P) holds an office in the Buddhist temple. He is also a member of the Japanese Co-ordinating Council, which seeks to improve relations between Nisei and Issei. (K ♀ 1 F₁), as before the war, is not involved in organizations. (N ♂ 4 F₁) does not attend church, and (N ♂ 5 F₁)'s affiliation with his prewar Methodist church is nominal. The boys take relatively little interest in either ethnic or interethnic organizations.

The relationships with other families in the neighborhood are friendly and not markedly different from the prewar days. The neighbors' attendance at (N ♀ 3 F₁)'s funeral created warm bonds, and when the family returned after the war, neighbors whom they did not know came to the house to welcome them back. As before the war, however, daily contacts with Caucasians are limited to occupational and school situations.

V. Interpretation

Participation.—The family looked to the Japanese community for their more continuous and primary associations. Through (I ♂ P)'s successful business, they enjoyed a position of prominence. (I ♂ P) was considered a leader and was active in various organizations, none of which were interethnic in character. Through (I ♂ P)'s membership the family participated in organizational activities, which the children utilized to establish their own informal associations. They subordinated cultural aspects to opportunities for sociability, although in some instances, such as jūdo and kendō, conservative cultural attitudes were undoubtedly imparted. The parents simply exposed the children to their native culture rather than systematically inculcating them with Japanese values.

---

* Information recorded at the time of the last interview is reported in the present tense.

(I ♂ P)'s economic career in the United States was characterized by an enterprising spirit. As early as 1910 he established himself in the hotel business in an ethnic community, and by 1915 he had been successful enough to make a trip to Japan. Despite the temporary setback he faced upon his return in 1916, (I ♂ P) soon invested in a second business. By 1941 he had made it the source of a comfortable middle-class standard of living for his family.

Culturally, (I ♂ P) was less enterprising. After nearly forty years in the United States, his participation in the dominant society was largely limited to business contacts. Although the family moved into a non-ethnic area several years before the war, interaction of the family with Caucasians was confined to superficial contacts with a few immediate neighbors. The children had friends among their schoolmates, but here too relations were not extended to development of interfamily activities.

Family structure.—(I ♂ P) was not a dominating figure, but authority and initiative for action resided in him. His absence from the home during most of the day left little time for association with the children, and (I ♀ P) assumed the major socializing functions. Her relations with the children were not particularly close, although she was permissive enough to create a relatively strong bond of sentiment with them. She was ambitious for her children, encouraging them in their educational pursuits, but her own lack of acculturation and sophistication did not enable her to participate meaningfully in their individuative development.

The family environment was relatively informal and permissive, but group solidarity was not strong. The presence of (K ♀ 1 F₁) was probably a major divisive factor for her relative isolation from her parents as well as from her siblings induced strains within the family. She was in the group but not of it, and her siblings' failure to accept her activated (I ♀ P)'s guilt about her own inability fully to accept her Kibei child. Thus (K ♀ 1 F₁) was, so to speak, an embarrassment to both generations, reducing the possibility of a strong sense of family solidarity. The Nisei developed their individual interests and sought their recreational associations and activities outside the family, and (K ♀ 1 F₁) was left to find her friends among other Kibei.

(I ♀ 2 F₁)'s separation from the family further attenuated group solidarity, for she represented the familial tie to Japan kept alive by parental guilt and commitment. Consequently, the parents could not fully invest themselves in their life in America even after their decision in 1928 to leave her in Japan and return to the United States. Their sense of responsibility was not easily set aside, and the possibility of reuniting the family in Japan always remained a background thought. Thus, the parents were not "free" to participate in American society, although they were permissive toward their children's acculturation.

Wartime experience.—The immediate effect of the war was to remove (I ♂ P) from the group, an event affecting the adjustment of all the family. (I ♀ P) assumed the leadership role and the responsibility for decisions. These decisions, however, were informed by the children, who functioned as interpreters of the events of the war and the subsequent evacuation. This function forced the children to step out of their pre-war dependency to cope with events of vital concern. (I ♀ P)'s leadership was consequently more apparent than real and depended heavily upon the competence of the children's interpretation.

The crisis of (I ♂ P)'s internment mobilized affectional bonds of the family, and the children made up for (I ♀ P)'s inexperience by their coöperative response to the situational stress. They acknowledged (I ♀ P)'s authority out of sympathy for the strain imposed by the absence of (I ♂ P), her concern for (N ♀ 3 F_1), and her own health.

Conditions in the center, however, were not conducive to a strongly integrated family life. The center environment increased the independence of the children, and family relations became attenuated. The permissive atmosphere which prevailed in the prewar family provided conditions for a stressless transition into independent status by enabling the children instrumentally to adapt to center life.

The family's reaction to (N ♀ 3 F_1)'s death illustrates the relatively loose structure of the group which permitted a latitude of independent response and adjustment. (N ♀ 3 F_1)'s death was rationalized as a direct consequence of the evacuation and center conditions, but it had remarkably little effect upon the direction of family adjustment. The bitterness and resentment toward the environment as a result of this tragic event were not sufficient to counter the cumulative force of the family's prewar adjustment.

Although (I ♀ P) registered her protest against the Administration in the loyalty questionnaire, this was apparently no attempt to force an "anti-American" position upon the family. (N ♂ 4 F_1), whose support would have been necessary for a decision to segregate and repatriate, was against such a move. He interpreted his sister's death within its situational context and did not generalize his resentment to the larger evacuation experience. He rejected center life as purposeless, and this appraisal led him to seek a way out of the center through relocation. Had his resentment been directed against the Administration, he might well have polarized the family toward segregation and repatriation.

Character of adjustment.—In spite of the critical nature of this family's wartime experiences, the group remained relatively unchanged. Their adaptability underlines the significance of parental permissiveness and informality in fostering the individual growth of the children. This atmosphere was not productive of a clearly defined structure of authority or a high degree of integration, but accommodation between its members was strongly developed. The relatively loose integration of the family made the group less vulnerable *as a group* to major crises. Its members responded differentially to them, permitting one member to assume responsibility and leadership when another had been incapacitated. This kind of flexibility allowed adaptive reorganization in crisis situations without loss of individual freedom which may accompany overidentification. The consistency of the family's adjustment toward American society in the face of adverse circumstances becomes more explicable in this light. The group perceived the different crises in terms of the interests of the members to whom the crises were most relevant. $(I \female P)$ was most seriously affected by $(N \female 3 F_1)$'s death, and the children accommodated to her. Registration and relocation were issues that concerned $(N \male 4 F_1)$ most directly, and the parents did not impose their will upon his decisions.

The family structure which emerged from the wartime experience is what might have been expected if the war had not intervened. Despite the economic loss with its consequences for the parents' old-age security, the members of the family have maintained their independence. This case suggests that a highly integrated family has most to win or lose when faced with environmental stress. The decisions and actions of the leader implicate the whole group, and success or failure is dependent upon his ability to assess correctly problems and group resources. A loosely integrated family is less likely to be committed to one member's decisions, permitting greater freedom for the exercise of individual choice and action.

Cultural Data

PREWAR

Religion:
$(I \male P)$ and $(I \female P)$ were Buddhists. $(K \female 1 F_1)$ was Buddhist, and $(N \female 3 F_1)$ and $(N \male 5 F_1)$ attended Methodist services. $(N \male 4 F_1)$ had no church affiliation.

POSTWAR

Religion:
Parents' affiliation with Buddhist temple more tenuous. $(N \male 5 F_1)$'s interest in church has declined.

Holidays:
New Year's Day observed according to
Japanese custom. Emperor's birthday
observed by parents. Boys' and Girls'
Days celebrated. *Obon*, a Buddhist holi-
day, observed by parents at the temple.
American holidays conventionally cele-
brated.

Diet:
Both Japanese and Western dishes were
served, the former predominating.

Reading matter:
Subscriptions to three Japanese vernacu-
lar papers and the Los Angeles *Times*.
Periodicals: *Life, Outdoor Life, Sports
Afield, Vogue, Reader's Digest*. Japanese
and English novels.

Language school:
Only (K ♀ 1 F$_1$) among the children able
to read and write Japanese with facility.
(N ♀ 3 F$_1$) 6 yrs. Bk. 12 (6th gr.)
(N ♂ 4 F$_1$) 6 yrs. Bk. 11 (6th gr.)

Holidays:
Holidays not important family occasions. Only token observances of American and Japanese holidays.

Diet:
Slight change in diet toward Western
dishes.

Reading matter:
Prewar library remains intact. Family
subscribes to one local newspaper and
one vernacular paper.

Language school:
During the war, (N ♂ 4 F$_1$) trained in
Japanese at the Army Military Intelligence School. (N ♂ 5 F$_1$) has not attended language school.

CASE 7

I. PREWAR FAMILY

(I ♂ P), the younger of two sons, was born in 1901 to a poor farming family of the *heimin* (commoner) class. In 1912 the whole family migrated from Japan to America and settled in southern California. The migration of whole families was atypical for Japanese immigrants to the United States.

(I 11 ♂ P) was enrolled in a public school where he completed the sixth grade. At the age of seventeen the boy quit school and began working in the produce industry where he soon established a business hauling vegetables.

In 1920 (I 19 ♂ P)'s marriage was arranged with a girl from a village near his own in Japan. (I ♀ P)'s father was a fairly prosperous farmer.

In 1923 (I ♂ P) went into partnership with his elder brother in the wholesale produce business. In 1933 and 1934 (I ♀ P) managed a vegetable and fruit stand in a retail food market to provide an outlet for the surplus handled by her husband. When business conditions improved, she quit the stand and went back to the management of her home. During the late 1930's the wholesale produce business was quite successful. (I ♂ P)'s business interests were divided between wholesale produce marketing and trade with Japan, and he made trips of six months' duration to Japan in 1937 and 1940 when he arranged for the exporting of home appliances and knitting machinery. While in Japan, (I ♂ P) invested in Japanese stocks and bonds.

The first child, (N ♀ 1 F_1), was born in 1923, (N ♀ 2 F_1), in 1925, (N ♂ 3 F_1), in 1927, (N ♂ 4 F_1), in 1928, and (N ♂ 5 F_1), in 1938. The family may be classed as patriarchal in form, although (I ♀ P) had a high degree of freedom in matters of the household. There is evidence that she was a resourceful woman (e.g., her management of the produce stand) and shared an interest in her husband's business. (I ♂ P) spent a good deal of time with the children, taking them to movies, golfing, and other types of recreation. He treated them without favoritism, but his judgments were decisive and did not brook argument. The children's relations with their mother were more permissive. The children got along congenially with each other, and the family was closely knit. This integration was built upon an affectional relationship between the parents. Having come to America at an early age, (I ♂ P) may have acquired more tolerant attitudes toward women than did most Issei men. The relationship also benefited from the fact that only three years

[159]

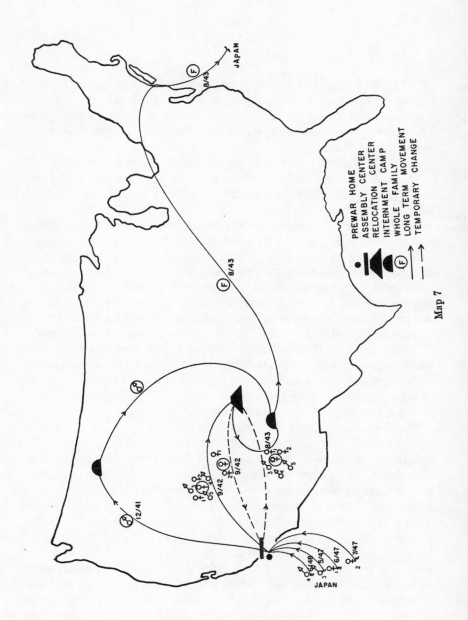

PREWAR HOME
ASSEMBLY CENTER
RELOCATION CENTER
INTERNMENT CAMP
WHOLE FAMILY
LONG TERM MOVEMENT
TEMPORARY CHANGE

Map 7

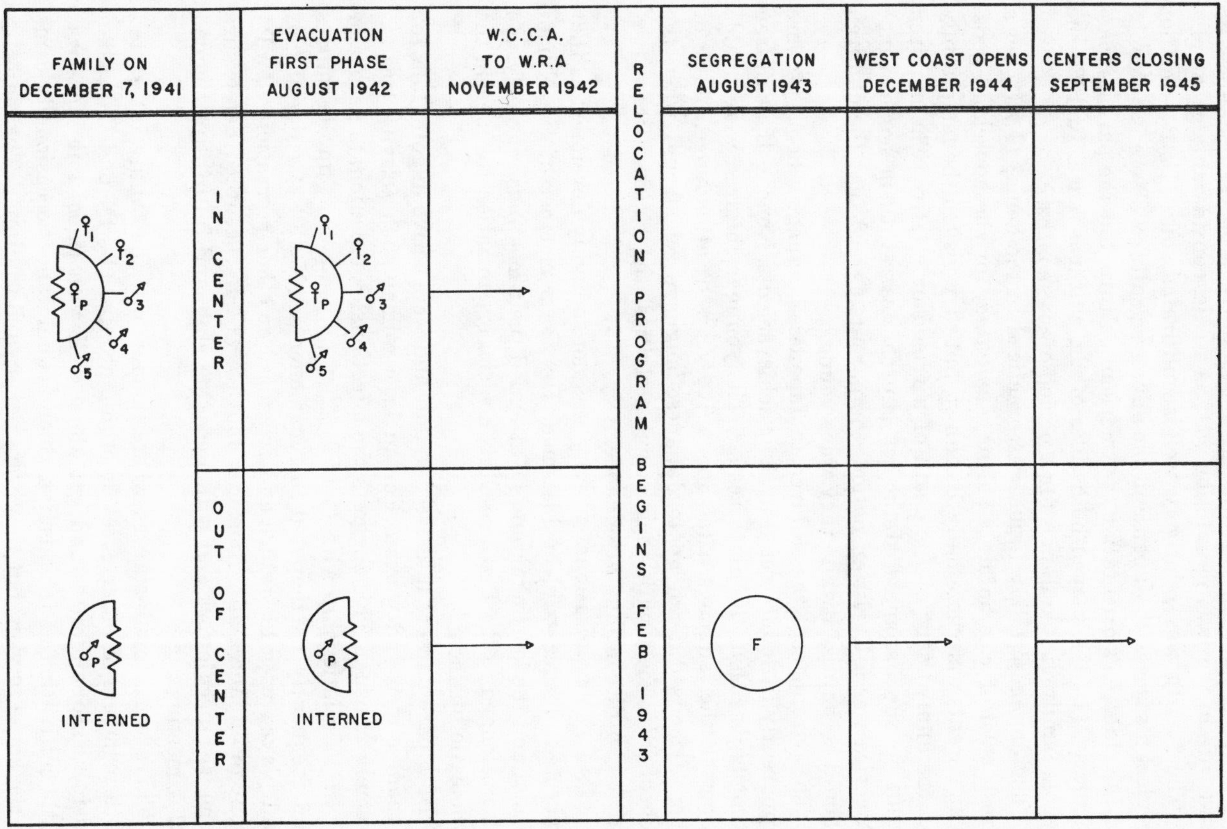

FAMILY ON DECEMBER 7, 1941
EVACUATION FIRST PHASE AUGUST 1942
W.C.C.A. TO W.R.A NOVEMBER 1942
RELOCATION PROGRAM BEGINS FEB 1943
SEGREGATION AUGUST 1943
WEST COAST OPENS DECEMBER 1944
CENTERS CLOSING SEPTEMBER 1945
IN CENTER
OUT OF CENTER
INTERNED
INTERNED
F

Chart 7

separated the husband and wife. The age differential between husband and wife in the Issei population was, as a rule, considerably greater.

The family was relatively well acculturated, but (I ♂ P) did not neglect his ties with Japan and the Japanese culture. There is no doubt of the children's orientation to American culture, but the parents, particularly (I ♂ P), played both sides of the cultural fence. In 1929 the whole family visited Japan for a period of six months.

The Japanese folk religion was practiced in the home; (I ♀ P) set a fresh bowl of rice before a shrine, *kamidana,* for the household gods. The parents were nominally Buddhist, but they visited the temple only on the anniversary of the death of a friend or relative. The children went to the Japanese Methodist church nearest their home. Since America was a Christian nation, the parents agreed that the children should be baptized while they were young.

The parents sent the children to Japanese-language school but were apparently little interested in their achievements. None of the children went higher than the ninth reader. The younger children were unable to speak the language after about five years of attendance. Many of their friends did not go to Japanese-language school and when the school interfered with their social activities, the children were permitted to discontinue attendance.

(I ♂ P)'s organizational activity was not so highly developed as that expected of successful businessmen. He was a member of the Nihon-jinkai and the kenjinkai, and he attended their meetings regularly. He also belonged to the Produce Club, a social organization for men in the wholesale business.

Both parents were interested in golf and were active in golf clubs for Japanese men and women. For an Issei woman such activity was extremely unusual. This suggests the affectional companionate nature of (I ♀ P)'s relationship with (I ♂ P). They played golf at public courses and frequently participated in tournaments. (N ♂ 3 F₁) enjoyed golf and played with his father and friends. For other recreation, (I ♂ P) went to Japanese and American movies. (I ♀ P) occupied her leisure time with needlework and with a cooking club, and faithfully attended PTA meetings.

There were few instances where members of the family interacted with members of other races or ethnic groups. (I ♂ P) had Caucasian business acquaintances and got along well with them, but there was little cultivation of friendships. Such acquaintances occasionally came to the house to visit, but they were not invited to dinner. The majority of the children's friends were Japanese, and only rarely did they join Caucasians in social activities.

II. Preëvacuation and Center Experience

At the outbreak of war the family owned a seven-room frame house. The furniture in it was valued at $5,000. The family had two cars, a new one used by (I ♀ P), and a 1937 coupé (I ♂ P) used for business. The family was composed of (I 40 ♂ P), (I 37 ♀ P), two daughters— (N 18 ♀ 1 F_1) and (N 16 ♀ 2 F_1)—and three sons—(N 14 ♂ 3 F_1), (N 13 ♂ 4 F_1), and (N 3 ♂ 5 F_1). All the children were still attending the public schools.

On December 7 (I ♂ P) and his brother were taken into custody by the FBI. The family learned that some Issei were being held on Terminal Island and went there to see him, but they were not allowed to speak to him. He was transferred inland, but they received no news from him for a month.

The assets of the produce company and (I ♂ P)'s bank account were frozen by the government immediately after the two brothers were taken into custody. Office and business equipment was impounded by the Alien Property Custodian. The two cars, which had been registered in the name of the company, were also impounded. A loss, including accounts receivable, of perhaps $100,000 was involved in the interruption of business.

(I ♀ P) drew approximately $300 per month for living expenses from her own account. She was left to assume responsibility for all family decisions and activities but was unable to secure a license to operate the market because she was an alien. Although the eldest daughter was eighteen, she did little to share (I ♀ P)'s burden.

The Caucasian neighbors were sympathetic, and the family experienced neither discrimination nor intimidation. On the contrary, the girls found that at the high school the Caucasian students were more friendly to them, and even the FBI men who came to their house to investigate (I ♂ P) were considerate of their distress. The family tried to keep up their normal activities despite the curfew restrictions. (N 18 ♀ 1 F_1) was graduated from high school in February; the other children continued at school until April, 1942.

In May they were evacuated to Santa Anita Assembly Center. (I ♀ P) had to make all the decisions in preparing for evacuation, although the physical problems were relatively simple. Most of the furniture was stored in an upstairs room, and a few possessions were left with

Caucasian neighbors. The house was left in the care of a neighbor.

At the center the family was assigned to a room about twenty feet square. Several hundred dollars were spent during the five-month period on small pieces of furniture (e.g., card tables, chairs, drapery material, etc.), ordered from a Los Angeles department store. Cots, tick mattresses, and blankets were furnished by the government.

(N 17 ♀ 2 F_1) and (N 18 ♀ 1 F_1) worked as waitresses in one of the messhalls, for which each received $8 per month. (I ♀ P) did not work while in the assembly center but attempted to keep her family unified and spent much of her time caring for (N 4 ♂ 5 F_1). Her leadership in the family was repected by the children. The members were well integrated in their relations with each other.

(I ♂ P) proposed that the family repatriate to Japan, probably while the family was in the assembly center, but (I ♀ P) did not immediately tell the children. The arrangements she made for the family possessions indicate that repatriation had not been considered at the time of evacuation.

It is uncertain if this move to repatriate was stimulated by (I ♂ P)'s detention or whether he believed the future of his family lay in a victorious Japan. The U.S. government had impounded most of the family's assets, and to begin anew after the war appeared too great a task to him. The advantages of going to Japan were many: (I ♂ P) had made a number of business acquaintances, and he had property, investments, and potential earning power there. The family did not know when he would be released to join them if they remained in the United States, but repatriation promised a reunited family immediately.

In October the family was transferred to the Granada Relocation Center. When the children were told about (I ♂ P)'s plan to repatriate, the older ones objected strenuously. Even (I ♀ P) did not support the plan. In order to work out an agreement, (I ♀ P), (N 19 ♀ 1 F_1), and (N.16 ♂ 3 F_1) went to Santa Fe where (I ♂ P) was interned. Touched by his loneliness, they agreed the family should go to Japan but that the children's American citizenship should not be renounced. When (I ♀ P) and the two children returned from their visit with (I ♂ P), the family applied for repatriation. In the course of the hearing (I ♀ P) said that she would permit the boys to be inducted into the armed forces, but she insisted that they owed a loyalty to the family also and should accompany their parents to Japan.

At Granada, (N 20 ♀ 1 F_1) worked as a secretary in the administration office and earned $19 per month. (N 18 ♀ 2 F_1) returned to high school in the relocation center and graduated in June, 1943, after which she worked for a short period in the administration offices. (N 17 ♂ 3 F₁) and (N 16 ♂ 4 F₁) resumed school. Anticipating repatriation, the family spent substantial sums for clothing, appliances, food, and furnishings, and money was invested in jewelry because they would be able to take only $600 in cash. The girls answered the loyalty question positively, for they identified with the United States. The three sons were under age and were not required to register. None of the children renounced his citizenship.

The family was notified in August, 1943, that their application for repatriation was approved, and they were informed that they would leave from New York in September. Furnishings they had accumulated during their stay in the center were given away. They left on a special train for repatriates and were reunited with (I ♂ P) en route. On the *Gripsholm* they had excellent dining, lounging, and recreational facilities. At Goa, India, they were transferred to the Japanese ship *Teia-maru,* on which the food and facilities were inferior. The ship was crowded and without recreational facilities, and the last half of the journey was not enjoyable. After seventy-five days at sea, they reached Yokohama in November, 1943.

III. RELOCATION (WARTIME JAPAN)

Upon arriving in Japan the family stayed in a Yokohama hotel until two houses, begun before the war, were completed on adjoining lots. The family purchased furniture and occupied both houses. (I ♂ P) became vice-president of a manufacturing concern. The family almost immediately recognized that repatriation was a mistake. They felt out of place in Japan, and even the relatives whom they knew through correspondence seemed strangers. This sense of isolation drew the family together; the children depended heavily upon the parents, who had to accompany them to enroll in school and to perform their routine tasks. In order to become less obtrusive, the daughters put away their more obviously American clothes and braided their hair. The attitudes of the children, and in some respects of the parents, remained American. They did not feel at home in Japan, where their speech marked them as foreign. The children's adjustment at school was difficult, and it was only when they found themselves among other Nisei that they felt at ease.

Through a friend, (I ♂ P) was introduced to the principal of a school operated by a Methodist mission, and he arranged to have the two girls enrolled. Interestingly enough, (I ♂ P) did not want his daughters to go to a school with "narrow-minded policies" and favored the mission school because the classes were taught in English. Subsequently the girls worked as clerks in the Foregin Office of the Japanese government.

(N 16 ♂ 3 F₁) and (N 15 ♂ 4 F₁) were enrolled in the boys' section of the Methodist school, but after six months they transferred to a residential school for Nisei. (N 6 ♂ 5 F₁) attended a Japanese school where he was accepted after a period of initiation. After a year, he could no longer speak English fluently. Like all foreign citizens, the children were required to carry travel permits and to report to the police every six months. They felt that they were constantly under surveillance and suspicion, and this made them resentful of the Japanese people in general. The feeling of discrimination strengthened their pro-American sentiments, and their relations with Japanese became strained.

When Tokyo was attacked by Allied bombers, the parents and the three boys were evacuated to the country. The two daughters preferred to stay in Tokyo, where they found the people more tolerant. In Japan, where male supremacy was an unquestioned fact, Nisei girls experienced severe deprivation of the personal liberties to which they were accustomed and were under greater pressure to conform to their new role than were Nisei boys. Nisei girls who persisted in retaining their American manners were considered *namaiki* (insolent).

When the armistice was declared, (N 20 ♀ 2 F₁) applied for passage to the United States. (N ♀ 1 F₁) and (N ♀ 2 F₁) found employment with one of the American military agencies in Tokyo. The sons applied for work as interpreters and were assigned to the medical corps. The colonel under whom they worked took an interest in them, and at his suggestion they joined the Army.

(N 20 ♂ 3 F₁) was sent to the United States for discharge in May, 1947. He found a place to live in Los Angeles and made a trip to Chicago for his father's projected export-import business. When he returned to Los Angeles he enrolled in a veterans' high school program. Both sons eventually attended college on the G.I. Bill.

(N 23 ♀ 1 F₁) was married in November, 1946, to a Nisei whom she met while working in the Foreign Office of the Japanese government. When the young couple applied for readmittance to the United States, (N 24 ♀ 1 F₁)'s application was approved first, and she returned to America where she gave birth to a child in August, 1947. (N 22 ♀ 2 F₁) left Japan in July, 1947, to join (N ♂ 3 F₁), who was staying with their maternal aunt in Los Angeles. (N 19 ♂ 4 F₁) reënlisted in May, 1947, and returned to the United States in 1950 to live with his two unmarried siblings. The parents were willing to let their children return to America even though they could not return. The repatriation and the attempt to establish the family in Japan were admitted failures. (N 9 ♂ 5 F$_1$) remained with his parents and attended a school for American G.I. children, arranged by listing him as a dependent of (N ♂ 3 F$_1$). The parents expect him eventually to return to America.

IV. Postwar Family

In March, 1950, the living group in America comprised (N 25 ♀ 2 F$_1$), (N 23 ♂ 3 F$_1$), and (N 22 ♂ 4 F$_1$). They shared their prewar house, of which (N 23 ♂ 3 F$_1$) was the legal owner, with three cousins whose parents were also repatriates in Japan. The relations between the siblings were casual, and in the household composed only of young people, there were few integrating functions.

V. Interpretation

Participation.—In this case we have documented the adjustment of an urban entrepreneurial family of Buddhist-Christian background and high socioeconomic status. The five children were spread over a fifteen-year age range and were provided with a family environment favorable to acculturation.

Before the war (I ♂ P) could expect continued success in his established business and in a contemplated new enterprise. His aggressiveness in business had carried him far, and he was able to deal competently with Caucasians as well as Japanese. He was not faced with the anxieties of a dependent old age, common among Issei.

(I ♂ P) was ambivalent toward adopting America as his home and place of business. Although with his brother he had built up a highly successful enterprise in America, he saw greater opportunity for his talents in Japan. His ambitions carried him twice to Japan within a period of two years, and there he tasted the prestige and status accorded to a man of his means. (I ♂ P)'s investments in Japan and the two houses he built there suggest an attempt to hedge against the risk of war.

As a large-scale wholesale produce merchant (I ♂ P) had acquired many American characteristics. However, his status aspirations were primarily and perhaps realistically oriented toward the ethnic community and his acculturation was used to enhance his ethnic status. This orientation limited the alternatives of familial adjustments to the consideration of the relative prospects of a future in the ethnic community as opposed to a future in Japan.

Family structure.—(I ♂ P) maintained a separation between his business and family life. He had freed his family of economic responsibilities, although, of ocurse, (I ♀ P) had contributed to her husband's early economic efforts. (I ♂ P) provided a comfortable middle-class standard of living. The affectional relations within the family were integrated through positively toned informal recreational activities. The parents' active interest in sports and other forms of entertainment in which they could participate with their children minimized intergeneration conflict and strengthened group solidarity.

Wartime experience.—The evacuation and (I ♂ P)'s internment precipitated his choice of a future in Japan. That his decision was opportunistic rather than nationalistic is reflected in his attitude in Japan during and after the war when he and the family kept themselves aloof and avoided organizational involvements. It is also interesting that (I ♂ P) kept his children in schools where English was spoken.

Although (I ♂ P) clearly acted as the head of his family, his power was not so great that an irrational and personal decision could have been imposed. He had to appeal to his family to support him by drawing upon affectional resources and defining the situation in broad family interests. The dependence of the children upon the parents and the strength of the affectional bonds limited their ability to oppose (I ♂ P)'s decision if they had wished to do so.

Character of adjustment.—The adjustment of this family was set by (I ♂ P)'s manipulative character, but the family he led through the difficult decision of repatriation was a highly integrated one with strongly supportive affectional bonds. (I ♂ P)'s internment set arbitrary limits of overt adaptation, for he thought he could not be released until the end of the war. He, therefore, decisively chose repatriation, effectively appealing to his family to endorse his choice. He did not obscure the problem or impose needless strains by asking his children to renounce their American citizenship. A less rationalistic or sophisticated person might well have done so, with possibly disastrous consequences for the capacity for collective action. Even when repatriation turned out unfavorably, (I ♂ P) and (I ♀ P) were able to redirect the children toward their American identification and release them to return to the United States. This, too, was accomplished without damage to familial solidarity.

Cultural Data

Religion:
Parents were Buddhist but were inactive. The children attended a Japanese Methodist church.

Holidays:
Japanese New Year elaborately celebrated. Boys' Day observed. American holidays family occasions.

Diet:
Japanese and Western dishes served.

Reading matter:
Two sets of encyclopedias in English, sets of history and Dickens, novels and children's books, Japanese encyclopedia. Subscriptions to Los Angeles *Times*, two vernacular papers, *McCall's, Ladies Home Journal, Life, Saturday Evening Post*, the Japanese publications *Kodankurabu, King*, and *Fujinkurabu*. Business journals for (I ♂ P).

Language school:
None of the children advanced beyond the 9th reader, roughly equivalent to the 5th grade in the Japanese grammar school.

Religion:
Church attendance has declined for both children and parents.

Holidays:
Japanese holidays no longer celebrated and American holidays not family occasions.

Diet:
Diet has become predominantly Western.

Reading matter:
Little change. Subscriptions to magazines have been discontinued.

Language school:
As a result of their residence in Japan the children have gained some facility in speaking Japanese.

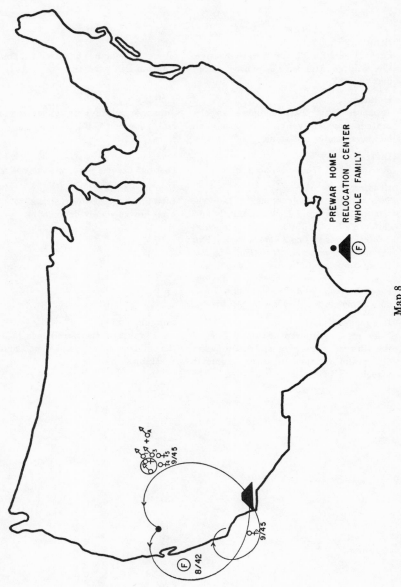

PREWAR HOME •

RELOCATION CENTER ▲

WHOLE FAMILY Ⓕ

Map 8

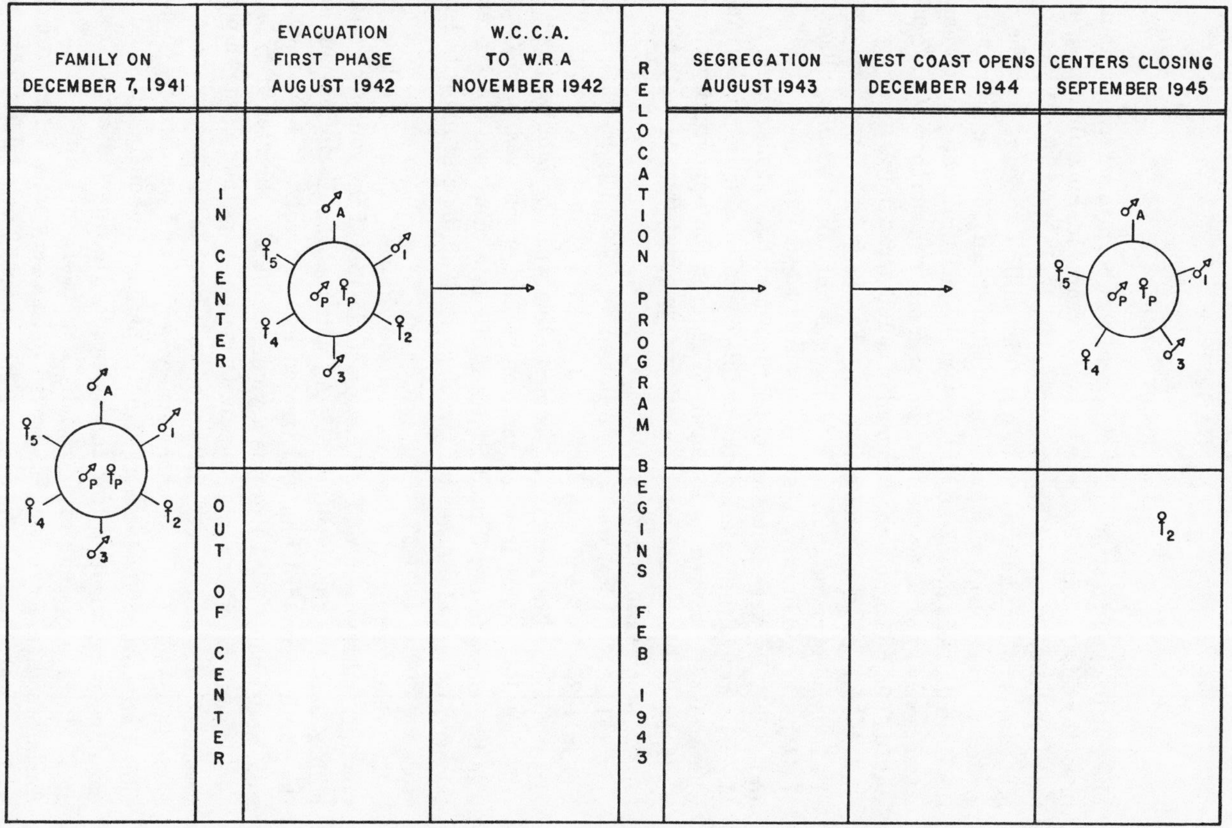

FAMILY ON DECEMBER 7, 1941	EVACUATION FIRST PHASE AUGUST 1942	W.C.C.A. TO W.R.A NOVEMBER 1942	SEGREGATION AUGUST 1943	WEST COAST OPENS DECEMBER 1944	CENTERS CLOSING SEPTEMBER 1945
	IN CENTER				
	OUT OF CENTER				

RELOCATION PROGRAM BEGINS FEB 1943

Chart 8

CASE 8

I. Prewar Family

(I ♂ P), the youngest of eight children, was born to a farming family in southwest Japan. When he was twelve years old, his father died, and his attendance at school became irregular. In 1896 (I 16 ♂ P) went to Manchuria, where he worked in a lumber mill. Two years later he migrated to Hawaii as an agricultural laborer. In 1900 he migrated to the United States mainland and first worked as a railroad section hand. After several years, he returned to farm labor in northern California, and in 1906 he became the foreman of a 160-acre vineyard.

In 1918 a picture-bride marriage (*shashin kekkon*) was arranged. (I ♀ P) was born in 1892 to a farming family in the same village as (I ♂ P). She had but two years of formal education in Japan. (I 38 ♂ P) and (I 26 ♀ P) were somewhat older than most Issei at marriage. After (I ♀ P)'s arrival in America, the couple occupied a house on the ranch where (I ♂ P) worked as foreman. Whenever the opportunity offered itself, he took contract work on other farms and then (I ♀ P) cooked for the laborers in the work camps.

In 1919, (N ♂ 1 F₁) was born, followed by (N ♀ 2 F₁) in 1923, (N ♂ 3 F₁) in 1925, (N ♂ 4 F₁) in 1929, and (N ♀ 5 F₁) in 1935. About 1920, (I ♂ P)'s elder brother (I ♂ A) came to live with the family. (I ♂ A)'s wife had died in Japan when their only child, a son, was quite young. The boy came to the United States in his late teens and worked as a farmer in Colorado. After his marriage in 1930, he and his wife lived with the family for a year.

The relationship between (I ♂ A) and the rest of the family is important. In his presence (I ♂ P) assumed the role of the younger brother rather than the family head. (I ♂ A) acted as the disciplinarian, and the children avoided him and treated him formally. (I ♀ P) resented him, and when (N ♂ 1 F₁) was a young child, she threatened to leave (I ♂ P) and take her son to Japan. Over the years the relationship between (I ♀ P) and (I ♂ A) improved to a level of mutual tolerance.

On the ranch, (I ♂ P) managed the vineyard and was directly responsible to the owner for his work. He was paid on an hourly basis and his earnings were adequate for family needs. He directed a year-round crew of three or four men (usually Japanese) and hired extra help during the harvest season. He proved to be a very satisfactory foreman and was well liked by the owner of the ranch. Their relationship was one of mutual trust and their daily contacts were friendly. Frequently the boss had dinner with (I ♂ P) and his family.

When the owner died in 1931, his wife turned over the management of the ranch to her son but retained (I 51 ♂ P) as the foreman. The new boss, although considerate and fair in his dealings with the family, was inexperienced in working with Japanese. He had special difficulty dealing with (I ♂ P) because he planned to mechanize the farm with equipment with which (I ♂ P) was unfamiliar. The new boss came to rely upon (N 14 ♂ 1 F_1) as an intermediary with (I ♂ P).

When (N 18 ♂ 1 F_1) graduated from high school in 1937 he chose not to continue his education at the local state college but instead went to work full time on the ranch, despite his parents' wish for him to attend college. Although (I 57 ♂ P) was healthy and an able worker, he had begun to rely upon (N 18 ♂ 1 F_1)'s assistance.

The owner was pleased to have (N ♂ 1 F_1) work full time on the ranch and proposed that he become the foreman. (N ♂ 1 F_1) relieved (I ♂ P) of the major responsibilities, especially those concerning the equipment. (I ♂ P) was displeased with the new arrangement. He did not fully understand the changes in procedure and equipment, but he was aware that (N ♂ 1 F_1) was better qualified. This change in roles marked the beginning of (I ♂ P)'s inkyo status.

In 1939 the family bought a 20-acre ranch located several miles from the one on which they were living. Because (N 20 ♂ 1 F_1) was a minor, the land was purchased in the name of a third party (quite probably the employer) and was legally transferred one year later. (N ♂ 1 F_1) continued to work as foreman, but (I ♂ P) went to tend the vineyards at the new family ranch. He failed to produce a crop of any consequence because the land was unsuited to viniculture.

Unlike the classic family farm enterprise, the work on the ranch was not a joint economic activity. The children were not given regular duties after school and on week ends. Only during the rush of the harvest season did they work on the ranch, and then it was as hired labor earning cash wages that went to the family. The shifting of the major economic burden from the father to the son did not substantially affect their respective statuses within the family because the work relationships were not closely integrated with the family activity.

In 1941 (I 61 ♂ P) was still the head of the family, and his decisions were final in family affairs, although (I ♀ P) was allowed to discuss problems with him. (I ♂ P) was formal and arbitrary with his children, but they did not find him inaccessible. (N 18 ♀ 2 F_1) and the younger children were still economically dependent upon the family when war was declared. They relied upon their parents for funds, but they did not receive regular allowances.

In contrast to (I ♂ P), who was silent and retiring, (I ♀ P) conversed freely and informally with the children on whom she impressed the Japanese behavior patterns and attitudes. The family achieved a *modus vivendi*, but there was little affectional unity even in the relations between mother and children. (I ♂ P) and (I ♂ A) were authority figures who introduced constraints even into the daily family routine. None of the children was closely identified with either parent, nor were there strong bonds between any two siblings.

(N ♂ 1 F₁), separated by four years from (N ♀ 2 F₁), was particularly isolated. Although he was not without social skill, he was not active in Nisei organizations except for sports groups. He read widely and did well in school, and there were no signs that he experienced stress because of the cultural differences between school and home. He assumed an attitude of passive dependence toward his parents which tended to reduce intergenerational conflict. (N ♂ 1 F₁) was also passive toward the dominant society and therefore failed to operate as an acculturational agent for his siblings.

The group had few familial activities. On occasion they went to the mountains for a week end, but (N ♂ 1 F₁) usually would stay at home or go off by himself. The individuality of the family members was such that none was completely at ease in the family circle, and group spirit was rarely achieved. (N ♀ 2 F₁), who appears to have been the most socially outgoing of the children, often persuaded her younger brother to take her and (N ♀ 4 F₁) to the movies and to affairs at the Buddhist temple.

In their rural environment the majority of age-group activities were organized at the public schools. There was little time for informal groups except at recess periods and noon hours. After school most of the students went home to farms separated by several miles. There were no Nisei clubs at the high school, but the Japanese-American students formed cliques and occasionally Nisei were nominated to run for offices in the student government.

At the time of Pearl Harbor the three youngest children were still in the public schools, and (N 18 ♀ 2 F₁), who had graduated from high school in 1941, was attending sewing classes conducted by a Japanese woman in a neighboring city. Although (N ♀ 2 F₁) resisted when the school was first suggested by (I ♀ P), it was not long before she found the classes pleasant. She attended willingly until several months before the evacuation.

This prewar family was isolated from both the Japanese community and the larger society. There was no community organization in which the family participated as a group. Although they were nominally Buddhist, (I ♂ P) and the sons rarely attended religious services or other activities, and (I ♀ P) was not an active member. (I ♀ P) did not belong to any organizations, but when a local group sponsored a Japanese movie, benefit show, or other activity, she was usually present. (I ♂ P) did not care for such affairs, but it was customary for the head of the house to make the *kifu* (donation), and he would attend if it were a benefit show.

The Nisei were also weakly integrated into the community organized around the Buddhist temple. (N ♂ 1 F₁)'s tendency to withdraw and (N ♂ 3 F₁)'s disinterested attitude toward the church isolated them. They had few opportunities for group activities; they shared few experiences with the other children in the family.

The parents were not well educated in Japanese and were indifferent about the achievements of the children at the language school. They were, however, very interested in what they did with their studies at the public school, placing much emphasis on the report card. (I ♂ P) used to tell the children that he would not sign the report cards if the grades were not satisfactory to him. Although the parents were impressed by the importance of education, they did little to direct their children's ambitions. There was no unified support for the education of the children, nor did the children themselves seek academic goals.

II. Preëvacuation and Center Experience

(N 18 ♀ 2 F₁), (N 16 ♂ 3 F₁), and (N 12 ♀ 4 F₁) were at the language school when they learned from the teacher about the attack on Pearl Harbor. The first reaction was one of fear that the Mexicans around the school might harm them. The teacher dismissed the class and told the children to go directly home. The family's home was quite isolated, more than a city block from the nearest neighbor, a Caucasian attorney. They were, therefore, somewhat insulated from the reactions of the greater community, but when they went into town for their marketing, they found that the townspeople who had been friendly had not changed their attitudes.

The younger children continued to attend school, and although they felt conspicuous they experienced no discriminatory acts. (N ♀ 2 F₁)

felt insecure about continuing with her sewing class, but she had transportation to the school in a fellow-student's automobile and therefore
continued to attend. Other students, who rode into the city by bus, did
not attend classes for a time until they became confident of public sentiment. The area was placed under curfew, but this had little effect on
the family's life.

The language school was closed immediately after the outbreak of
hostilities, and when four Buddhist priests from a neighboring city
were arrested by the FBI, the church was closed. The community was
torn by a rumor that a prominent Nisei had been responsible for the
arrest of an Issei rooming-house operator.

The area in which the family lived was designated as Military Area
No. 2, a free zone into which the Army encouraged voluntary evacuation. It was presumed this area would not be evacuated. During the
next few weeks many voluntary evacuees moved in from the coastal
zone and the number of Nisei in the schools increased noticeably.

A neighboring area was evacuated in May to the Turlock Assembly
Center nearby, and the Japanese in the free zone were permitted to
visit friends in the center. (I ♂ P) and the children once went to see
friends at the center and heard rumors there that the free zone would
also be evacuated. Although the rumors of the evacuation of Military
Area No. 2 persisted, (I ♂ P) would not believe them. An old family
friend reported that he had heard from a Navy commander that Area
2 would not be evacuated. (I ♂ P) was convinced by this counterrumor,
and he made no preparations for the eventuality of evacuation. Even
when the orders were issued, (I ♂ P) would not believe that the family
would have to evacuate, and it was only after the friend again talked
to him that he was convinced that the Army had made the decision.
When Area 2 was ordered evacuated, many in the zone blamed the
JACL and the Turlock Assembly Center evacuees. It was believed that
these two groups resented the freedom enjoyed by the Japanese in Area
2 and had succeeded in precipitating their evacuation.

The attorney who owned the adjoining ranch opposed the evacuation.
The owner of the ranch was also distressed at the news and sympathized
with the family but apparently took no positive steps. However, he did
permit the family to store their possessions, and this made them feel
less pressed than other evacuees who had to dispose of their property.
The parents and (N 22 ♂ 1 F$_1$) discussed their problems, and only three
days before the evacuation (N ♂ 1 F$_1$) was charged with selling the 1936
Ford from which they realized the Blue Book price (about $200) and

a newly purchased refrigerator for which they received $100. When the family returned in 1945, they found the stored property intact. This family's preparation for evacuation was orderly and economically far better than most evacuees who enjoyed no such favorable conditions.

In Military Area No. 2, unlike Area 1, there was almost two months' notice before evacuation, and the family was relatively well prepared. They registered at the local high school in the latter part of July with (I 62 ♂ P) listed as the head. Guided by their brief observation of center life, the family did not buy quantities of unnecessary items, as many early evacuees did. They regarded suitable clothing as most important and prepared themselves for the hot Arizona climate at Gila Relocation Center.

There was no disagreement within the family about the evacuation. The young children could not act independently of the parents if they would and (N 23 ♂ 1 F_1) had no desire to do so. By this time the evacuation and its disruptive consequences were old stories, and they took the event as a matter of course. The family was among the last evacuees and left on August 7, 1942.

There were nine members in this family when it moved to the relocation center, and seven in the primary group, plus (I ♂ A) and his son who joined them at the time of the evacuation. The family crowded into a room about 25 by 30 feet which afforded little privacy for the three girls. The family met these new circumstances with its characteristic acquiescence.

In the process of housing assignments, the family became separated from their friends, who were quartered at the opposite end of the center. The other residents of the block were from the Turlock Assembly Center, and they resented the newcomers because they were "reserving" the block for Turlock friends. Feelings remained strained for several months before the block developed a sense of harmony. In the meantime, the children walked half a mile across the center to visit their old friends. As we shall see, the ecological position of the family had consequences for later adjustments, particularly the Army registration.

Although (I ♂ P) was the formal head of the family, (I ♀ P) managed family affairs from day to day just as she had done before the war. (I 62 ♂ P), who had been gradually slipping into retirement on the ranch, assumed the role of the patriarch relieved of his responsibilities, but he adjusted with difficulty. For a short time he worked as an agricultural laborer on the center farms, but he did not work as he had done on his own farm a few months before. For most of his three years in the center (I ♂ P) did no assigned work but spent his time as did many old men—in search of odds and ends of tree trunks, roots, and stones, which were ground and polished.

Although (I ♂ P) took a smaller part in family affairs, important family decisions were still cleared through him. In practice, (I ♀ P)'s decisions were important, particularly when they pertained to the children. She could influence (I ♂ P) as the children were unable to do.

About three months after evacuation (N 23 ♂ 1 F₁) and two friends arranged to share a room in the same block but several barracks away from the family. Although the parents did not oppose this move, the significance of this action must not be overlooked. This is an instance of the breakdown of familial control and the development of age-graded associations among Nisei who had previously been isolated from their peers. (See cases 2 and 10.) (N ♂ 1 F₁) became independent of the family and spent much of his time in his room. He occasionally visited the family barracks, but he entertained his friends in his own quarters. The two older daughters looked after the bachelor quarters, cleaned, and did the laundry.

Two months after (N ♂ 1 F₁) moved, (I ♂ A), his son, and (N 17 ♂ 3 F₁) moved into another room, leaving the parents and the three daughters in the original room. (N ♂ 3 F₁)'s move seems to have been a matter of convenience rather than an assertion of independence, for he continued to regard the family room as his "home."

After (I ♂ A) moved into his own quarters, he interacted less with the family and his influence declined. He did not enter into family discussions about such problems as the loyalty issue and made his decisions independent of his former relation to the family.

When the family entered the center, the three younger children were enrolled in the school. (N 17 ♂ 3 F₁) worked on the garbage crew for a short time. (N 23 ♂ 1 F₁) worked at the messhall until several months after the Army registration, when he took a job in the radio shop operated by the coöperative. Some time after arriving at the center, (N 19 ♀ 2 F₁) took a job as a waitress in one of the dining halls for a year and then for two months as a canteen cashier. When one of her friends relocated, (N ♀ 2 F₁) took over her job as a domestic in the house of one of the appointed personnel. She worked four hours per day at a wage of $16 per month. (I ♀ P) worked for a short period as a janitress and then as a messhall helper in one of the kitchens.

In the center the children felt less dependent upon the parents. They did not give their earnings to the parents as they had done before the war. In the center it seemed "only natural" that the children spend their money as they pleased.

None of the family took part in organizational activities. The girls danced and played games and went to Buddhist services regularly with other girls in the block. The sons and (I ♂ P) did not attend church during their stay in the center, although (I ♀ P) occasionally attended. (N ♂ 1 F₁) had a clique which met at his barracks, and (N ♂ 3 F₁)'s informally organized group devoted itself to athletics.

(I ♀ P) saw that the children were becoming more independent, and she castigated them about late hours, playing cards, and the like. She did not attempt arbitrarily to restrict them, however. When the Army registration issue was raised, (I ♀ P) aggressively made decisions for the family. She was determined that the family should be segregated and impressed upon (N 24 ♂ 1 F₁) that he must answer the questions negatively. At least two considerations underlay this decision. Since her immigration to the United States, (I ♀ P) had wanted to visit Japan. Her mother was presumably still alive, and (I ♀ P) wanted to see her once more. More importantly she wanted to save her sons from conscription.

Both (I ♂ P) and (I ♂ A) were indifferent to the Army registration, and (I ♂ A) decided against segregation. They had been in the United states for over thirty years and had nothing to return to in Japan. (I ♀ P) persisted, however, and was able to win her husband to her point of view. By their answers, the necessary conditions for segregation were established.

(N 24 ♂ 1 F₁) realized that (I ♀ P) was trying to protect him from the draft, and he objected to this. He was not impressed by the importance of the registration issue and compliantly gave negative answers but changed them several months later when he began to discuss plans for relocation to Chicago with one of his roommates. (N 17 ♂ 3 F₁) was also directed by (I ♀ P) to answer negatively to the loyalty questions, and he complied. (N 14 ♀ 4 F₁) and (N 8 ♀ 5 F₁) had little to say about the matter, although they did not want to go to Japan.

(N 20 ♀ 2 F₁) was less compliant with (I ♀ P)'s demands than her siblings. About half of the population in the block gave answers that indicated disloyalty, and group pressures encouraged a disloyal position. Most of (N ♀ 2 F₁)'s group associations, however, were with friends who lived outside the block and were "yes, yes" people. This was in contrast to (N ♂ 1 F₁)'s co-workers in the block messhall. (N ♀ 2 F₁) argued strenuously with (I ♀ P) about the registration issue. She told

(I ♀ P) to go to Japan alone if she were determined to and to let the others do as they wished. (I ♀ P) replied that she was trying to keep the family together. (I ♀ P) was so adamant that (N ♀ 2 F₁) finally let (I ♀ P) assume that she would answer negatively. (N ♀ 2 F₁), however, answered the questions positively, thus making herself eligible for relocation. (Note that pressures on daughters for negative answers were less strong than on sons eligible for the draft.)

The segregation program moved slowly, and as weeks became months without any notification of the date of the family's segregation, (N 24 ♂ 1 F₁) began to wear down (I ♀ P)'s initial refusal to consider plans for relocation. Finally she consented to let him go to Chicago only to have the friend, with whom (N ♂ 1 F₁) was to relocate, segregate to Tule Lake. (I ♀ P) used this as a new pretext to resist; in spite of his urgings, (I ♀ P) would not again give her consent. (N ♂ 1 F₁) became sullen and silent, but he could not bring himself to defy her. He remained in the center until the day it closed.

The family was never segregated, and they never learned why. (I ♀ P) became increasingly distressed as the days passed and other families were segregated. Inquiries at the administration offices brought no results, and it was well into 1944 before (I ♀ P) finally gave up the idea of segregation. It may well be that covertly both (N ♂ 1 F₁) and (N ♂ 3 F₁) gave positive answers to the loyalty questions, even though they were directed to answer negatively, or the family's orders may have been lost in the administrative machinery.

When the family learned of rescission, they had no plans for relocation. (N 25 ♂ 1 F₁) had given up his relocation plans, but (N 21 ♀ 2 F₁) was anxious to relocate. Although not many of the girls in the block were relocating, (N ♀ 2 F₁)'s friends in other blocks were leaving or had already left for the east. (I ♀ P) had been so opposed to (N ♂ 1 F₁)'s relocation plans that (N 21 ♀ 2 F₁) did not dare to ask her consent. However, a girl from a neighboring family had returned to Los Angeles, and through correspondence (N ♀ 2 F₁) made plans to join her.

The parents displayed no concern when WRA announced on June 22, 1945, that the center was to be closed by October 1, 1945. Unknown to (I ♀ P), (N 22 ♀ 2 F₁) applied for terminal leave. Fearfully she told (I ♀ P) what she had done and was surprised to learn that neither (I ♂ P) nor (I ♀ P) objected. It would appear that although the announcement of June 22 did not precipitate relocation activity on the part of the parents, it produced a marked change in their attitudes toward relocation.

III. RELOCATION

By early 1945 (I ♀ P) had given up the idea that the family would be segregated, but she had no plans for relocation. She thought she would remain in the relocation center for the duration of the war, and (I ♂ P)'s poor health made it seem doubly advisable to remain in the center. In 1944 (I 64 ♂ P) became ill with an undiagnosed ailment and never fully recovered.

In September, 1945, (N ♀ 2 F₁) left the center for Los Angeles and stayed with a friend for about a week after which she moved into the home of a Caucasian family. Here she worked for her room and board as a "school girl" while she attended dressmaking classes. When she had completed the year's course, she took a part-time summer job in a dress shop. During this period she and a friend from the center worked together in the home of another Caucasian family. Then in the fall of 1946 she returned to school to study dress designing for one semester. Upon the completion of this course she obtained a job in a custom-dressmaking shop in Beverly Hills and worked for her room and board in another Caucasian home closer to the shop.

(N ♂ 1 F₁)'s registration status affected the family's relocation. Disloyal individuals, even when they were not segregated, were not qualified to relocate, but after rescission nonsegregated residents were given a blanket release. Facing the prospect of forced relocation, (N ♂ 1 F₁), who had been corresponding with the lessee of their farm, arranged to return to their home. (I ♀ P) reluctantly was convinced of the wisdom of this decision and on September 20, about three weeks after (N ♀ 2 F₁) left the center, the family relocated to their former home. They stayed several days with Japanese friends and then moved into the barn on their 20-acre ranch. The housing was primitive, of course, but in a few months the boys had partitioned the building into rooms.

The former employer wanted the family to return, but (N 26 ♂ 1 F₁) preferred to farm his own land; (I ♂ A) took the job instead. The family's ranch was not suitable for vineyards and before any other produce could be planted, the grapevines had to be dug up and farming equipment had to be bought. To finance the purchase the two boys and occasionally (I ♀ P) went to work in the local vineyards as laborers. Their wages were about $1 an hour.

In the fall of 1946 and again the following year the family planted cantaloupes. Both crops yielded well in a good market.

IV. POSTWAR FAMILY*

In the postrelocation period (N ♂ 1 F₁) assumed the major economic burden of the family. (I ♂ P)'s health had not improved and he was unable to work. (N ♂ 3 F₁) worked with his brother, and although the two discussed the problems of the farm, (N ♂ 1 F₁) was considered the boss. (N 20 ♂ 3 F₁) took the produce to market, for he was the better bargainer. (I ♀ P) had little to do with the farm.

The crop in 1949 was a failure both in yield and price, and the profit of the two preceding years was lost. (I ♂ P)'s health was rapidly failing, and the family was careful that he should not see their concern about the poor prospects for the year. In December, 1949, (I 69 ♂ P) contracted pneumonia and died within a few days. Funeral services were held at the Buddhist temple and (I ♂ P)'s cremated remains were placed in a shrine.

After (I ♂ P)'s death, (N 30 ♂ 1 F₁) failed to assume his role as acknowledged head of the family, and when the Issei of the Japanese community requested that the head of the family attend some function, (I ♀ P) usually represented the family. (N ♂ 1 F₁)'s relations with the rest of the family were distant except perhaps for (N 14 ♀ 5 F₁), who was his favorite.

The influence of (I ♂ A) declined in the postwar days and he was no longer a person to be feared by the children nor an object of hostility for (I ♀ P). He returned to the family after about a year but has not worked on the farm. He was seventy-three years old in 1950 but in active good health.

(N 27 ♀ 2 F₁) remained in Los Angeles, and in 1950 was sharing an apartment with two friends. Many of her friends had relocated to Los Angeles, and she became a part of an active group of young Buddhists. (N ♀ 2 F₁) visits her family, who live about 200 miles away, two or three times a year. She corresponds with them casually and is rather independent of them.

There is almost no contact with Caucasians by the family as a group. (N ♂ 1 F₁) had a few friends before the war from his high school days, but he no longer sees them. The harvest season brings (N 25 ♂ 3 F₁) into greater contact with the dominant group, but a contact limited to business relations. The other members of the family tend to restrict themselves to associations with the ethnic group.

---

* Information recorded at the time of the last interview is reported in the present tense.

V. Interpretation

Participation.—After forty years' residence in the United States, (I ♂ P)'s participation in American society was limited to the ranch on which he worked as foreman and the Caucasian owner of the ranch. His lack of interest in the dominant culture extended to indifference toward the acculturation of his children. His conservatism impaired the performance of his duties as foreman, for the job required a mastery of changes in large-scale farming procedures. Consequently his lack of knowledge of modern equipment and agricultural practices exposed him to changes in his status, both on the ranch and within the family. (N ♂ 1 F₁)'s training in American schools enabled him to function more adequately with the Caucasian owner than (I ♂ P) could, and by 1937 he had assumed major responsibility for the operation of the ranch.

The participation of family members in ethnic community activities was largely a consequence of the children's membership in the Buddhist church. There were, however, few occasions when the family was represented as a group at community affairs, for none of the organizations claimed the interest of all the members. The Nisei had little cohesion, and there was a minimum of group-oriented activity.

Family structure.—The most remarkable characteristic of this family was the dominant role of (I ♂ A), who displaced (I ♂ P) as the authority figure and economically exploited the family. The rigid and formal tone was set by the presence of (I ♂ A), whose authority was not tempered by affection. In this role he took the rights and privileges of the family head without discharging its responsibilities. (I ♂ P)'s submissive adaptation to this situation set the pattern for the rest of the family. This was particularly important for (N ♂ 1 F₁), who was strongly impressed by his obligations to (I ♂ A) and his parents, and he habitually yielded to them. So mild was his resistance that issues were rarely explicitly defined or discussed, and he did not assume his culturally prescribed role as an alternative leader in his family. He became foreman of the ranch in the place of (I ♂ P) without gaining an authority consonant with his responsibilities, perhaps because (I ♂ P) had no authority to surrender and perhaps because (N ♂ 1 F₁)'s training in practiced passivity could not be so simply changed.

Under these conditions it is not surprising that group feeling between the children was weak, intergenerational conflict was absent, and the attitudes of submission were rationalized as Japanese filial piety. The rural setting of the family insulated it from acculturational influences which might have challenged the pattern of authority and submissiveness. As noted above, the family was loosely articulated to the community and therefore these external resources were not utilized by the group. The farm enterprise did not call for the work of the several individuals and therefore even this source of integration was lacking. Nor did the family suffer those economic difficulties that so often gave rise to the projection of ambitious goals upon the children.

We have learned to expect to find that even in rather weakly organized families the mother provides an affectional center reducing tensions, ameliorating formality, and providing a resource for future action. This cannot be discovered in this case. The most that can be said is that (I ♀ P) mediated the day-to-day relationships and helped order short-term objectives and responsibilities.

Wartime experience.—For this family the evacuation experience was not traumatic. They moved to the center with the maximum amount of preparation and, although living conditions were crowded at first, there is no evidence that this created an undue amount of strain. (N ♂ 1 F$_1$) achieved a modicum of autonomy when he was able to make living arrangements with two other Nisei. In this he was utilizing an opportunity afforded by the extemporized character of barracks housing and an opportunity for individuative action, which in this case took the form of informal peer-group associations. This did not extend, however, to decisive independence on such matters as the loyalty registration and relocation. It must be borne in mind that none of the other children was nearly so important as (N ♂ 1 F$_1$) in the possible reëstablishment of the postwar family economic unit. In the long run, (I ♀ P) became the head of the family and maintained effective control over him because of his habituated compliance.

(N ♀ 2 F$_1$), however, achieved a notable degree of independence in adjusting to relocation, and this affected her postwar relations with the family. She drew on peer-group associations that had a different orientation to relocation. Most of her friends lived at the opposite end of the center, and she spent a great deal of time with them. Few among this group were disloyal, and although the positive faction was less militant than the negative group, there was nevertheless opposition to disloyal Nisei.

Character of adjustment.—This case shows individuals being subjected to the by-product pressures of administrative policy: chance associates at work and in the barracks who were strongly committed to one or another action became significant factors in the lives of all but the most independent and decisive personalities. For example, note the achieved independence of (N ♀ 2 F₁) and the segregation pressures on (N ♂ 1 F₁). These were some of the unanticipated consequences of WRA housing policy and the segregation-relocation program.

Cultural Data

PREWAR

Religion:
Parents nominally Buddhist but neither active. (N ♂ 1 F₁) and (N ♂ 3 F₁) indifferent to religion; (N ♀ 2 F₁), (N ♀ 4 F₁), and (N ♀ 5 F₁) active in a church group. A *butsudan* in the home but no home rituals.

Holidays:
New Year's Day casually observed. Family attended *Obon* festivities. Christmas and Thanksgiving observed.

Diet:
Predominantly Japanese. Very conservative even for rural residents.

Reading matter:
Mostly (N ♂ 1 F₁)'s book-club selections. Subscriptions to two vernacular newspapers, *Shonen,* a Japanese monthly magazines, a local newspaper, and *Saturday Evening Post* and *Liberty* magazines.

Language school:
Attendance and level of achievement:
(N ♂ 1 F₁) 12 yrs. Bk. 12 (6th gr.)
(N ♀ 2 F₁) 12 yrs. Bk. 11 (6th gr.)
(N ♂ 3 F₁) 10 yrs. Bk. 10 (5th gr.)
(N ♀ 4 F₁) 4 yrs. Bk. 4 (2nd gr.)

POSTWAR

Religion:
Little change. (N ♀ 2 F₁), (N ♀ 4 F₁), and (N ♀ 5 F₁) active in the Young Buddhists Association.

Holidays:
Observances remain unchanged.

Diet:
Fare is less Japanese. Western dishes prepared by (N ♀ 4 F₁).

Reading matter:
Fewer Japanese-language publications.

Language school:
None has returned to a language school.

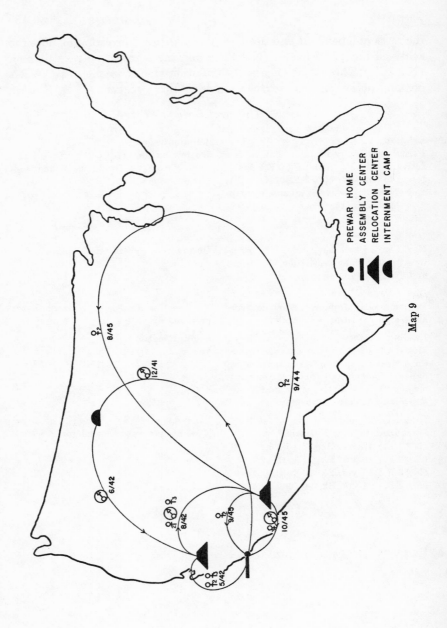

PREWAR HOME

ASSEMBLY CENTER

RELOCATION CENTER

INTERNMENT CAMP

Map 9

Chart 9

CASE 9

I. Prewar Family

(I ♂ P) was born in 1877 in a rural community in southwest Japan. At the age of twenty-five he migrated to Portland, Oregon, and at first worked for a Japanese farmer at a wage of $18 per month. Two years later he became a delivery boy for a liquor store, a job he held for six years. He then started his own liquor store and sent for the bride who had been selected for him by his parents.

(I ♀ P) was born in 1880 in the same village as (I ♂ P). (I 33 ♂ P) and (I 30 ♀ P) were married when she arrived in Portland in 1910. (I ♀ P) helped in the store until the birth of (K ♀ 1 F₁) in 1914. (K ♀ 2 F₁) was born a year later.

In 1916 the family moved to San Francisco where (I ♂ P) opened another liquor store in partnership with his brother and (I ♀ P)'s two brothers. Their monthly income, estimated at $500, provided support for (I ♂ P)'s family and the partners. (K ♀ 3 F₁) was born in 1917 in San Francisco.

In 1921 (I ♀ P) died in surgery, and (I ♂ P) took the children to Japan and placed them in the care of their paternal grandparents. (I ♂ P) remained with the children a few years, but returned to the United States in 1923. He moved to southern California and opened a vegetable stand in partnership with his brother. Several years later the brothers opened two branch stands, but these were liquidated in the 1929 depression. Leaving the main store in charge of his brother, (I ♂ P) went to Japan to visit his children in 1929, remaining for two years, during which time he studied electrotherapy. When he returned to the United States in 1931, the main store had gone bankrupt, and he opened an office to practice electrotherapy. He soon moved again to a small city in southern California, where he married for the second time.

In 1933 (I ♂ P) sent for (K 18 ♀ 2 F₁) to join him and his new wife. (K ♀ 2 F₁) had graduated from high school in Japan and wished to continue her education at an American university. In February, 1934, the stepmother died following an automobile accident. (K 22 ♀ 1 F₁) returned to the United States in 1936, and she was followed by (K 21 ♀ 3 F₁) in 1938.

The two older daughters taught in the Japanese-language school, and their earnings were included in the common family fund controlled by (I ♂ P). Personal expenses such as clothing, tuition fees, and the like were disbursed by (I ♂ P), and monthly expenses for the family averaged about $200. The family lived comfortably in a large house, and children from the language school were frequently invited to picnic in their spacious yard. The daughters cultivated a middle-class Japanese style of life with scroll paintings and floral arrangements (*ikebana*) decorating their rooms. As Japanese school teachers, (K ♀ 1 F₁) and (K ♀ 2 F₁) were looked upon by the parents of their pupils as models of "Japanese womanhood." (K ♀ 2 F₁) was asked to sponsor a girls' club and to give lessons in Japanese etiquette.

Although (I ♂ P) was the final authority, family problems were freely discussed. (I ♂ P) was a benevolent but at times authoritarian father. When (K ♀ 2 F₁) graduated from a junior college, (I ♂ P) insisted that she stay at home rather than continue her studies at a university. However, she was adamant and enrolled at a local university in spite of his objections. (I ♂ P) again came into conflict with (K ♀ 2 F₁) about her relations with men. At first he forbade the girls to associate with men, but later he relaxed this prohibition to the extent that he allowed his daughters to entertain friends in their home. Even then, (I ♂ P) interfered with (K ♀ 2 F₁)'s dates and would not allow her to be unchaperoned.

(I ♂ P) was frequently approached with marriage proposals for his daughters. Discussion of these proposals lasted for days or weeks, and at their conclusion (I ♂ P) had to perform the difficult task of "politely refusing" with such excuses as, "She wishes to continue her study," or, "She wishes to go back to Japan." The girls were, in fact, planning to return to Japan, and they would consider only exceptionally attractive proposals. (I ♂ P) often persuaded his daughters to consider the proposals but never demanded that they accept them. The girls' resistances to marriage were largely based on their observation of the job ceiling for Nisei males. They noted that even with college degrees most Nisei could find work only as vegetable-stand clerks, nurserymen, or gardeners. In Japan, the girls felt they would be able to marry men with greater opportunity for economic advancement and social prestige.

Affectionally, the family was closely knit, although (K ♀ 2 F₁)'s independent attitude weakened her relationship with her father. Although she was willing to sew for him, her sisters were more attentive; they laid out his clothes and went with him on business and social calls. The patriarchal structure of the family was ameliorated by these strong affectional bonds, and the group tended to be conservative in its adjustment to the dominant society. There was no self-conscious effort toward acculturation; indeed the family was primarily oriented toward the

Japanese culture. (K ♀ 2 F₁) opposed (I ♂ P)'s wishes, for example, not because he impeded her adjustment to American society but rather because he obstructed her plans for a career in Japan. She considered her American experience as "broadening" and "cultural" rather than an adaptation to a new society.

(I ♂ P) was a nominal Buddhist and occasionally attended memorial services. In the home there were Buddhist shrines, ancestral tablets, and scriptures. (K ♀ 2 F₁) attended a local Japanese Baptist church, but the two other sisters had no religious affiliation.

For many years (I ♂ P) had been active in the Japanese community, but he usually eschewed responsible offices because of his age. He was a member of the Japanese Veterans Association and held a nominal membership in the kenjinkai. He made regular contributions to the Community Chest, Red Cross, and other charities. The girls were not active in community organizations. (K ♀ 1 F₁) and (K ♀ 2 F₁) joined the Japanese School Teachers' Association, and for about two years the latter was a member of the Kibei division of the JACL.

The family had several Caucasian friends and acquaintances whom they had met through (I ♂ P)'s practice. The postmaster and the fire chief were former patients. They were acquainted with several Mexicans, but they had no friends among them or among Negroes. The family was known in the business section, and they were received in a friendly manner by shopkeepers. They exchanged gifts with a few of their Caucasian friends at Christmas and sent greeting cards to a large number. The family's relations with non-Japanese were pleasant, a state of affairs they attributed to (I ♂ P)'s respected status.

II. Preëvacuation and Center Experience

In 1938 (K 24 ♀ 1 F₁) returned to Japan to study at a university. Early in the summer of 1941 she wrote to the family urging them to return to Japan, and (I 64 ♂ P) talked seriously of doing so. (K 24 ♀ 3 F₁) responded enthusiastically. (K 26 ♀ 2 F₁) suggested that her father and sister join (K ♀ 1 F₁) in Japan and she would follow them after she graduated from an American university. (I ♂ P), however, would not leave her behind, and the family decided they would wait for her to complete her education.

On the evening of December 7 (I 64 ♂ P) was taken into custody by the FBI. He was held in Los Angeles until December 19, but the girls were not allowed to see him. He was sent to Missoula, Montana, and they received his first letter after Christmas. They then wrote to him frequently.

The Japanese school was closed, and there was no source of income for the girls. (K 26 ♀ 2 F₁) withdrew from the university. Sympathetic friends and members of the Baptist church visited the girls often. Four Caucasian friends prepared affidavits testifying to (I ♂ P)'s character, and they were sent to Missoula for (I ♂ P)'s hearing, together with affidavits prepared by the girls.

After residents of a nearby community were evacuated with only forty-eight hours' notice in February, 1942, the girls began preparing for a similar order. On the advice of friends and the minister of the church, they burned all papers that might be construed as suspicious. Japanese magazines and phonograph records were also burned. When short-wave radios and weapons were banned, the living-room radio and a shotgun were entrusted to a Caucasian friend and a Japanese sword was taken to the police station. The short-waveband was removed from another radio.

In the latter part of February (I ♂ P) wired the girls to sell everything and go to his brother's house in Los Angeles. (K 27 ♀ 2 F₁) was reluctant to burden her uncle with two more people, but (K 25 ♀ 3 F₁) was lonely and insisted that they act according to their father's instructions. (K ♀ 2 F₁) then agreed to move and placed advertisements in the local newspaper for the sale of the car and furniture. Following is a list of some of the items sold and the prices obtained:

1938 four-door sedan...........................$385.00	
six dressers ....   5.00 and $7.50 each
six beds ....   10.00 each
nearly new living-room suite.................   35.00
davenport 10.00
RCA eight-tube radio........................   15.00
hardwood dining-room suite..................   35.00
electric washer 22.50
vacuum cleaner 12.50
hardwood office desk and chair..............   10.00
miscellaneous tables ....   1.00 to $5.00
rugs ....   5.00 to $17.50
refrigerator 95.00
piano 35.00

The girls kept only a minimum of furniture and (I ♂ P)'s electrotherapy equipment.

(K ♀ 2 F₁) and (K ♀ 3 F₁) lived with their uncle for two months, during which time they corresponded frequently with (I ♂ P) and sent him packages. Changing regulations allowed them to correspond in Japanese through a close censorship. As days passed into weeks and rumors of evacuation mounted, (K ♀ 2 F₁) became embarrassed about accepting the hospitality of their uncle, and in order to avoid a direct payment of money, she bought food and other goods to repay him. The contents of the safe-deposit box, sealed at the outbreak of the war, were released, and (K ♀ 2 F₁) transferred them to a bank in Los Angeles.

In May, 1942, evacuation notices were posted in the Los Angeles area, and (K ♀ 2 F₁) registered as the head of a family of two. After two months the evacuation order was a relief rather than a shock for her. It meant that the period of doubt was at an end and they were ready to go. They picked through their possessions once more to stay within the limits of two hand cases and made arrangements to store most of their property in the Japanese Christian church in Los Angeles. The day before they were to be evacuated, the girls received a telegram from (I ♂ P) informing them that he was to be released with the first group of men and he was being transferred to the Santa Anita Assembly Center, but the girls were evacuated to the Tulare Assembly Center. Each evening they went to the central office expecting (I ♂ P)'s return, and he was finally transferred to Tulare in June.

When (I 65 ♂ P) rejoined his family, the WRA record listing (K 27 ♀ 2 F₁) as head of the family was not changed, but he resumed leadership and imposed stringent rules upon his daughters. On one occasion (K 27 ♀ 2 F₁) returned to the barracks shortly before midnight from a dance sponsored by the Social Welfare Department in which she was then employed. It was an occasion especially planned to bring Nisei and Kibei together, and she had walked home with one of the boys in the block. When she entered the room, (I ♂ P) began berating her in a loud voice, accusing her of immorality, i.e., dancing. Although (I ♂ P)'s behavior was not new to her, she suffered the humiliation of having the neighbors hear him scold her.

The family was transferred to the Gila River Relocation Center in August, 1942, and (K ♀ 2 F₁) found employment teaching in the center school, frequently serving as interpreter and translator for the Administration, and teaching a Japanese-language class for the Caucasian staff members. In the summer of 1944—at the request of the block residents—she began a Japanese-language class for the young children but discontinued it when the Administration opposed language classes.

(K 25 ♀ 3 F₁) was in poor health and did not work during most of her stay in the center. (I ♂ P) was elected block manager several months after their arrival in the Gila River Relocation Center, and (K ♀ 3 F$_1$) worked for a short period as his assistant. (I ♂ P) and (K ♀ 2 F$_1$) received the "professional" salary of $19 per month, and although (K ♀ 3 F$_1$) was working, she was paid on a half-time basis. The clothing allowance for the family amounted to $10 per month, and (I ♂ P)'s investments brought an annual dividend of about $50. Expenses frequently exceeded this small income when such items as an electric hot plate, a cooler, a suit for (I ♂ P), and a watch for (K ♀ 3 F$_1$) were purchased.

The family considered the Army registration primarily as a question of repatriation and expatriation, and loyalty was weighed in terms of attachment to one culture as opposed to another and not as a matter of national obligation. For (K 28 ♀ 2 F$_1$), who felt equally attached to both cultures, this was a difficult decision. Her strong ambitions for educational achievement were directed toward a career in Japan, where opportunities were not obstructed by racial discrimination. However, she found the American climate ideologically more compatible with her individualistic point of view.

(K 26 ♀ 3 F$_1$) had never been able to adjust herself to life in America; she thought constantly of her happy and secure life in Japan. She made few friends in America and withdrew into a dependent role of the baby of the family. When one of (I ♂ P)'s brothers wrote the family urging them to file application for repatriation, she was enthusiastic in her response and appealed to (I ♂ P)'s desire to return to Japan. Her efforts were reinforced by (K 29 ♀ 1 F$_1$)'s communications through the Red Cross suggesting that the family join her in Japan.

(K ♀ 2 F$_1$), however, was determined to complete her college education in America and would not consent to repatriate. She argued that if they were to repatriate, they would have to abandon the property they had stored and their investments. It would also entail another move, this time to Tule Lake, and another indeterminate period of waiting before the move to Japan. She described the discomfort and possible dangers of transoceanic travel under wartime conditions. With these considerations in mind, (I ♂ P) decided against repatriation, and (K ♀ 3 F$_1$) was unhappy and resentful. Data regarding the answers to the loyalty questionnaire are lacking, but it is probably safe to assume that all three registered "yes, yes." We make this assumption in the light of (I ♂ P)'s status, an interned alien released to center custody. Since the family decided against repatriation, (I ♂ P) would have made his status more insecure and limited his freedom had he given a negative answer. As for $(K ♀ 3 F_1)$, her dependence upon the judgment of both $(I ♂ P)$ and $(K ♀ 2 F_1)$ would have made it improbable that she should answer the questions negatively.

Although the family decided against repatriation, they did not consider family relocation. $(I 67 ♂ P)$ strongly opposed relocation, probably in an attempt to prevent $(K ♀ 2 F_1)$ from making definite arrangements for attending an eastern university. In the summer of 1942, when $(K ♀ 2 F_1)$ first brought up the subject of relocating to continue her education, $(I ♂ P)$ reacted violently and refused to listen to her, but for two years she periodically broached the subject. In 1944 she applied for a position as an instructor in Japanese at Chicago and also applied for admission as a student. She was accepted to begin work in the fall semester, and in the face of her persistent efforts $(I ♂ P)$ finally gave his consent. In September, 1944, $(K 29 ♀ 2 F_1)$ left for Chicago on indefinite leave.

Although $(K ♀ 2 F_1)$ was happy to be able to complete her college work, she felt guilty at leaving her family. However, it was not feasible to take them with her, for $(I ♂ P)$ was old and $(K 26 ♀ 3 F_1)$ was in poor health. During her first few months in Chicago, $(K ♀ 2 F_1)$ exchanged letters with her family every day and periodically sent gifts. Later, correspondence was less frequent. $(I ♂ P)$ also sent gifts to $(K ♀ 2 F_1)$, sometimes ordering Japanese confections from Denver.

When $(K ♀ 2 F_1)$ learned of the opening of the West Coast to the Japanese, she was completing her last year's work at the university. She wanted to pursue graduate work there, and $(I ♂ P)$ and $(K ♀ 3 F_1)$ were not interested in relocation. The Army release order required no immediate action.

III. RELOCATION

However, when the closing of the centers was announced in July, 1945, the family had not yet chosen its course. $(K 30 ♀ 2 F_1)$ had graduated and continued to work at the university. She wished to remain there, and urged $(I ♂ P)$ and her sister to join her in Chicago. $(I ♂ P)$, however, preferred to return to the familiar and milder climate of California, and he refused to relocate to Chicago. $(K ♀ 2 F_1)$ yielded to $(I ♂ P)$ and returned to the center during the summer to prepare the family for their return to California.

$(I ♂ P)$ sent $(K ♀ 2 F_1)$ to look for a house in Los Angeles, but she was unsuccessful. However, she was able to find two rooms, without private bath or kitchen, which she rented for $36 per month. In view of the housing shortage in Los Angeles, (K ♀ 2 F₁) considered herself fortunate, although she knew the rent was above OPA ceiling prices. She felt that the landlady, who was renting all her apartments and rooms to Japanese, was taking advantage of their circumstances, but neither she nor the other tenants cared to involve themselves in a report to the OPA.

Upon their arrival in October, 1945, (K ♀ 2 F₁) again looked for suitable apartments, but none could be found, and they were forced to consider buying a house despite inflated values. They settled upon an income property that consisted of five three-room units, each complete with bath and kitchen facilities. The OPA ceilings on the rentals were very low, ranging from $15 to $17.50, and the monthly income from the property amounted to $79. The family purchased the property at $7,500, paying $3,200 down and monthly installments of $65. The property was recorded in (K ♀ 2 F₁)'s name, and (I ♂ P) left negotiations entirely to her, although he always accompanied her to the bank where the property was in escrow. With the purchase of some furniture, for which they paid several times the price they had received for the furniture sold in 1942, the family moved into the house in January. The property stored before evacuation was reclaimed in good condition. The family minimized expenditures during this period when they depended almost entirely on their savings. (K ♀ 2 F₁) had hoped to find a job as a Japanese-language instructor in one of the local colleges or universities, but there were no openings.

IV. Postwar Family*

(I 70 ♂ P) has relinquished much of the control in the family and relies heavily upon (K 32 ♀ 2 F₁). He takes no important action without discussing it with her. When he sold stock to finance the house, they discussed the matter. Before the war (K ♀ 2 F₁) took no part in deciding upon investments. (I ♂ P) continues, however, to scold and monitor (K ♀ 2 F₁).

In February, 1946, they renewed (I ♂ P)'s electrotherapy license. He is in good health and occupies himself with his profession. In his leisure, (I ♂ P) takes care of the garden and is happily anticipating the growth of the fruit trees he has planted. He speaks occasionally of Japan. (K 30 ♀ 3 F₁), however, constantly talks about going to Japan. She has not forgiven (I ♂ P) and (K ♀ 2 F₁) for deciding against repatriation, and this is a source of unhappiness in the family. They tell

---

* Information recorded at the time of the last interview is reported in the present tense.

($K ♀ 3 F_1$) that Japan is no longer the Japan she remembers, but she remains unconvinced and resentful. ($K ♀ 2 F_1$) attempts to placate her by promising an early trip.

The postwar family has not reëstablished the prewar atmosphere of Japanese culture in their home. Holidays are passingly observed, and there is less interest shown in Japanese cultural objects than before the war. Their diet is about the same, but less elaborate and formal. Subscriptions have been reduced to the Los Angeles *Times,* the vernacular Colorado *Times,* and the *Rafu Shimpo.* There has been a general retrenchment in their standard of living. The family has reëstablished relations with their prewar friends. Shortly after their return, the family was visited by two Caucasian friends who welcomed them back; when the family returned the visit, they were warmly received.

V. INTERPRETATION

Participation.—This incomplete family of an Issei and three Kibei was closely integrated by well-defined relations between ($I ♂ P$) and his daughters. They were strongly oriented toward Japan. ($I ♂ P$)'s semi-professional practice included Caucasian as well as ethnic patients, and through the former he had established informal associations with the nonethnic community. ($K ♀ 2 F_1$)'s schooling constituted another major avenue of communication between the family and the dominant society. She quite deliberately sought to participate in American society and frequently discussed her experiences with her family. These anecdotes and attitudes comprised a liberalizing influence counteracting ($I ♂ P$)'s traditional Japanese orientation.

As teachers in the local language school, both ($K ♀ 1 F_1$) and ($K ♀ 2 F_1$) participated in the affairs of the ethnic community and had the prestige attached to sophistication in conservative culture. ($I ♂ P$) had the status of respected age in the small community.

Family structure.—Despite separations the family formed a strongly integrated unit. ($I ♂ P$) enjoyed the affection and respect of his three daughters, and there was little of the alienation of parent and child which frequently accompanied the return of Kibei to the United States. The fact that all the children were Kibei and ($I ♂ P$) was culturally conservative did much to create a solidary atmosphere.

Ordinarily, Nisei girls sent to Japan at an early age absorbed well the attitudes and manners befitting the role of a Japanese wife— obedience and submissiveness, sometimes to the point of docility. However, it is clear that ($I ♂ P$)'s daughters were not ordinary girls, and they were not amenable to his suggestions about marriage. $(K \female 1 F_1)$ and $(K \female 2 F_1)$ were ambitious for higher education, and $(K \female 3 F_1)$ was unhappy in the United States and wanted to return to Japan.

Wartime experience.—The threat of war precipitated discussion of an immediate return to Japan. This move was blocked by $(K \female 2 F_1)$'s insistence on completing her education, which effectively prevented $(I \male P)$'s and $(K \female 3 F_1)$'s return to Japan.

$(K \female 2 F_1)$'s independence and competence served the family well when war broke out and $(I \male P)$ was interned. She assumed the leadership role and discharged her responsibilities capably. Throughout the experience $(K \female 2 F_1)$ maintained a family identity even when they joined their relatives. It is significant that $(K \female 2 F_1)$ did not herself decide to join their relatives or sell the family possessions. Rather, she was the agent of $(I \male P)$'s decisions and a temporary agent. When $(I \male P)$ returned from the internment camp, he resumed his status, insisted upon his authoritarian role, and refused to grant $(K \female 2 F_1)$ the right to manage her own affairs, even though her ability to do so had been demonstrated.

The strength and persistence of $(K \female 2 F_1)$'s personal ambitions defined the repatriation as well as the relocation issues for the family. The registration issue reopened the prewar plans for returning to Japan. The war, the evacuation, and $(K \female 1 F_1)$'s encouraging letters from Japan were strong arguments for repatriation. $(K \female 2 F_1)$ nevertheless resisted a family decision that would deter her from her educational goals, and despite $(K \female 3 F_1)$'s pleas, she was able to convince $(I \male P)$ of the advisability of postponing the trip.

The repatriation issue settled, $(K \female 2 F_1)$ gradually presented her plans for relocation to $(I \male P)$. He could never fully accept her educational ambitions, and he opposed her at every turn, but she persisted until she finally gained his consent. Although $(K \female 2 F_1)$'s ambitions were strong, the decision to relocate was apparently not an easy one. She considered $(I \male P)$'s age and $(K \female 3 F_1)$'s poor health and dependence. Although $(I \male P)$ berated her for her independent attitudes and presumed the right to dominate her, she was aware that he was dependent upon her. On the other hand, she required $(I \male P)$'s overt consent before she could finally act.

Character of adjustment.—The traditional orientation of this family defined the wartime crises as problems which called for group rather than individual adjustment. This is particularly notable in the light of $(K \female 2 F_1)$'s strong ambition, which played such a dominant role in the decision-making process. In spite of her independent attitude and personal motivations, her sense of filial obligation and the strong affectional bonds of the family constrained her from making a more individualistic adjustment. She always worked within the formal definitions of familial obligations and required (I ♂ P)'s approval to legitimize her action.

(K ♀ 2 F₁)'s ambitions, however, were not so individualistic as they appeared. The evacuation had hastened (I ♂ P)'s dependency by destroying his established practice and aggravated (K ♀ 3 F₁)'s weak physical condition. Thus (K ♀ 2 F₁) was faced with the responsibility of providing for two dependents. With such a prospect the completion of her eduaction could provide an economic base for the postwar family. Hence, (K ♀ 2 F₁)'s actions may be interpreted as essentially group oriented and as maintaining the unity of the family.

Cultural Data

PREWAR

Religion:
(I ♂ P) nominally Buddhist. (K ♀ 2 F₁) attended a Japanese Baptist church. Other two siblings unaffiliated.

Holidays:
Japanese New Year elaborately celebrated. Girls' Day observed. American holidays celebrated; gifts exchanged with Caucasian friends on Christmas.

Diet:
Meals predominantly Japanese.

Reading matter:
Large and diversified library including classics from Japanese and Western literature. American and vernacular newspapers and both Japanese and American magazines: *Newsweek, Saturday Evening Post, McCall's, Fujin Kōron, Fujin Kurabu, Chuo-Kōron, Kaizo,* and *Kōdan Kurabu.*

Language school:
All children had graduated from high schools in Japan.

POSTWAR

Religion:
Family inactive.

Holidays:
Observances inconsequential.

Diet:
Diet same as prewar except simpler.

Reading matter:
Subscriptions to one American newspaper and two vernacular publications.

CASE 10

I. Prewar Family

(I ♂ P) was born in southwest Japan in 1874 to a farm family whose ancestors were of the samurai class. He attended school for four years, after which he was put to work on the farm. In 1911 a marriage was arranged through baishakunin with (I 22 ♀ P), who was also from a farm family of samurai stock. A year after their marriage (I 39 ♂ P) emigrated to the United States, and (I ♀ P) joined her husband in California in 1913. He hoped to earn enough money in the United States to retire comfortably in Japan. (I ♂ P) had been working as a lumberjack, but because there were no Japanese with whom his wife could associate, the couple moved to central California where they worked sugar beet and onion farms on a crop basis.

In 1914 and 1916 (N ♀ 1 F_1) and (N ♀ 2 F_1) were born, followed by (N ♂ 3 F_1) and (N ♂ 4 F_1) in 1918 and 1920, respectively; but the older daughter and son died, the first after three years and the other as an infant. In 1920 the family of four moved to another farm community. With good yields and prices the family netted about $2,000 annually while farming 15 acres. By 1924 they had saved approximately $7,000 and, planning to return to Japan, they quit operating their farm. It was customary among Japanese to ask debtors to settle debts when creditors planned a trip to Japan. The family waited in vain for $600 they had loaned, and after six months they returned to farming, lost money, and were never able to finance their trip.

(N ♂ 5 F_1) and (N ♂ 6 F_1) were born in 1922 and 1924, respectively, and in 1926 (N 6 ♂ 4 F_1) died in an accident. Only three of the six children had survived.

In 1926 the family moved to an 8-acre farm, which they leased in the name of a Nisei friend who was of age. The family lived in crude quarters simply furnished, and during the depression of the early 'thirties the farm barely supported the group.

In 1927 (I 53 ♂ P) developed a cancer, and knowing he could not survive many months, he advertised in a Japanese newspaper for his brother's son (I ♂ A).* The "uncle," as he was called by the children, had been working in central California and immediately joined the family. (I ♂ P) died within five months after his arrival, and a short time later, in 1928, the youngest child (N ♀ 7 F_1) was born.

---

* Although he was not biologically an "uncle" to the family, this was his social status and we shall therefore designate him by the symbol (I ♂ A).

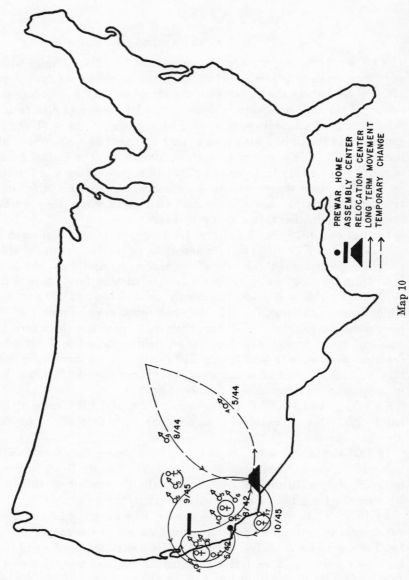

PREWAR HOME
ASSEMBLY CENTER
RELOCATION CENTER
LONG TERM MOVEMENT
TEMPORARY CHANGE

5/44

8/44

9/45

10/45

5/42

Map 10

Chart 10

The children had never been affectionally close to their father. They were, in fact, afraid of his bad temper, which was frequently aggravated by drinking. He scolded, broke furniture, and mistreated his wife, who met his abuse passively. (I 43 ♂ A) took the place of (I ♂ P), and was temperamentally similar. (I 38 ♀ P) was submissive to (I ♂ A), as she had been to her husband. (I ♂ A)'s role as the leader of the family was clearly defined for the children but there does not appear to have been any filial or affectional bond between them. (I ♀ P) got along well with all her children, who thought she was understanding and tolerant of American customs. (I ♂ A) opposed social dancing, movies, dating, etc. The children were quite close to each other and went together to movies, the amusement park, and the homes of friends.

In 1937 (N 21 ♀ 2 F₁) married a twenty-two-year-old Nisei whose Buddhist family operated a nursery and florist shop in suburban Los Angeles.† Friends of the family acted as go-betweens (*nakōdo*). After the Buddhist wedding over three-hundred guests attended a reception at a Chinese-style restaurant. The groom took (N ♀ 2 F₁) to live with his family, and she was happy to leave the drudgery of the farm. However, the adjustment to the marriage was burdened by the care of her invalid mother-in-law and a husband who had been pampered by indulgent parents. Occasionally (N ♀ 2 F₁) would return to her mother and weep for sympathy and understanding.

In 1939 the family was evicted when the land on which they were farming was sold. They moved to another plot, owned by a Caucasian who offered the family a 60–40 deal. The landowner paid for half of the expenses, labor excluded, and received 40 per cent of the profits. The three remaining children helped on the farm after school hours. The truck gardening was not very successful, but no debts were incurred. The year 1940 was moderately successful and they could afford to purchase a small 1935 sedan for $300; by 1941 they had saved about $1,500. During this period the family lived in the buildings they had moved from their previous farm.

Acculturation was not a vital force in this family. (I ♀ P) did little to support or resist the acculturation of her children, and (I ♂ A) apparently had little interest in them as individuals. Six years separated (N ♂ 5 F₁) from (N ♀ 2 F₁). Large differences in age between siblings decreased the impact of acculturation on the family, for it decreased the solidarity of the agents of acculturation, i.e., the children.

† This new family unit is not considered a part of the primary family and does not appear on the family chart or map.

Acculturation was further hampered by the fact that the eldest child was a female. In this environment there was a lack of support for acculturation and an absence of a positive interest in Japanese culture; the orientation of the children was neither American nor Japanese.

The religious affiliations of the family were tenuous. Both (I ♀ P) and (I ♂ A) were from Buddhist families, but they were not active members of any temple. They attended the temple annually on the anniversary of (I ♂ P)'s death. The children had no religious affiliations, although (N ♀ 7 F₁) had attended a Caucasian Methodist church when she was seven or eight years old. The children did, however, attend a Japanese-language school affiliated with the Buddhist temple. About a hundred students were taught by a priest from a Los Angeles temple, with the help of two Nisei college students. Classes began with the singing of hymns, and instruction was given in reading, *kanji* (Chinese characters), penmanship, ethics, and Japanese history. Attendance at the school was almost universal among the Japanese children in their locality, and the children were enrolled as a matter of course. With the exception of (N ♀ 2 F₁), the children did not read or write Japanese well, and there was no apparent increased understanding of the parents or of their culture through the study of the language.

The Japanese-language school record is as follows:

Child	Years attended	Grade reached
(N ♀ 2 F₁)	10	Third year, high school
(N ♂ 5 F₁)	8	Sixth year, grammar
(N ♂ 6 F₁)	7	Fifth year, grammar
(N ♀ 7 F₁)	6	Fourth year, grammar

There were few family ties with Japan. (I ♀ P), whose parents were dead, had no formal education and very rarely wrote to her sister. (I ♂ A) seldom wrote to his father. (N ♀ 2 F₁)'s language training enabled her to write Japanese, and she corresponded several times each year with relatives and friends in Japan. The other children never wrote letters to Japan.

(I ♂ A) was active in a number of Japanese organizations. He was a member of the Nihonjinkai, kenjinkai, California Farmer's Association, and the Japanese school association, and he donated to the Japanese Army. (I ♀ P) belonged only to the ladies' club of the Japanese school.

In high school, (N ♀ 2 F₁) was the president of the Japanese Club and a member of the JACL as well as the girls' club at the language school. Her special interest was flower arrangement. (N ♂ 5 F₁) belonged to the Future Farmers of America in high school, the Japanese school boys' club, and was a football fan. The two younger children did not take part in any organizations.

Associations with Caucasians were confined largely to school friendships. The girls seem to have been more intimate with their Caucasian friends, exchanging dinner invitations and attending movies with them. The boys' activities with their friends were of a more casual, athletic character. (I ♀ P)'s incompetence in English isolated her from Caucasians. (I ♂ A) chatted with his two hakujin neighbors and gave them Christmas gifts.

The Japanese children were discriminated against in the use of the municipal swimming pool, where Negroes were also excluded, although Mexicans were admitted. (N ♀ 7 F_1) remembers having been called a "dirty Jap" by a little boy while visiting in the home of a Caucasian friend.

II. Preëvacuation and Center Experience

The outbreak of war brought no change in the attitudes of the Caucasian neighbors; they remained friendly and visited the family occasionally. In April, 1942, shortly before the evacuation, one of (N 14 ♀ 7 F_1)'s friends came to visit and brought her some dresses. Because so many Issei men were being detained by the FBI, (I ♂ A) had a suitcase packed; but he was not arrested.

At the time of Pearl Harbor the family consisted of (I 51 ♀ P), (I 56 ♂ A), and three children: (N 19 ♂ 5 F_1), (N 17 ♂ 6 F_1), and (N 13 ♀ 7 F_1).

The family continued to plant until March and they had haulers take produce to the market until two or three days before the evacuation. Most of the family's farm equipment was sold or abandoned. There was little discussion about the evacuation, and (I ♂ A) disposed of the property. The 1935 automobile was sold for $100, a planting machine and a cultivator were left on the farm, and miscellaneous items such as seeds, hose, etc., were sold for nominal sums. A Mexican family was allowed to live rent free in the furnished buildings which the family arranged to leave on the farm. With a minimum of preparation, the family was evacuated to Tulare Assembly Center in May, 1942, with about $700 in their possession and an additional $1,000 in the bank.

During their four months in the assembly center neither (I 58 ♂ A) nor (I 53 ♀ P) worked. Their newly found leisure was spent visiting with neighbors and friends. (N 20 ♂ 5 F_1) and (N 18 ♂ 6 F_1), however, found employment in the messhalls as cooks and each was paid $12 per month. This was probably the first time they had earned money outside the family farming enterprise, and they spent it on small luxuries such as cakes, soft drinks, and candy, which were not served in the messhalls. Besides these small expenditures, the family spent about $200 of the cash for clothing and various household items.

Although numerous organizations for teen-agers and young people mushroomed in the center, the children did not join any of them. (N 14 ♀ 7 F_1)'s recreational needs were met among the children who were enrolled in the summer school she attended. The boys occasionally participated in informally organized athletics, but most of their leisure was spent with a gang of Kibei who roamed the center late at night. They were silent about the activities of the gang.

The family was transferred to the Gila River Relocation Center in August, 1942. They were assigned to an apartment 25 by 25 feet which they had to themselves. (I ♂ A) fixed up the barracks by making benches, cupboards, a table, closet, etc., but no money was spent on these furnishings. The boys apparently took little part in making the room livable, although such projects usually involved all members of other families.

In the relocation center, (I ♂ A) worked as a messhall cook for $16 per month, and (I ♀ P) occupied her time with handicrafts and the few housekeeping duties. The boys worked at various jobs: (N ♂ 5 F_1), as a timekeeper, cook, and bookkeeper; (N ♂ 6 F_1), as cook, then pantry clerk, truck driver, and warehouse loader. (N ♀ 7 F_1) was in school from 1942 to 1945, but worked one summer as a timekeeper.

As in the assembly center, the children did not join recreational organizations but went to the movies, dances, sports, and other activities singly or in small groups. The boys, however, joined the Young Buddhist Association, which undoubtedly reflects the influence of the Kibei groups with which they were associated.

The influence of the Kibei upon the attitudes of the two boys was dramatically highlighted in their response to the Army registration in February, 1943. There were dissenting opinions and conflicts within the family on this issue, but as was characteristic of this family, there were no strong convictions. In the beginning of 1943 the outcome of the war was far from clear, and many Kibei propagandized their friends and enemies with prophecies of what Japan would do when the United States was defeated. The pressures were supported by, and in turn reënforced by, the bitterness of the evacuation experience. Nevertheless, the boys' attitudes did not crystallize, and in their indecision they answered questions 27 and 28 "yes, no."

(I ♀ P) also gave "yes, no" answers. This is significant because (I ♂ A) answered both questions positively. It is unclear whether or not his decisions implied a willingness to dissolve his part in the family.

The married daughter, (N 27 ♀ 2 F_1), answered "yes, yes," as did her husband. She was not close either to (I ♀ P) or to the boys, and her opinion had little effect on them. (N 15 ♀ 7 F_1) was not required to register, but when the boys and (I ♀ P) moved toward segregation, she was carried along.

When the boys learned that their Kibei friends who had given "no, no" answers were to leave for Tule Lake, they changed their answers to "no, no." To further support this change, they applied for expatriation; (I ♀ P) asked for repatriation, since she was in favor of the move. At the hearings on their applications for expatriation, the family members were not decisive, and the applications were neither granted nor rejected. This left the boys in an unstable situation, but they left their answers to the questionnaire unchanged.

In 1944 (I 60 ♂ A) was granted a seasonal leave to work in sugar beet fields in Colorado. After three months he returned to the center with about $100. None of the family, except (I ♂ A), was eligible for relocation because of their answers to the loyalty questionnaire.

In 1945 (N 23 ♂ 5 F_1) proposed marriage to a Kibei girl, but (I ♀ P) protested violently. She was dissatisfied with the information she was able to get about the girl's family, and was suspicious that they were of the eta group. (N 23 ♂ 5 F_1) refused to give up the girl, and (I ♀ P) threatened to disown him if he went through with the marriage. However, a go-between was sent by the girl's family to (I ♂ A) to seek the family's consent. Although (I ♀ P) attended the wedding and the bride's family tried to mollify her, she remained negativistic throughout the whole affair.

In the late spring of 1945, about two years after the sons had requested to be expatriated, they changed their loyalty answers to "yes, yes." Japan's defeat appeared certain, and the move seemed senseless considering both of them knew so little about the country and its language. The Kibei had been long gone from the center, and the boys found little support for their shaky and irrational position. It is possible that the rescission was the precipitating cause of the change, but it is more probable that they were increasingly aware that their answers had little to do with their loyalty to the United States.

III. Relocation

The boys' change in position was supported by (I ♀ P), who had always said that if she were to stay in the United States she would go only to California. The possibility of being able to return to the vicinity in which they had formerly lived introduced a symbolic security into the situation. (I ♀ P) also had her registration answer changed to "yes, yes."

In June, 1945, (I ♂ A) went on indefinite leave to work for a Chinese on a California farm. There was an extra house on this farm, and in August, (I 56 ♀ P) and (N 17 ♀ 7 F_1) went to join him. (N ♂ 5 F_1), his wife, and (N ♂ 6 F_1) had applied to return to California at that time, but because of their former answers to the registration questions, they were not granted leave. However, on August 30 there was a blanket release of all evacuees still in the relocation center in order to facilitate the closing of the center.

In October, 1945, (I ♂ A), (I ♀ P), and (N ♀ 7 F_1) moved to a farm in Los Angeles County to sharecrop with the Caucasian with whom they had farmed before the war, and three remaining members of the family joined them.

The family moved into the houses they had lent to tenants at the time of evacuation, and arrangements with the landowner were reëstablished. The family contributed all of the labor and the equipment; the landowner supplied land, water, and one-half the cost of seeds, fertilizer, etc. The family received 60 per cent of the profit. When they resumed truck gardening, the family bought equipment amounting to $2,500 and purchased a 1937 sedan from the landowner for $700.

(N 18 ♀ 7 F_1) was graduated from high school in June, 1946, and enrolled at a Los Angeles university in September of that year. She took a job in which she earned board and room plus $15 per month in a private home. She was dependent upon the family for the rest of her spending money, tuition, and books. During the summer of 1947 she worked on the farm for two months and then moved to one of the coöperative houses near the campus.

IV. Postwar Family*

A growing conflict between (I 66 ♂ A) and (N 28 ♂ 5 F_1) has broken into the open. Since the family's return to the West Coast, (I ♂ A) has been increasingly resentful of (N ♂ 5 F_1)'s dominance, particularly in the affairs of the farm; but because he is the legal head of the family, the

* Information recorded at the time of the last interview is reported in the present tense.

power is weighted in (N ♂ 5 F₁)'s favor. Most of the farming decisions are made independently by (N ♂ 5 F₁), and most of the returns from it are in his name. As an expression of his insecurity, (I ♂ A) has proposed that the family finances be transferred to the name of a third party, presumably (N 22 ♀ 7 F₁), who is apparently on better terms with him. However, the family works as a unit for the enterprise, and the proceeds are deposited in the common fund over which (N ♂ 5 F₁) has legal control.

In his separate residence, (N ♂ 5 F₁) is dominant; his wife is passive and acquiescent. This is in contrast with her behavior before their marriage when (I ♀ P) complained that she did not display the reserve characteristic of Kibei girls. She has a degree of affectional control over her husband, but there appears to be some culture conflict. His wife lacks the responsiveness and cultural facility that he might have been able to find in a Nisei. Since bearing two children (1947 and 1949), (N ♂ 5 F₁)'s wife has gained more acceptance in the family. Tensions between the family and the "outsider" have decreased, and she is integrated into the group through common affection for the grandchildren.

Both (N ♂ 5 F₁) and (I 66 ♂ A) are looking toward the future. The older man wants security for his old age and proposes buying land and building on it. (N ♂ 5 F₁), however, wants to continue to amass some capital with a view to acquiring a business. (N ♂ 5 F₁) feels neither obligation nor affection toward (I ♂ A). (I ♀ P) cautions her son against rash handling of this problem, not because she thinks (I ♂ A) is necessarily right, but because she wishes to avoid unpleasantness. In an overt struggle it is probable that (I ♀ P) would side with (N ♂ 5 F₁), just as she did on the segregation issue. Although (I ♀ P) is submissive to (I ♂ A), she agrees with (N ♂ 5 F₁) that (I ♂ A) "talks big" about farming but actually is very hesitant about taking a chance. (N ♂ 5 F₁) and (I ♀ P) hold that profitable farming involves risk-taking. This basic issue tends to split the family.

(N ♂ 5 F₁) and (N ♂ 6 F₁) are quite close, and the latter can be counted upon to support his brother in a disagreement with (I ♂ A). The boys have never been, and are not now, affectionally close to (I ♂ A). (N 22 ♀ 7 F₁) is more sympathetic with (I ♂ A)'s insecurity.

The farming enterprise has been moderately successful, and in 1949 the family operated their farm on a contract basis, growing spinach for a packaging concern, a type of farming involving little risk and a steady income because of the assured market. The estimated net profit for 1949 was about $10,000 and the family has recently bought new furnishings.

Early in 1949, (N 25 ♂ 6 F_1) was drafted into the Army. He dislikes Army life intensely and his letters express dissatisfaction and loneliness.

The family members have not affiliated with any organizations since their return. As contrasted with his active participation before the war, (I ♂ A) attends few community activities. (I ♀ P), as before the war, has joined no groups, although she regularly attends Buddhist services.

There has been some increase in correspondence with individauls in Japan. (I ♀ P) does not write letters but sends packages to her sister and repatriated friends. (I ♂ A) has never sent anything. The children write in English about once a month to their friends and cousins who were expatriated.

The frequency of social interaction with other races has decreased since their return. Some of the boys' old friends visit them once in awhile, but there is very little activity. (I ♂ A) visits with his neighbors as before.

V. INTERPRETATION

Participation.—The demands of the farming enterprise left little time for the family's participation in the larger community, and their contract with the white landowner was the major factor that related the group to the dominant society. By mediating between the family and the American society in their economic activities, the landowner limited their volume of out-group contact.

With minor exceptions, only the children's school relations were consequential for the family's acculturation. Apart from the school, contact with the dominant culture and society was largely confined to the indirect channels of mass media.

(I ♂ A)'s participation did not integrate the family with the Japanese community. His and (I ♀ P)'s organizational affiliations were nominal and were not used as a means of family interaction. The children attended the language school as a formality, but Issei were indifferent to their scholastic achievements and associations, and peer-group contacts were subordinated to the pressing demands of the farm.

The family's leisure time was atomized and individualistically consumed with few occasions for group activities, either in or out of the home. The pronounced isolation of this family from both dominant and ethnic communities affected its acculturation and its adjustment to the wartime experiences.

Family structure.—Before the war serious strains underlay the apparent integration of the group. The conditions of sharecrop farming united the family in a common economic effort even in the absence of affectional relations. At the outbreak of the war (I ♂ A) had full control of the farming enterprise, and his strong control forced (N 19 ♂ 5 F_1) into a role of responsibility without power or status. The relationship between the two brothers and (I ♂ A) was strictly formal and, at least in the case of (N ♂ 5 F_1), strongly colored by resentment and hostility.

The relationship between (I ♀ P) and (I ♂ A) is obscure. It is not clear whether (I ♂ A)'s early assumption of responsibilities as the head of the family was balanced with sexual privileges. Although (I ♂ A) was (I ♀ P)'s nephew, he was five years her senior. Nor is it clear how the children perceived this relationship, which may have been a further source of antagonism between (N ♂ 5 F_1) and (I ♂ A).

(I ♀ P)'s role in the family did not ameliorate this tension. Her husband had thoroughly imbued her with the Japanese concept of the place of the woman, and her only response to the abuse she received at his hands was to accept completely the definition of her role. The children were afraid of (I ♂ P). (I ♀ P)'s attitude toward her husband carried over into her relationship with (I ♂ A), who apparently did not abuse her but whose attitude toward women was much the same as (I ♂ P)'s. (I ♀ P)'s isolation from the ethnic community as well as from the dominant society provided few opportunities that would expose her to alternate definitions of the woman's role in the family. Her passivity and acquiescence toward the dominance of the male head minimized her influence in the adjustment of her children to their status in the family. Although the children thought (I ♀ P) understood their problems, it would seem that she merely sympathized without comprehending.

Nor was (I ♀ P) a positive force in the acculturation of the children. She provided no active support for their participation in either the ethnic community or the dominant society. In the general absence of a significant cultural orientation in the family the children must have found it difficult to move toward either the Japanese or American culture.

Wartime experience.—If we have evaluated the prewar family structure correctly, the evacuation broke in upon a strained situation. (N ♂ 5 F_1) was able to escape the necessity of working under (I ♂ A) and of being party to the rule of a cousin over a family that was rightfully his own. Soon after the family moved to the assembly center,

(N ♂ 5 F₁) sought out the dissident Kibei element in the center. Their revolt gave direction to (N ♂ 5 F₁)'s aggressive feelings. Belonging to a gang also reduced the frequency of interaction in a family situation that he found distressing. (N ♂ 5 F₁) and his younger brother spent most of their time with the Kibei group.

Kibei associations directed a negative response to the loyalty questionnaire. It is noted that on this issue (N ♂ 5 F₁) was in opposition to (I ♂ A), who answered positively. (I ♀ P) sided with (N ♂ 5 F₁), perhaps reflecting a realization on her part of the legitimacy of (N ♂ 5 F₁) as family head. (I ♂ A) appears to have had little influence, if indeed he attempted to exert any. It is significant that a schism appeared in the family on this question. (N ♂ 5 F₁) expressed his conflict through it and freed himself from the control of (I ♂ A).

There was undoubtedly strong pressure put upon him by his Kibei friends to give a "no, no" answer. Despite this, his original answer was "yes, no," a response that perhaps reflected his unwillingness to pay the price of national alienation for his familial rebellion. In the light of this indecision, the changing of his answer to "no, no" probably was less an expression of his convictions than a measure of his insecurity. When group support for his position was gone (i.e., the segregation of his Kibei friends), he sought to hasten his own segregation and thus achieve the security of closure.

The marriage of (N ♂ 5 F₁) to a Kibei girl was the climax of his rebellion and a partial resolution of his conflicts. His determination to marry the girl in spite of, indeed, perhaps, because of, family disapproval symbolized the assertion of his independence. By refusing to submit, (N ♂ 5 F₁) assumed a mature status within the family.

(N ♂ 5 F₁)'s assumption of the control of the farming enterprise in the postwar period shifts the conflict from the problem of independence to that of leadership. He aggressively took over leadership, including the control of the family finances, and (I ♂ A) reacted in defense of his waning power by attacking the personal habits of (N ♂ 5 F₁). (N ♂ 5 F₁)'s ambivalent attitude toward (I ♂ A) is reflected on the one hand by his willingness to let him "take it easy," and on the other by his wish that (I ♂ A) would go away.

Character of adjustment.—In the analysis of this family, we have focused on (N ♂ 5 F₁), who clearly was the central figure in the adjustment to wartime experiences. This case illustrates one of the ways in which the institutional manipulations gave dramatic expression to strains in the prewar structure of the family. The center provided a new setting for the resolution of familial conflicts; administrative acts created issues that precipitated conflicts and provided a medium for their expression.

The apparent contradictions in ($N \,\male\, 5 \, F_1$)'s behavior on the loyalty issue had little, if anything, to do with loyalty. The primary problem was one of authority and dependence, and within the context of attenuated familial controls and enlarged peer-group associations the family would have been faced with conflict on some other issue if not the registration one. It must be noted, however, that it may well have been only a matter of administrative red tape that the family escaped grave consequences from ($N \,\male\, 5 \, F_1$)'s action in the loyalty registration.

It seems safe to conjecture that even if the war had not intervened, some kind of restructuring was inevitable. However, the evacuation and particularly the registration issue afforded ($N \,\male\, 5 \, F_1$) an opportunity to assert his independence in a relatively secure setting. In ordinary circumstances this would have been more difficult to achieve and ($N \,\male\, 5 \, F_1$)'s status probably would have changed gradually and less disruptively.

Cultural Data

PREWAR

Religion:
Parents were from Buddhist families but were not active members.

POSTWAR

Religion:
($I \,\female\, P$) attends services regularly. In the center the brothers were members of the Young Buddhist Association, but do not now belong to any church group, nor does ($N \,\female\, 7 \, F_1$).

Holidays:
New Year's Day elaborately celebrated. Boys' and Girls' Days and the Obon passingly observed. The American holidays recognized though not always observed. Holiday festivities usually individual rather than family-centered except for Thanksgiving and Christmas.

Holidays:
Holidays observed as before the war. Boys' Day and Girls' Day, which among Nisei are minor holidays, are still celebrated. Obon observed by ($I \,\female\, P$) and ($I \,\male\, A$). All American holidays observed as before.

Diet:
Predominantly Japanese.

Diet:
Minor changes in diet

Reading matter:
Encyclopedias, children's books, and a few textbooks; subscriptions to a Japanese-language paper, *Newsweek*, *Life*, *Modern Screen*, *Reader's Digest*, and *California Cultivator*.

Reading matter:
Subscription to the Los Angeles *Examiner*, *Rafu Shimpo*, *Life*, *Holiday*, *True Detective*, comics, *Reader's Digest*, and *Sports Afield*.

Language school:
Attendance at language school and the levels of achievement:

(N ♀ 2 F₁) 10 yrs.   (3rd yr. h.s.)
(N ♂ 5 F₁) 8 yrs. Bk. 12 (6th gr.)
(N ♂ 6 F₁) 7 yrs. Bk. 10 (5th gr.)
(N ♀ 7 F₁) 6 yrs. Bk. 8 (4th gr.)

Language school:
None of the children has returned to a language school.

GLOSSARY

GLOSSARY

assembly centers ....temporary housing centers, administered by WCCA, near the localities of original residence, to which the evacuees were removed

baishakunin ....a go-between for marriage arrangements; a match-maker (*see* nakōdo)

butsudan ....Buddhist household shrine

engeikai ....an entertainment club, usually composed of local amateurs interested in Japanese drama, music, and dance; also the programs presented by the club

eta ....a pariah caste

evacuation ....removal of Japanese population from West Coast states and western Arizona to assembly and relocation centers—March to November, 1942

gisei ....a sacrifice; (*gisei ni naru:* to sacrifice oneself)

go ....a form of checkers

hakujin ....Caucasians

haiseki ....expulsion; (*haiseki suru:* to exclude); to discriminate in the sense of status discrimination

hanamatsuri ....Buddha's birthday festival

heimin ....a commoner in the feudal caste system

hinamatsuri ....Girls' festival (in March) commemorated by the display of dolls

ikebana ....flower arrangement

inkyo ....an institutionalized status of retirement from the headship of a family

internment camp.......center administered by Department of Justice for persons deemed security risks

inu ....informer, eavesdropper, spy; literally "dog"

Issei ....first generation immigrant

jūdo ....jūjutsu

junyōshi ....a younger brother adopted as a son and heir-apparent

Kaigun Kyōkai ....Navy Association

kamidana ....a household shrine

kana ....Japanese phonetic alphabet

kanji ....Chinese ideographic character

karuta ....Japanese playing cards

keigo ....respectful terms; honorific titles of address

kendō ....Japanese fencing

kenjinkai ....Japanese prefectural association in the United States

Kibei ....American-born Japanese, educated in Japan and returned to the United States

kifu ....donations to various community associations

koimatsuri ....Boys' festival (in May) commemorated by the flying of paper carps

koshōgatsu ....Little New Year celebration

koshu ....the head of a family

koto ....a long Japanese zither-harp of thirteen silk strings

Meiji ...."enlightened"; refers to the reign of Emperor Mutsuhito (1867–1912)

meshiya ....restaurant with Japanese menu; chop house

nakōdo (or nakaudo)....a go-between; a match-maker (*see* baishakunin)

namaiki ....insolent; impertinent

Nihonjinkai ....Japanese Association

Nisei ....American-born Japanese; literally "second generation"

no, no ....negative replies to registration questions no. 27 and no. 28 (see pp. 26–30 and 225)

nōgyōkumiai ....farmers' association

obon (or bon)..........a Buddhist festival commemorating the ancestral spirits (similar to All Souls' Day)

omochi (or mochi)......a festive rice cake, served especially during the New Year's celebration

omanjū (or manjū).....festive rice cake, a bean-jam bun

osekihan (or sekihan)...a steamed rice and red bean (*azuki*) mixture served on Boys' Day and Girls' Day and other festivals

osonae ....a pyramid of round omochi cakes of graduated sizes, displayed during the New Year season

oyakōkō ....filial piety; also one who practices filial piety

ozōni (or zōni)........a rice-cake soup (rice cakes used as dumplings) served during the New Year festivities

registration ....a combined WRA and Army policy requiring all center residents seventeen years or over to answer loyalty questions

relocation ....the removal of the evacuated population from WCCA assembly centers; also the resettlement of evacuees, principally to communities in the Midwest

relocation centers ....WRA administered centers for evacuated population

rescission ....the rescinding of the order excluding Japanese population from West Coast states and western Arizona

sake ....rice wine, the chief alcoholic beverage of the Japanese

samisen (or shamisen)..Japanese lute with three strings

Sansei ....child of Nisei parents; literally "third generation"

segregation ....WRA policy which separated "disloyal" evacuees from the "loyal"

Seichyō no Iye ....a medicoreligious cult

shashin kekkon ....a marriage arranged by an intermediary through the use of photographs; literally "photograph marriage"

shochikubai ....a New Year's display of an arrangement of sprigs of bamboo, plum blossoms, and pine

sōryō ....the eldest son

tenchōsetsu ....Emperor's birthday

yes, yes ....affirmative replies to registration questions no. 27 and no. 28 (see pp. 26–30 and 225) yobiyose . . . . American-born child who has lived in Japan and subsequently returned to his family in the United States (Yobiyose applies to the kibei as well as to a child who spent only his preschool years in Japan)

yōshi . . . . an adopted child (son) ; a son-in-law who has assumed the name of his wife's family

NOTES

NOTE TO PREFACE
(Pages iii–iv)

[1] An early effort to develop by statistical procedures a typology of Japanese families foundered on the reef of costs which prevented the accumulation of a sufficiently large sample. See Leonard Bloom, "Transitional Adjustments of Japanese-American Families to Relocation," *American Sociological Review*, 12, no. 2 (April, 1947), 201–209.

NOTES TO CHAPTER I
(Pages 1–11)

[1] S. F. Miyamoto, "Social Solidarity Among the Japanese in Seattle," *University of Washington Publications in the Social Sciences*, 11 (Dec., 1939), 84

[2] *Ibid.*

[3] J. F. Embree, "Acculturation Among the Japanese of Kona, Hawaii," *Memoirs of the American Anthropological Association*, no. 59 (1941); W. A. Caudill, "Japanese-American Personality and Acculturation," *Genetic Psychology Monographs*, 45, pt. 1 (1952). Our discussion is informed by a theoretical statement outlined in L. Broom and J. I. Kitsuse, "The Validation of Acculturation: A Condition to Ethnic Assimilation," *American Anthropologist*, 57 (Feb., 1955), 44–48.

[4] See Broom and Kitsuse, *op. cit.;* and L. Broom and E. Shevky, "Mexicans in the United States: A Problem in Social Differentiation," *Sociology and Social Research*, 36 (Jan.–Feb., 1952), 150–158.

[5] L. Bloom and R. Riemer, *Removal and Return* (Berkeley and Los Angeles: University of California Press, 1949), pp. 32–123.

NOTES TO CHAPTER II
(Pages 12–36)

[1] M. Grodzins, *Americans Betrayed* (Chicago: University of Chicago Press, 1949), pp. 1–15; War Relocation Authority, *Impounded People* (Washington: U.S. Government Printing Office, 1946), pp. 2–4.

[2] See War Relocation Authority, *Wartime Exile* (Washington: U.S. Government Printing Office, 1946), chap. 5.

[3] Grodzins, *op. cit.*, Appendix 1, See also *Impounded People*, p. 32.

[4] *Wartime Exile*, p. 98. A distinction must be made between *internment* of individuals viewed as security risks who were arrested and mass *evacuation* of the whole population. Interned persons were held in camps administered by the Department of Justice.

[5] Grodzins, *op. cit.*, chap. 2.

[6] *Ibid.*, pp. 194–196.

[7] *Impounded People*, p. 34.

[8] Grodzins, *op. cit.*, chap. 3.

[9] *Ibid.*, p. 77.

[10] *Final Report, Japanese Evacuation from the West Coast, 1942* (Washington: U.S. Government Printing Office, 1943), pp. 33–38.

[11] Grodzins, *op. cit.*, pp. 183–184.

[12] *Wartime Exile*, p. 144.

[13] *Ibid.*, pp. 145–147.

[14] *Ibid.*, p. 147.

[15] Grodzins, *op. cit.*, chap. 9.

[16] *Wartime Exile*, p. 148.

[17] L. Bloom and R. Riemer, *Removal and Return* (Berkeley and Los Angeles: University of California Press, 1949); J. tenBroek, E. N. Barnhart, and F. W. Matson, *Prejudice, War and the Constitution* (Berkeley and Los Angeles: University of California Press, 1954); Grodzins; A. H. Leighton, *The Governing of Men* (Princeton: Princeton University Press, 1945); D. S. Thomas, *The Salvage* (Berkeley and Los Angeles: University of California Press, 1952); D. S. Thomas and R. S. Nishimoto, *The Spoilage* (Berkeley and Los Angeles: University of California Press, 1946); *Final Report, Japanese Evacuation from the West Coast, 1942;* War Relocation Authority, *Final Report* (Washington: U.S. Government Printing Office, 1946–1947).

[18] "In the war in which we are now engaged racial affinities are not severed by migration. The Japanese race is an enemy race and while many second and third generation Japanese born on United States soil, possessed of United States citizenship, have become 'Americanized,' the racial strains are undiluted. To conclude otherwise is to expect that children born of white parents on Japanese soil sever all racial affinity and become loyal Japanese subjects, ready to fight and, if necessary to die for Japan in a war against the nation of their parents. That Japan is allied with Germany and Italy in this struggle is no ground for assuming that any Japanese, barred from assimilation by convention as he is, though born and raised in the United States, will not turn against this nation when the final test of loyalty comes. It, therefore, follows that along the vital Pacific Coast over 112,000 potential enemies, of Japanese extraction, are at large today. There are indications that these are organized and ready for concerted action at a favorable opportunity. The very fact that no sabotage has taken place to date is a disturbing and confirming indication that such action will be taken." [*Final Report, Japanese Evacuation from the West Coast, 1942*, p. 34.]

[19] *Ibid.*, p. 66.

[20] *Ibid.*, p. 77.

[21] *Ibid.*, p. 78.

[22] *Ibid.*, p. 245.

[23] War Relocation Authority, *Community Government in War Relocation Centers* (Washington: U.S. Government Printing Office, 1946), p. 2.

[24] *Ibid.*, p. 4.

[25] War Relocation Authority, *WRA, A Story of Human Conservation* (Washington: U.S. Government Printing Office, 1946), p. 33.

[26] *Community Government in War Relocation Centers*, p. 7.

[27] *Ibid.*, p. 4.

[28] *Ibid.*, p. 10.

[29] *Ibid.*, p. 11.

[30] *WRA, A Story of Human Conservation*, p. 76.

[31] *Ibid.*

[32] *Ibid.*

[33] Quoted in *ibid.*, pp. 77–78.

[34] *Ibid.*, p. 78.

[35] *Ibid.*, p. 82.

[36] *Ibid.*, p. 81.

[37] *Ibid.*

[38] *Community Government in War Relocation Centers*, p. 12.

[39] *Ibid.*, p. 5.

[40] *Ibid.*, pp. 7–8.

[41] *Ibid.*, p. 26.

[42] *Ibid.*, p. 27. This betrays a theory of social causation quite at variance to that held by General DeWitt. See n. 18.

⁴³ See *WRA, A Story of Human Conservation,* p. 49.

⁴⁴ The so-called "loyalty" questions were no. 27 and no. 28.

Question no. 27: "Are you willing to serve in the armed forces of the United States on combat duty, wherever ordered?"

Question no. 28: "Will you swear unqualified allegiance to the United States of America and faithfully defend the United States from any or all attack by foreign or domestic forces, and forswear any form of allegiance or obedience to the Japanese emperor, or any other foreign government, power, or organization?"

Affirmative answers to both questions ("yes, yes") were presumed to indicate "loyalty" to the United States, and negative responses were considered indicative of "disloyalty." Mixed answers (i.e., "yes, no" and "no, yes") were given by evacuees to express a variety of objections, resentments, and qualifications. (See chap. iii, and case materials.)

⁴⁵ *Community Government in War Relocation Centers,* p. 39.

⁴⁶ War Relocation Authority, *The Relocation Program* (Washington: U.S. Government Printing Office, 1946), p. 23.

⁴⁷ *WRA, A Story of Human Conservation,* p. 56. For a discussion of the registration program at Tule Lake Relocation Center, see pp. 57 ff; also, Thomas and Nishimoto, *op. cit.*

⁴⁸ *WRA, A Story of Human Conservation,* p. 57.

⁴⁹ "This rumor was a contributing factor to the large number of people who sought refuge by staying at Tule Lake during segregation and to the large number of repatriation requests made at other centers by families, who, to avoid enforced relocation, sought haven with the 'disloyals.'" [*Community Government in War Relocation Centers,* p. 52.]

⁵⁰ *WRA, A Story of Human Conservation,* p. 63.

⁵¹ *Ibid.,* pp. 63–64. Of the 77,957 evacuees eligible to register, 3,254 did not register, 68,018 were "loyal," 1,041 qualified their answers, 5,376 gave "disloyal" responses, 234 did not answer, and the answers of 34 are unknown. These figures represent final registration results, which reflect changes from original answers submitted between date of registration and September, 1943. See *ibid.,* p. 199.

⁵² *Ibid.,* p. 69.

⁵³ War Relocation Authority, *The Evacuated People; A Quantitative Description* (Washington: U.S. Government Printing Office, 1946), p. 30.

⁵⁴ Roughly 65 per cent of those relocated by the end of 1943 were between the ages of fifteen and thirty-four. [*Ibid.,* p. 50.]

⁵⁵ It was a common relocation pattern for one member of the family, usually the eldest male Nisei or eldest Nisei, to relocate first as a "scout." This was often for the sake of economy as well as to facilitate the adjustment of the family.

⁵⁶ *WRA, A Story of Human Conservation,* p. 135.

⁵⁷ Presumably "new relocation procedures" refers to the facilitation of leave-clearance procedure through the administration of the mass registration.

⁵⁸ See chap. iii; see also *Community Government in War Relocation Centers,* p. 55.

⁵⁹ *Ibid.,* p. 56.

⁶⁰ *Ibid.,* p. 64.

⁶¹ *WRA, A Story of Human Conservation,* p. 122.

⁶² *Ibid.*

⁶³ *The Evacuated People,* p. 30.

⁶⁴ *The Relocation Program,* pp. 46–47.

⁶⁵ *WRA, A Story of Human Conservation,* p. 124.

⁶⁶ See *The Relocation Program,* p. 49.

⁶⁷ *Ibid.,* p. 50. The general lack of success of the relocation program in the east

indicated a need for a reëvaluation of the program, particularly for policies regarding West Coast relocation.

[68] *Ibid.*, p. 52.

[69] *Ibid.*, p. 36.

[70] WRA's reply to this recommendation stated: "On the West Coast ... there is not the same need for exploratory trips of this type that there is in other sections of the country. The evacuees, after all, have a first-hand knowledge of the coastal region—its agriculture, climate, and economic opportunities." [*The Relocation Program*, p. 58.] It should have been apparent to WRA that after the evacuation experience the evacuees were concerned about more than the agriculture, climate, and economic opportunities of the West Coast.

[71] *Ibid.*, p. 55.

[72] *Ibid.*, p. 76.

[73] *Ibid.*, p. 77.

[74] *Ibid.*, p. 79.

[75] *Ibid.*

NOTES TO CHAPTER III

(Pages 37–49)

[1] *Final Report, Japanese Evacuation from the West Coast, 1942* (Washington: U.S. Government Printing Office, 1943), p. 77.

[2] *Ibid.*, pp. 77–78.

[3] War Relocation Authority, *WRA, A Story of Human Conservation* (Washington: U.S. Government Printing Office, 1946), p. 102.

[4] *Ibid.*, p. 81.

[5] See D. S. Thomas and R. S. Nishimoto, *The Spoilage* (Berkeley and Los Angeles: University of California Press, 1946).

[6] See chap. ii, pp. 30–35; also J. F. Embree, "Resistance to Freedom: An Administrative Problem," *Applied Anthropology*, 2 (Sept., 1943), 10–14; and E. H. Spicer, "Resistance to Freedom: Resettlement from the Japanese Relocation Centers During World War II," in E. H. Spicer, ed., *Human Problems in Technological Change* (New York: Russell Sage Foundation, 1952).

[7] War Relocation Authority, *Community Government in War Relocation Centers* (Washington: U.S. Government Printing Office, 1946), p. 7.

[8] See n. 44, chap. ii, for wording of questions no. 27 and no. 28.